IS THERE LIFE
AFTER DEATH?

IS THERE LIFE AFTER DEATH?

The latest evidence analysed

**Professor
Robert Kastenbaum**

PRION

Revised edition published in 1995 by Prion
an imprint of Multimedia Books Limited
32-34 Gordon House Road,
London NW5 1LP

First published in 1984

A catalogue record of this book is available from the British Library.

ISBN 1-85375-188-X

Cover & text design by Tamasin Cole
Cover illustration © Galaxy Picture Library
Typeset by Type Technique, London W1
Printed in Great Britain by
HarperCollinsManufacturing, Glasgow

CONTENTS

ACKNOWLEDGMENTS

I would like to thank Arthur Berger, J. D., Steven Bridge, Robert Ettinger, Erlendur Haraldsson, Ph.D., Raymond A. Moody, M.D., Ph.D., R. Michael Perry, Ian Stevenson, M. D., and Marilyn Wilson for sharing their work and experiences with me. They are by no means responsible for the way their contributions have been used (and occasionally abused) in this book. My appreciation also is extended to Multimedia/Prion for giving me this opportunity to revisit the borderlands of life and death. Marsha Dunstan has been a model editor even if I have not invariably been a model author.

Bunny, Honey, Spirit, Ulysses, Serena, Snowflake and Pumpkin have in their various ways kept me anchored contentedly in this life while contemplating the next. Indeed, the underlying spirit in this book has been Spirit, the ancient among our cats, who now spends much of his time lying under my computer desk and snoring away the time between sorties to the food dish. Despite his age and wisdom, Spirit does not seem to have reached the stage of renouncing all desire and achieving nirvana. But, then, neither have I.

INTRODUCTION:
"A CURIOUS WILD PAIN"

A dead-end street in New York City (the South Bronx, to be specific) pretty much defined what I knew about the universe as a young child. The survival question took a very narrow but intense form for all the rambunctious urchins of Bonner Place. We did not ask if the human spirit and personality survives death. Instead, we were preoccupied with surviving each day in our obscure microcosmos. City streets and crumbling tenements were not yet as dangerous as they were to become some years later when drugs and gang activity took over and neighborly support diminished. Nevertheless, life was dangerous enough, and we all knew it. This was a life that one lived personally, rather than vicariously through the television and computer screens (no credit to us; these tempting devices had not yet arrived from the devil's workshop).

Even a child in such a place, however, had moments that granted a hint or glimpse of a wider, deeper, richer, and more mysterious world. I remember standing on the fire escape on chill evenings, eager to escape the confines of a stuffy tenement apartment. What was up there? The night sky, stars. But what was *out* there? Were there other worlds with other little kids wondering about us? Was there an ENORMOUS god? Was there nothing, nothing, nothing at all? Had all of everything been there all the time? Was it all going to last forever or vanish one night with a blink? More personally, I wondered if there really were angels and spirits looking down on me, checking to see if I had cleaned my room and desisted from teasing my little brother.

Eventually I would clamber back inside the apartment, not knowing any more than I had before about the mysterious and remote vastness that surrounded Bonner Place. Already I had learned from disappointing experience that none of the books on our shelf and none of the Really Smart People in our neighborhood had a convincing answer for my questions. And yet I was not ready to give up on the possibility of answers that would satisfy both mind and heart.

I'm still not ready to give up. Over the years I have had the opportunity to learn from the many gifted contributors to physics, biology, psychology, philosophy, history, literature, and the arts. The continued vitality of humankind's quest for understanding has helped me to grow up a little and even to dare contribute something of my own from time to time. I hope you are not ready to give up either. I hope that you are ready and willing to explore one of the greatest and most persistent questions that ever formed itself in the human mind. If the men and women – and probably the little kids – at the dawn of history could address themselves to the question of survival, why should we not also accept this challenge, having at our disposal an impressive accumulation of experience, knowledge and, on occasion, even wisdom? It is a foregone conclusion that we do not have all the answers. We should, however, be in a superior position to ask the question and evaluate the contending answers.

Our first task is syntactical and punctuational. A great many people march through their lives with this formulation of the central issue:

There is life after death!

Quite a few other people unflaggingly endorse a slightly different formulation:

There is no life after death!

Although these statements differ markedly in substance, their common form suggests that both represent minds that have locked their doors and tossed away the keys.

May I suggest we try it this way instead:

Is there life after death?

This formulation is more in keeping with the limits of our knowledge, the fallibility of our reasoning, and the temptation to believe what we want to believe, knowledge and reasoning be damned. We will, then, be dispensing with the exclamation point and following the question mark wherever it may lead us.

The book you are scanning is intended for those who judge that the survival question is no less important than the thousand little decisions and conclusions we reach in daily life. It will be most useful for those who can resist quick and easy answers to difficult questions, and who are aware that new developments continue to occur in our investigation of the survival question. Do you have an opinion or a feeling about survival that you would like to check against the available evidence? Have you heard of recent research and wondered about its validity? Has some hard-to-explain phenomenon entered your own life, raising new questions and possibilities related to survival? Are you someone who is often called on to comfort people in distress, or those with urgent concerns related to dying, death, grief, and survival? I must respond affirmatively to all these questions myself and so I admit to having written this book for myself as well as for you.

The possible survival of death is our central concern. Other compelling questions arise along the way, however. What difference does or should the answer make to how we live between now and death? What are the implications not only for our personal lives, but for government, religion, commerce, and the entire paraphernalis of society? And what should be our rules of evidence? Keep an eye (actually both eyes!) on the last-mentioned question, even though at first it may seem the least interesting. We will see that in pressing for acceptable survival evidence we must also question some dominating views in the general scientific enterprise.

In the first edition of this book I tried out a new method that might be called "experimental belief". I tried to believe whole-heartedly in every position that was examined; and then to believe just as whole-heartedly in an unsparing critique of every position. This approach worked, so it is called upon again in this revised edition. I first present the position as though its most ardent advocate, although taking more care for accuracy than one always finds from a partisan. After this spell of enthusiasm, I do my best to undermine the position, again, playing fair with the facts. This advocate/critic approach is taken until we reach the final chapter in which we can reflect on what we have been through together and where this leaves us.

There is significant new material in the revised edition. Most obvious are the two completely new chapters. Reincarnation was discussed briefly in the first edition, but now richly deserves its own chapter, both for the continued upsurge in belief and for the interesting new observations that seem to support the belief. All the traditional survival beliefs assume a dead body. The chapter on cryonics describes a radically different alternative, one that bears the marks of today's high-tech society. Whether one is attracted or repelled by the cryonic option, it can help us to achieve a fresh perspective on the survival question and the conflicting motives involved.

The channelling movement has become more salient in recent years, along with its share of claims and critiques. We have therefore added a section on channelling in our exploration of mediumship and survival. Raymond Moody, Jr., who opened the fascinating realm of near-death experiences to the world, has recently re-opened a long-neglected chapter of human experience. His rescue of the *psychomateum* from the ruins of antiquity and his own attempt to establish communication with the dead also has its own new section. Throughout the book there are numerous additions and revisions in the light of new information and the author's opportunity for a critical review.

One further thought before beginning ...

True, the survival question must lead us in to problems of evidence and logic. But we will never lose sight of passionate humanity. The sense that there is – or should be – something more than the life we know on earth has captivated many people from ancient times to our own. Somehow we must do justice to the depth and character of this "immortality feeling" that at times appears to critical human experience. Consider but one brief example here. Bertrand Russell employed his towering intellect to address the major problems of philosophy and society in the twentieth century. Russell could usually be counted upon to be on the opposite side to popular and traditional opinion. If one were to assemble a legion of believers in the hereafter, Bertrand Russell would not be summoned, and yet he writes to his "Colette":

> *Do you know how sometimes all the barriers of personality fall away, and one is free for al the world to come in – the stars and the night and the wind, and all the hopes and passions of men, and all the slow centuries of growth – and even the cold abysses of space grow friendly ... And from that moment some quality of ultimate peace enters into all one feels – even when one feels most passionately ... In some way I can't put into words, I feel that some of our thoughts and feelings are just of the moment, but others are part of the eternal world, like the stars – even if the actual existence is passing, something – some spirit or essence – seems to last on, to be part of the real history of the universe, not only of the separate person. Somehow, that is how I want to live, so that as much of life as possible may have that quality of eternity.*

In a later letter, Russell writes: "The centre of me is always and eternally a terrible pain – a curious wild pain – searching for something beyond what the world contains, something transfigured and infinite."

In these intimate passages, Russell, capable of the most aloof and critical thought, expresses a passion that was no less a part of his nature and which, as he himself confesses, was at the very core of his being. The fact that a critical mind and a heart searching for "something beyond" were both true of Russell puts us on notice that we will not succeed if we ignore either the critical intellect or the passions.

The purpose of this book might then be restated – a confrontation with a "curious wild pain," bringing both heart and mind to the challenge.

Robert Kastenbaum
Tempe, Arizona, 1994

1

THERE AND BACK:
THE NEAR-DEATH EXPERIENCE

It was in 1975 that a little known publishing company brought out a book by a philosophically-minded physician who was unknown to the general public. Raymond A. Moody, Jr.'s *Life After Life*[1] was primarily a collection of memories by people who had survived close encounters with death, usually in a medical emergency or severe accident. Moody also shared his attempt to make sense of these reports. The book astonished and intrigued its first readers. Through word of mouth, it became an international best-seller. Unlike many other topics that fascinate people for a while and then rapidly fade away, the Near-Death Experience continues to fascinate.

There is much that is exotic and even thrilling about NDE reports. What gives these reports their continuing fascination, however, is the belief that NDEs offer firm proof of survival after death.

Is this belief well-founded? We will examine the evidence pro and con throughout most of this chapter. There have been many reports of NDEs since Moody's first book, as well as a number of studies, theoretical interpretations, and critiques. Now is a good time to revisit the early reports and see what has been learned over the past two decades. In a moment I will divide myself into the advocate and critic of NDE reports as proof of survival. First, however, let's remind ourselves of just what is meant by a NDE.

THE CLASSIC NEAR-DEATH EXPERIENCE

Major surgery. She had been on the operating table a long time. At one point the surgeons thought they had lost her. She did recover, however, and one day confided something to her young son. "I was dead for a while. But it felt wonderful, so peaceful. I had no pain, no worries. I was floating in the sky, as free as can be. Now I know what death is. And I will never be afraid of death again. Death is beautiful."

I was a grade school child when my mother shared this experience with me. Neither of us–or the public at large – had ever heard of NDEs;

this was long before Moody's book. Through the following years my mother faced further medical crises, but, true to her word, never expressed any detectable fear of death. When her death did come into near prospect, she re-affirmed her freedom from fear of death and nothing in her words or actions ever challenged the veracity of that statement.

Other people around the world had similar experiences before NDEs came into vogue, and a few shared these experiences. By and large, however, NDEs did not come into focus as significant human experiences. Although my mother's report contains several elements of what has become the "classic" or "core" NDE, it is useful here to look at more detailed communications.

A VETERAN REMEMBERS HIS DEATH

Moody's interest in NDEs was aroused by several reports, especially one related to him by psychiatrist George G. Ritchie, M. D. The experience had occurred before the telling. At that time Ritchie was a premedical student who had been inducted into the army. He suffered a rapidly-developing case of pneumonia with very high fever. By the time a physician arrived in the barracks, Ritchie was dead, or so the physician judged by the absence of vital signs. It was during his "death" that Ritchie had his astounding and unexpected experience. Detailed accounts of this experience have since been given by Ritchie[2] himself and by Roszell[3] in consultation with Ritchie. Our summary here is based on these two accounts.

The dead or at least "deadish" Ritchie was shocked to see his own body in the hospital room. He was above the body, floating this way and that. He could float through walls, doors, and people. This unprecedented experience gave him a sense of "icy loneliness". Ritchie was having an out-of-the-body experience. Next he observed that the darkened hospital room was becoming brighter and brighter until it was filled with a light of dazzling brilliance. His report of bright, dazzling light is another NDE component that would be included in many other survivor's memories.

> At that point, what appeared to him as the shape of a man of light stepped toward him from out of the light. This figure of light stood by his side while a panorama of his life passed before his eyes in complete detail, and all the thoughts of his mind were laid open to this figure, whom he now calls his guide.

Here were the spiritual encounter and the panoramic memory that would also be mentioned in many subsequent NDE reports. Ritchie was deeply affected and, again, as many others would later report, felt that his life had been enriched by his mysterious spiritual experience.

"MOUSEY" MAKES IT THROUGH

Let us take another example, one of the first that was related to me during the course of my work. The person who shared this experience is a nurse of many years experience.

Martha N. was a crumpled, motionless object thrown clear of her car after it had been struck by a truck whose brakes failed. The first bystanders who came to the scene directed their attention to her young son who was still in the car, injured but conscious. The woman's condition appeared too serious for any but trained medical personnel to approach. Even the ambulance squad responded at first as though Martha was beyond help, and concentrated instead on the child.

But Martha was not in that crumpled, motionless body. She was hovering above the scene, more an observer than a participant. Later she would report an extraordinary sequence of events. First, there was concern for her son. This took precedence over everything else. Martha drifted away from her own body to float above the car. She could see that her boy was more frightened than injured. Martha did not know whether she was actually speaking to her child, or beaming thoughts to him. "Everything will be all right, Donnie. Just a little accident. Everything will be all right." She saw another motorist, a woman, get out of a car and speak comfortingly to Donnie, although she couldn't get the door open. After a while – it was hard to judge time – Martha saw that her boy was receiving effective attention and did not seem in danger.

She soon began to feel curious about herself, or, rather, about that body she had become accustomed to inhabiting and which now lay on the side of the road. Drifting back to hover above her own body, she saw that it had now been partially covered by a blanket. Blood had dripped down her chin, probably from her mouth. A uniformed person – it looked like a woman, but she couldn't be sure – seemed to have taken charge of Martha's body, and was bending over her.

At this point Martha found herself becoming more interested in her new condition than in the body down below. She remembered feeling a little guilty about the messy scene – the broken glass, the two damaged vehicles, the traffic tie-up, all those people involved, and, of course, her own dishevelled body. Not at all the way she preferred to appear in public! Nevertheless, Martha felt there was not much to be done about here. Why stay around, then?

The most enticing part of her new state was the sensation of weightlessness. "I felt so incredibly light. There was just no effort at all to anything I wanted to do, no resistance, I didn't have to drag my heavy old body along with me!" Actually, Martha's body prior to the accident had been neither "heavy" nor "old", but she had long been struggling to keep her weight under control.

Martha started to experiment with this new situation. She

discovered that simply by thinking – "not really even thinking, just sort of having a whim to move this way or that" – she could change her position. For a while she felt completely caught up in this new-found ability to move effortlessly through space. "The closest thing was to swimming, but this was even better, there were just no limits at all." Feeling free, relaxed, and serene, Martha had temporarily lost her sense of attachment to the world below. "I could have gone on like this forever."

Nevertheless, Martha knew very well what had happened, that her body, emptied of self, was lying back there in the ordinary world, once the only world she herself had known. And the experience did not continue forever.

> I heard my [deceased] grandmother speak my voice. I was sure it was her. She had that way of being teasing and serious at the same time. Grannie scolded me in a very loving way. "Now you get back. You get back where you belong, Mousey!" Mousey had been her name for me when I was little. I didn't speak to her, but I was thinking to myself, "No I won't go back! It's so much nicer like this!" Grannie seemed to hear me anyhow and told me again to get back, that Donnie needed me and I still had a lot to do on earth.

Martha remembers hesitating. For a moment she felt stubborn, just the way she had been as Mousey, wanting to have her own way and enjoying the freedom of her new situation. But then she realized that Grannie was right. "To tell the truth, I still didn't really want to go back, but I knew it was my duty to." And back she came. Martha does not remember actually re-entering her body, although that was her intention. She does, however, remember part of the ambulance ride, although she passed out again before reaching the hospital.

Like many others who have had this kind of experience, Martha came away with the conviction that there was no reason to be frightened of death. "If that's what death is, how could anybody be scared of it?"

THE ADVOCATE'S CASE

Enough of preliminaries! We proceed now to our major business, namely establishing the truth and meaning of NDEs beyond a reasonable doubt.

DEFINING THE NDE

The experiences of my mother, George Ritchie, and Martha N. had particulars of their own, but were similar in important respects to what many others have reported. We will now review some of the major compilations and studies of NDEs and see why these provide good evidence for survival of death.

THERE AND BACK: THE NEAR-DEATH EXPERIENCE

Let us first dispose of one objection that critics have enjoyed waving about. They suggest that the popularity of Moody's first book stimulated suggestible people to offer over-imaginative reports. So appealing were these experiences that almost everybody wanted to hear one, if he couldn't have one of his own, and supply soon increased to meet the demand – or so goes the criticism.

Not so! First of all, this objection does not account for the first set of NDEs that Moody collected and shared: they had not read his book! More importantly, similar experiences have been related by people in many cultures over the centuries. Frederick H. Holck, [4] for example, a professor of religious studies, has found numerous examples of NDE-like accounts in religion and folklore. Reports given to Moody in the 1970s and incidents that occurred many centuries ago and in diverse places are comparable. Among Holck's examples is the Dream of Scipio in Cicero's treatise *On the Republic*. In this episode, Scipio not only hears majestic music (as happened in one of the reports cited by Moody) but is also given a 'music of the spheres' explanation by one of his dead ancestors.

Other examples are found in *Bardo Thodol*, better known as *The Tibetan Book of the Dead*, in sacred Zoroastrian and Buddhist writings, in St Paul's vision, and in a number of citations from American Indians, the Dayaks of Borneo, the Maoris, and so on. There are correspondences between the experiences of people in our own time who have returned from the borderlands of death and what has been told by other men and women long before Moody and his book.

Holck discovered four especially common similarities between the new wave of NDEs and previous reports:

- The experience of leaving one's body – accompanied by the sense of having a 'spiritual body'.
- A meeting or reunion with departed friends and ancestors.
- An experience with a light of dazzling brightness.
- Discovering a dividing line or border between two worlds of experience.

Martha's experience clearly included the first two of these, and implied the fourth. She did not report the experience with a bright light, but it is found in many cases collected by Moody and others.

In addition, some contemporary people with NDEs had no previous knowledge of this phenomenon. This was true of most of the people who confided their experiences to Moody, and also of many who have since been studied by physicians and behavioural scientists. Despite the media attention that followed the publication of Moody's book, there are still people who could not invent an NDE even if they wanted to for the simple reason that they have never heard of one.

To claim that NDEs are somehow manufactured or are embellishments of more ordinary experiences also ignores how most such experiences are shared. Typically, people who have had an NDE keep it to themselves. This is partly because of fear that others will think it a bizarre and 'crazy' episode, and partly because it is too precious to share with those who are not prepared to value it properly. Those who would acquire NDE reports must usually first establish a relationship of trust, making it clear that it is safe to share this experience just as it happened. Perhaps more people are now willing to share their experiences as a result of recent public attention to the phenomenon, but the experiences themselves must be reckoned with.

The fact that NDEs have been reported from antiquity right up to the present time indicates that we are in the presence of something substantial. Now we add the important fact that there is such great commonality among these reports. Despite differences of culture and circumstances, people who have been brushed by death tend to return with similar memories. The similarities are even more remarkable when we consider how difficult it must be to find the right words to convey such exceptional experiences; our ordinary language and set ways of thinking often falter before the highly personal and unusual.

Moody has described for us an 'ideal' or 'complete' NDE. In practice, most reports include some but not all of these elements, yet they are all relatively common. In a complete NDE, you would actually hear yourself being pronounced dead by the physician. This would be followed by an uncomfortable noise of some kind, usually a loud ringing or buzzing. While hearing this noise, you would sense yourself moving rapidly through a long dark tunnel. Next, you find yourself outside your own body but still in the same physical environment. You would observe your body as though a spectator while resuscitation attempts are being made. Eventually, you would become more accustomed to your new condition and learn how to function with a spiritual rather than a physical body. Still later, you would have company: visitations from the spirits of deceased friends and relations. They are all trying to help you.

At the peak of the experience is the glimpse of "a loving, warm spirit of a kind ... never encountered before – a being of light ... This being asks you to evaluate your life and helps you along by showing you a panoramic, instantaneous playback of the major events of your life." You find yourself approaching a barrier or border between earthly life and the life to come. You resist going back, even though you have learned that your time is yet to come. Finally, you do return to your physical body, and with intense feelings of joy and peace.

We do not have to rely on the reports gathered by Moody which, as he himself admits, were not obtained under controlled scientific conditions. Fortunately, there have been other independent investigations of the phenomenon. By and large, the portrait of NDEs other researchers have painted bears a close resemblance to Moody's reports.

CLINICAL DOCUMENTATION OF NDEs

One of the first to make an independent check was the University of Florida cardiologist Michael B. Sabom and his colleague, social worker Sarah Kreutziger.[5] They quickly learned that NDEs were unknown to most professional personnel who cared for critically ill people. Next, Sabom and Kreutziger carried out a preliminary study of 50 patients who had suffered a documented near-fatal episode. These people included an equal number of men and women, their ages ranging from 19 to 76. All had been unconscious during the crisis, which most commonly was cardiac arrest followed by resuscitation. Accidents, suicides and a variety of other life-threatening conditions were also represented.

The investigators were careful to avoid leading questions. They wanted the patients to tell their own stories in their own words.

Most of them remembered nothing during their period of unconsciousness. Eleven patients, however, had definite recollections, while unconcious, either of viewing their body from a detached position of height several feet above the ground (autoscopy) and/or of 'travelling' into another region or dimension (transcendence).[5]

All the patients were at first reluctant to discuss their experiences for fear of ridicule, and required assurance and the promise of anonymity before they would speak.

Who were these people with NDEs? Age, sex, religious affiliation, education, social background and psychiatric history proved to be useless information, failing to discriminate between those who did and those who did not have NDEs. It could not be said that only certain kinds of people have NDEs. This early finding (or non-finding, if you like) has been supported by later independent research.

Despite the severe stress and risk the patients were undergoing at the time, their experiences were marked by a predominant sense of calm. "Very cool and peaceful" is the way one person described himself. Another wondered what they were concerned about "because I knew I was all right ... No fear involved at all, in fact, I felt real peaceful ... just as calm as all get out."[5] Essentially, these experiences fit in very well with those told to Moody, neither adding nor subtracting anything substantial. Even though this first study by Sabom and Kreutziger was limited, it did add independent confirmation and a comparison of subjective reports with medical documentation.

Sabom and his colleagues continued their investigation over a five-year period, accumulating 116 documented cases of survival from unconsciousness and a near-fatal episode.[6, 7] Again, cardiac arrest was the most common life-threatening incident, being present in about four out of five cases. Near-death experiences of the Moody type were reported by 61 people, including 29 who felt they had visited a mysterious region of great beauty and meaning.

In this extended study, Sabom took an important step towards verifying NDEs. His new evidence strengthens the case for survival of death. He concentrated on people who had reported not only NDEs but also 'autoscopic' adventures -what others have more often called out-of-the-body experiences. Down there is the physical body, up here is an observing self with a 'spiritual' body, if any. How do we know that this really happens, and is not just a subjective impression? A person might think that he sees his body on the road or the operating table, as well as the actions of the people around him. Perhaps this is an illusion, although a vivid and fascinating one. The solution obviously – is to discover whether what the person thought he had witnessed actually did take place.

The researchers turned to the 32 survivors whose reports included autoscopic experiences. Carefully, they set aside all but six of these cases. Why? Because the reports were too general for close comparison with the actual events that happened during the crisis. In these precious six remaining cases the autoscopic memories were sufficiently detailed for an in-depth comparison. They concluded that "in each of these six cases, the autoscopic observations matched with the actual events, often with remarkable details." Incidentally, although the other 26 cases were considered insufficiently detailed to provide a firm test, their recollections were also in accord with the actual facts.

What shall the rest of us conclude, then? People who were 'dead to the world' in a state of unconsciousness were nevertheless able to give specific and accurate reports. Is this not confirmation that through the NDE one can function in remarkable ways? The validity of autoscopic reports having been demonstrated, one need no longer hesitate to accept the rest of the NDE for what it is – a most comforting visit to the realm of death. While Sabom's recent study may be the first piece of research to verify the accuracy of information gained during the NDE, anecdotal reports are also supportive. It is probable that every investigator of these phenomena has received reports in which the unconscious victim saw and heard things that turned out actually to have taken place. Certainly, there is nothing to stand in the way of further research confirmations except the energy and dedication required to continue these studies.

Sabom's expanded research project also found not only the prevailing sense of peacefulness as an outcome, but also the sense that people had been through a profound experience. He observed that "most commonly death anxiety was dramatically reduced, if not totally eliminated by the NDE. Associated with this decrease in death anxiety was the strong personal conviction that the NDE represented a privileged glimpse of what was to occur at the moment of final bodily death."[6]

Psychiatrists Bruce Greyson and Ian Stevenson[8] studied 78 NDE reports, making use not only of the narratives themselves but also of questionnaires, interviews and medical records. One of their most interesting findings was that people with NDEs had not made a habit of collecting 'psychic' experiences. In comparison with the general population. There were actually fewer episodes in their lives that suggested they were reading somebody's mind, dreaming of events that subsequently happened and the like. The experiences reported during a life-or-death crisis cannot be explained away as the creation of minds habitually tuned to exotic frequencies.

Psychologist Charles A. Garfield[9] has not limited himself to studying people with life-threatening illness. He founded a volunteer counselling service in Berkeley, California, known as the SHANTI project, and has also worked with patients of the University of California Cancer Research Institute. For three years he worked as a counsellor-therapist with 215 cancer patients who subsequently died, getting to know them well and spending three or four hours a week with them for periods ranging from a few weeks to almost two years. Some of these patients reported experiences of the type we have already encountered: seeing a powerful white light, hearing celestial music, meeting a deceased relative or a religious figure.

In keeping with the other studies, these patients described their experiences as "incredibly real, peaceful and beautiful". Others experienced either a tunnel, "the void" or both. Garfield then made a special point of interviewing 36 other patients who had been close to death. Often he was the first person to have a substantial interaction with them after their crisis, which gives his observations particular value. Seven of these patients reported NDEs of the Moody type – and their memories of these experiences remained constant after several more weekly contacts. These observations suggest that NDEs are remembered right away, and are not distorted or embellished later. This gives us even more confidence in such reports.

Information about the NDE continues to accumulate. Psychiatrist Russell Noyes and his colleagues have accumulated several hundred cases in the course of a variety of investigations [10-16]. While the Noyes group hesitates to draw conclusions about survival of death, they have added more cases to the total available for our consideration.

SYSTEMATIC RESEARCH CONFIRMS NDEs

Perhaps the most systematic researcher in this area is Kenneth Ring, a professor of psychology at the University of Connecticut. He has set himself the task of conducting NDE work that will meet all the standards expected of quality research. After publishing several articles on this topic, he brought his methods and findings together in *Life at Death* [17] and followed up with *Heading Toward Omega*.[18] Additionally, he founded The International Association for Near-Death Studies, dedicated exclusively to research and discussion on this topic.

This society publishes *Journal of Near-Death Studies* (previously titled *Anabiosis*).

Ring's findings confirm what we have already learned from other observers. We will concentrate on what he has added to previous knowledge. The particular manner of nearly dying does not seem related to having an NDE. This finding can be set alongside Ring's confirmation of what others have also found, namely, that age, sex, economic status and other individual characteristics likewise do not correlate with the NDE. It cannot be said that NDEs are experienced only by certain kinds of people, or only under certain very specific life-threatening conditions. For example, one does not have to be religious in any conventional sense in order to have an NDE. Taken together, these findings suggest that the NDE represents a phenomenon powerful enough to cut across the individuality of person and situation. Ring himself describes the phenomenon as "robust".

Ring developed a scale to assess the depth of an NDE, which makes it possible to do research in a standard and quantifiable manner. This scale is now being used by other investigators as well. This more refined approach has confirmed Moody's description of the basic NDE. Ring points to the "extraordinary similarity" between Moody's findings and his own. Those who might have hoped that Moody's observations would just go away, then, must now contend with confirmatory independent and systematic research.

One phenomenon mentioned by Moody fairly leaps off the page in Ring's report. The survivors often went through a critical moment of decision: return to life or continue in the new state of peace and joy? Usually the decision was made during a conversation either with God or with a deceased relative. The decision situation typically occurred near the end of the NDE and, in fact, seemed to be the concluding event. Going back to take care of one's family, especially young children, was the most common reason for the decision to return. Ring comments that "the decision whether to return to life is usually made in an atmosphere that has a very definite otherworldly ambience. A specifically religious interpretation is given to it by many, though not all, of the experiencers."[17]

SPIRITUAL REBIRTH WITHOUT FEAR OF DEATH

Through his interviewees, Ring has much to say about the consequences of the NDE. Most of the survivors returned with a heightened appreciation of life. There was a sense of rebirth and a new sense of purpose, although not always easy to put into words. Feeling stronger and more confident, the survivor is less disturbed by the small problems of everyday life and more compassionate towards others. While these changes were typical for all people who had had close calls with death, they were most pronounced for survivors who had had an NDE.

Does the survivor also become more religious? Yes, reports Ring, in the 'inward' sense of religion. This change in attitudes and values, however, occurred only among those who had had a substantial NDE – just coming close to death and returning was not enough to generate religiosity. The NDE experiencers felt no closer to the external forms of religion. In fact, they often observed that ritual and dogma now seemed to stand in the way of what they had learned to be true through their own experiences. The NDE seemed to awaken a sense of a cosmic religious feeling, rather than allegiance to any single established religion.

Belief in life after death increased tremendously among those survivors who had had an NDE. As a group, they went from an average position of 'not sure' to 'strongly convinced'. Survivors who had not had an NDE did not change their original beliefs. This shows, according to Ring, that "it is not 'merely' coming close to death that tends to convince one that there is life after death; it is, apparently, the core experience itself that proves decisive." [17] Similarly, there was a sharp decrease in fear of death among survivors with an NDE, but not among those who returned without such an experience.

THE NDE IS A DIRECT PERCEPTION OF UNIVERSAL REALITIES

And what does Ring himself make of the whole pattern of findings, his own and others? He interprets the NDE as a direct perception of reality that has been granted to the individual because of his temporary freedom from dependence on the physical body. In this condition, one escapes the routine perception of the world forced on us by our experiences and bodily limitations and can appreciate the basic structure of the universe. Ring makes use of a theory developed by the distinguished neurobiologist Karl Pribram.[19-20] Our brains function in a holographic manner. We are biologically equipped to register and interpret the complex frequencies which comprise the universe and 'translate' these into usable sensory experience.

In *The Holotropic Mind*,[21] Psychologist Stanislav Grof has demonstrated how our understanding of human consciousness must take into account spiritual as well as biological realities. Out-of-the-body experiences and other characteristics of the NDE are not freakish or pathological, but reveal to us some of the insufficiently appreciated potentials of the human mind.

Influential and up-to-date scientific theories such as those of Pribham and Grof can help us to understand the relationship between the NDE and ordinary experience. One does not have to dismiss the NDE as a peculiar, much less a faulty, view of reality. Rather, the NDE offers a strikingly realistic view of reality that eludes our usual perceptions.

Ring courageously examines all the major aspects of the NDE, including the perception of light at the end of the tunnel. His conclusion is that the light phenomenon might well represent "a glimpse of this astral reality".[17]

Indeed, light and spiritual revelation have been closely associated throughout the centuries. The NDE tunnel experience has much in common with mystical experiences that have transfigured the lives of those fortunate enough to have them. Take, for example, the Vision of Salvius, a medieval experience as recorded by Gregory of Tours and quoted by Carol Zeleski:

> *Four days ago, when the cell shook, and you saw me lifeless, I was taken up by two angels and carried up to the height of heaven, and it was just as though I had beneath my feet not the squalid earth, but also the sun and moon, the clouds and stars. Then I was brought through a gate that was brighter than our light, into a dwelling place where the entire floor shone like gold and silver;* **there was an ineffable light** *and it was indescribably vast. (my emphasis)*

"There is light at the end of the tunnel" is a common message of hope to people who are frustrated and discouraged. It is also the most salient message of both NDEs and similar experiences of a transcendent reality.

The NDE is one of the ways God or Nature employs to awaken us to the cosmic dimensions of our lives. This must surely be our conclusion.

CHILDREN, THE TEMPORAL LOBE, AND THE GLOW OF GOD

Impressive new evidence has been provided by a professor of pediatric medicine. Melvin Morse has studied NDEs in both children and adults. Furthermore, he has elucidated the interconnection between the spiritual experience and its accompanying brain activity.

Morse first answered an important question in a decisive manner. His daily work brought him into contact with children who were afflicted with life-threatening conditions. He was a physician trying to save lives and facilitate the healing process, not a researcher. Nevertheless, he found himself in the position to make significant observations, and these led to the conclusion that children as well as adults can have NDEs.

His first such observation occurred in dramatic circumstances. Morse was attempting to resuscitate Katie, a girl who had been found floating in a YMCA pool. She was unresponsive, and nobody knew how long she had been in the water or why the accident had occurred. Here is an excerpt from Morse's description of the episode:[23]

I was trying to thread a small catheter into one of her arteries so we could get an exact reading of the oxygen in her blood. The procedure, called arterial catheterization, is particularly difficult and bloody since an incision into an artery is required.

Morse suggested that her family wait outside until the line was inserted. They made a counterproposal: could they hold a prayer vigil around her bed?

Why not? I thought. She's going to die anyway. Maybe this will help them cope with their grief. The family held hands around her bed and began to pray. Katie lay flat and lifeless as breathing machines and monitors beeped and buzzed and several IV tubes gave her fluids and medications ...

One push of the needle and blood began spurting from the arterial line ... the calmest people in the room were the members of Katie's family. As the blood spurted out, they began praying out loud.

How can they be so calm? I thought. Isn't it obvious that she is going to die? Three days later she made a full recovery. (pp. 4-5)

The miraculously recovered girl had an astonishing memory for the medical procedures that taken place. Despite the fact that "her eyes had been closed and she had been profoundly comatose during the entire experience. She still 'saw' what was going on." When questioned about her experience in the swimming pool, she replied, "Do you mean when I visited the Heavenly Father?" Katie became embarrassed after making that statement and would say no more that day. Later she gave a more extended account of her NDE. This included her meeting with a guardian angel by the name of Elizabeth. Katie had wanted to stay with The Heavenly Father, but when Jesus asked if she wanted to see her mother again, she said yes, and then she awoke.

This compelling episode led Morse to be alert to other possible NDEs in children, and these he did find both in his own practice and in reports from others. The fact that children are capable of having NDEs and that their reports have much in common with those of adults adds much to the already powerful case for NDEs as proof of survival.

Morse and his colleagues next proposed a valuable theory regarding the biophysical correlates of the NDE.[24] Traditional scientists are not likely to be comfortable with verbal reports alone. They want to know how NDEs and other unusual states of being can take place within our central nervous system. This is the essence of his theory:

- Previous studies have found that stimulation of the temporal lobe of the brain produces the sensations of spontaneous memories, beautiful music, religious visions, and hallucinations. Out of the body experiences can also be produced by the electrical stimulation of neuronal connections within the temporal lobe.

- There are direct links between the temporal lobe and the midbrain area, especially the hippocampus. This is significant because structures in the midbrain play a key role in the processing of information, memories, and dreams. As Morse and his colleagues put it, this is the part of the brain "most associated with a sense of consciousness or soul".
- Neurochemical changes occur in the midbrain when the individual is under psychological stress or when psychoactive substances have been introduced into the body. The brain responds to these challenges through its serotonin system and possibly by other related changes as well. Serotonin is a substance that is involved in the transmission of signals within the central nervous system, technically, a monoamine neurotransmitter.
- Close brushes with death – and other emotional stressful situations – activate the brain's natural defense mechanism in which serotonin release figures prominently. This process includes the disinhibition of a specific set of neurons in the temporal lobe. It is this disinhibition or release of control that leads to out of the body experiences and hallucinations. The potential for NDEs and some other altered states of consciousness always exists within our brains.

Here, then, is a sophisticated scientific explanation for the physical side of the NDE. In his most recent book[25], Morse takes the next step. He reveals the connection between the physical and the spiritual facets. *Transformed by the Light* includes new case histories based on the largest study ever conducted of people with NDEs. The respondents ranged in age from 20 to 70 and over. The total of 350 respondents included several different samples: 100 adults whose NDEs had occurred in childhood, and 50 each in the following categories:

- NDEs when seriously ill in childhood.
- Seriously ill as children, but no NDEs.
- Interested in NDEs and New Age phenomena, but who had never been seriously ill or had a visionary experience.
- Simple out of the body experiences as children or adults.
- Visionary or mystical experiences as children, but not in the context of illness.
- Normal adults, mostly the white, suburban, middle-class parents of the children in his medical practice.

The respondents were given a set of measures concerned with their anxiety levels, coping styles, values, and related variables. It was found that the NDE was a transforming event. For example, "those who had childhood NDEs radiate well-being." Furthermore, the results made it clear that NDEs are a very special kind of visionary episode. "Ordinary visionary experiences" – if we can use that odd phrase – have their effects. According to Morse, these experiences can decrease death anxiety and hint that there is survival after death, in a vague sort of way. By contrast, the person who survives a NDE "is irrevocably altered for life."

Morse's findings serve as an impressive confirmation and extension of the early studies by Ring and other investigators: having a NDE is a profound and transfiguring personal experience, and in a very positive sense. With this fact well established, Morse's next task was to complete his explanation of the NDE process – and a further proof of survival.

> *When we reveal the right temporal lobe as the place in the brain where the NDE occurs, we are talking about the spot where the mind, body, and spirit interact. We are talking about the area that houses the very spark of life itself.*[25] (p.195)

The experience of "this loving white light" is the most significant element in the NDE, according to Morse. It demonstrates the reality of our dual nervous systems. During everyday life we use our basic biochemical nervous system. This is guided by the left side of our brain – with the left temporal lobe being especially important. We have another, more subtle nervous system as well, however. This is a "subtle, electromagnetic nervous system which is responsible for healing bone breaks, regeneration of body tissue, and the psychosomatic linkages between the brain and the body."

At the moment of death, the biochemical nervous systems ceases to function. This produces a disinhibition – a release – of the usually silent electromagnetic nervous system. Often this is the first time the person has experienced his or her alternative nervous system in operation. The right temporal lobe is now on the job. The light it shines upon us is what Morse calls "the glow of God". Actually, it was one of his patients who described the experience in this way, and Morse recognized that this was the perfect term.

The NDE, then, is a kind of premortem bonus. A stressful, life-threatening situation has activated a function of the nervous system that ordinarily does not operate until one is close to death. This is both a physical and a spiritual experience. The survivor is a happier, less anxious, and, it may not be going too far to say, better person. Understandably, Morse urges us to trust this vision.

And so what have we learned? We have seen that independent investigators verify not only the reality but also the specific characteristics of NDEs. We have seen that ordinary explanations for these experiences fail – they cannot be dismissed as a merely physical reaction to crisis or oddities produced by the personal and social characteristics of the individual. We have seen that these experiences are profound events that lead to a deepened appreciation of life and a heightened sense of one's place in the cosmos. We have seen that modern scientific theory can interpret the NDE as an astoundingly direct viewing of reality. We have seen behavioural scientists go as far as they can toward endorsing the NDE as proof of survival, and lending their own knowledge and beliefs to make up the difference. Perhaps most compellingly, we have learned from the survivors that 'death' is not to be feared, because, in some vital sense, 'death' is not 'death' after all.

THE CRITIC'S RESPONSE

Nothing! We have learned nothing about death from all the NDEs that have been reported, analysed and published. Furthermore, ten thousand additional cases, or ten million, would not alter this conclusion. We still would have learned no more about death than we knew at the start, little though that might be.

Does this conclusion seem harsh? Perhaps so. Those who prefer sweet illusion might as well return to slumber in their 'strawberry fields forever' and stop reading here. However, those are willing and able to exercise their "traditional biochemical brains" should certainly proceed. It will be seen that the negative conclusion is the only one that evidence and logic support.

WHY THE NDE TELLS US NOTHING ABOUT DEATH

The NDE is to be taken seriously – it is no hoax or fad. There is, however, an enormous difference between the experience as an experience and as supposed evidence for immortality.

Notice first that some people have close calls with death and yet do not return with a Moody-type NDE. In fact, most survivors fall into this category. To their credit, all the researchers report that the classic or core NDE is mentioned by only a fraction of those who have recovered from a life-or-death crisis. Ring had difficulty (which he acknowledges) in establishing his final sample, so his findings cannot be claimed as representative of all those who have survived close brushes with death. Within this unbalanced sample of respondents, Ring found that 48 per cent had the sort of NDE that interested him.

Sabom found 52 per cent in his extended sample, but only 22 per cent with marked NDE features in the original study. Only 22 per cent of Garfield's patients had NDEs and some of these were quite different from the Moody type. Dobson, Tattersfield and Adler[26] found only 5 per cent in a study carried out prior to the publication of Moody's book. Noyes and his colleagues found a "mystical" experience resembling the Moody type in 36 per cent of accident victims who had come close to death. The percentages themselves are not that crucial. The key point is that many people fail to report the Moody-type NDE. This point is particularly applicable to studies (e.g. Greyson and Stevenson[8]) that advertise for people who have had NDEs and which consider no other groups.

Two recent sets of researchers[27,28] made a determined effort to identify people with NDEs in carefully monitored hospital situations. These studies were intended to provide information that is more useful than memories that are recalled long after the event. Most NDE studies have relied upon memories of events that took place years before. Patients who survive cardiopulmonary resuscitation and other critical procedures should be excellent prospects for NDE reports. What happened? Neither team could find enough patients with NDEs to draw any conclusions – other than the scarcity of such reports when one is right there waiting for them.

If the NDE tells us something about death, why are so many people silent on this subject?

And shouldn't everybody have the same experience?

Several researchers have emphasized that characteristics of person or situation do not seem related to the occurrence of NDEs. This makes their non-occurrence just as hard to explain as their occurrence. A hard-pressed advocate might argue that everybody does have an NDE when life is in jeopardy, but that some people, well, they just forget. Such an excuse hardly recommends itself, especially when we bear in mind that the core NDE makes such a pleasant, even ecstatic, memory. The advocate would have to add to an already shaky excuse an explanation as to why people should forget pleasant rather than unpleasant events. The further one pursues this line of reasoning, the more unpromising it becomes. How much more convincing it would be if everybody came back from a near-death episode with a near-death experience!

"INVERTED" NDEs: ROUND-TRIPS FROM HELL?

The problem here is not just with the non-reports. It is also with different kinds of reports. Garfield, you will remember, in general had a closer relationship to the people he studied than did the other early investigators. He had the chance to know them better. Interestingly, he is also the most explicit in sharing NDEs of a less attractive variety. Some of the people he worked with experienced "demonic figures, nightmarish images of great lucidity". Still another group reported "dreamlike images, sometimes 'blissful', sometimes 'terrifying', sometimes alternating."[8] Obviously, there are 'bad trips' along with the more reassuring kind.

Concerned more with helping than with studying people, Garfield emphasizes this negative aspect again:

Not everyone dies a blissful, accepting death. My friend's tortuous, labored breathing during the twenty-four hours before she died hardly appeared blissful. I hope those who suggest that she was really 'feeling no pain' thanks to the 'immunity' provided by her comatose state or

*because she was really 'out of her body' are correct. However, **almost
as many of the dying patients I interviewed reported
negative visions (encounters with demonic figures and so
forth) as reported blissful experiences, while some reported
both.***[8] (emphasis added)

In working with people who were undergoing life-threatening crises, my
colleagues and I also observed some who were tormented rather than
comforted by their memories of these experiences.

Is it possible that Garfield's observations and mine were based on
unusual samples that do not represent the larger population of people
with NDE reports? Advocates liked to think so. They did not deny the
occurrence of occasional "bad trips", but thought these to be rare. It is
no longer possible to persist in this belief. An accumulation of more
recent reports makes it clear that negative NDEs – which are now
starting to be called "inverted" – are rather common. People just did
not want to talk about or listen to these frightening accounts.

"Inverted" NDEs are now being taken seriously.[29] The Fall, 1994
issue of *Journal of Near-Death Studies* is devoted to this topic. In the lead
article, Ring defines the inverted NDE as:

*... merely an experience that has exactly the same form as the classic
NDE, but is perceived in terms of a negatively-toned affective filter.
That is, the person reports all the usual events – having an out-of-the-
body experience, going through a tunnel, encountering a light, and so
on – but responds to these features from a standpoint of fear rather than
peaceful acceptance.*[30] *(p. 7)*

I like best the "merely" part. Recognition that hellish experiences are
common "merely" explodes the wish-fulfilling inference that death is a
lovely place to be as proven by NDEs. If Moody and other early NDE-
gatherers had given us a reasonable helping of hellish reports I doubt
there would now be such as thriving industry that is devoted to selling
us on the NDE as proof for survival of death.

What are advocates to do, given that inverted reports have now been
acknowledged? Let us not underestimate the true believer. This is what
they are doing: blaming the victims.

*... the answer already seems clear ... The person who responds this
way is likely to be terrified by the prospect of losing one's ego in the
process. As a result, the experience of dying is resisted strenuously
rather than being surrendered to. It is this very resistance that creates
the filter of increasing fear that comes to pervade the entire experience.
(op. cit.)*

The message is clear. If we are dead for a while and don't enjoy it, why,
it's clearly our own fault! We should surrender to the dying process if
we want to be blissfully dead. How unenlightened, how crude it would

be of us to resist dying! If Ring's logic rings a bell with you, then please inquire about certain highly desirable Arizona desert property that I might let you purchase for a pittance of its true worth.

The blaming-the-victim strategy is only part of the effort that is being made to rescue the politically correct version of the NDE from irksome contrary reports. For example, Ring is pleased to announce that inverted NDEs have a tendency to turn themselves right side up over time. (This reshaping to accord with socially desirable expectations would not surprise nor especially impress memory experts.) There was still a bit of awkwardness to deal with, though. Some NDEs are not only inverted but *hellish*. The experiencer feels as though he or she had actually been undergoing the terror and torments of a demon-ridden hell. From the advocate's standpoint, what is really disturbing about such reports is that they do not seem to change to a more peaceful experience. Ring felt that he must challenge this conclusion, even though it was offered by one of the most respected NDE researchers, Bruce Greyson. He certainly works hard at this task. After labyrinthian assertions he emerges with this gem:

> *Frightening NDEs, therefore, though they are by definition scary, aren't real. Only the Light of the NDE is. In fact, the only thing that is keeping you from the Light right now are your illusions about what is real (op. cit. p. 16)*

Well done, oh, Ring-leader! You have already concluded that it is our own damn stupid fault if we do not enjoying dying and death. Now you leap into the middle of our lives and condemn our ideas about what is real as "illusions."

What is really scary here? Not the hellish NDEs because, according to Ring, they are not real, although they are reported as intensely and sincerely as the politically correct NDEs. The really scary thing is that the person who first attempted to bring scientific method and logic to the study of NDE reports is now blinded by the glare of his own beliefs and insists upon imposing them on others no matter what strange turns of thought and persuasion might be required. We had all better buy into Ring's conception of eternal bliss – or else!

WE DON'T NEED TO DIE FOR AN NDE

The case for the NDE as evidence of survival is further weakened by a fact readily acknowledged by many investigators and scholars: the mental state characteristic of the core NDE also occurs under other circumstances. One does not have to be on the verge of physical death to witness the blinding light, encounter spirit beings or have the sense of wandering away from one's body. Such a state often occurs in the sacred literature of both the East and the West and among individuals who have attained a 'mystical' experience independent of any particular religious belief. Furthermore, people have often sought and attained such a state through hallucinogenic drugs (as well as through fasting, withdrawing into the wilderness and other actions). Medical psychologist Ronald Siegel[31] has shown that imagery similar if not identical to the NDE can be produced by commonly used anaesthetics in the operating room as well as by peyote and other known hallucinogens.

It is clear that altered states of consciousness can have the characteristics associated with the NDE. Additionally, the autoscopic or out-of-the-body experience has been observed in the absence of any danger to life, and has also been 'made to order' through guided imagery. Karlis Osis,[32] one of the world's most respected parapsychologists, has for years conducted controlled experiments in which a few people with special talents along this line seem to acquire information by somehow transcending their physical location in space. Osis' research on this subject has not been fully accepted by the scientific community, and understandably so. To accept his work as valid might require a radical re-examination of what we think we know about physics, physiology and psychology.

Nevertheless, Osis' research is a model of its kind. The experimental controls he exerts in his laboratory are certainly superior to what has been available to NDE hunters in their complex, uncontrollable clinical situations. Scientists are still not ready to accept Osis' well controlled studies of the autoscopic experience within the laboratory and with no assumptions about life everlasting. Why, then, are some of us so quick to credit observations made and reported catch-as-catch-can in uncontrolled clinical situations?

The case for the NDE as evidence of survival is weakened by Osis' research – whether or not we are ready to accept his findings. If we reject his findings, then how can we turn round and accept the autoscopic reports from clinical studies that begin after the fact (after the supposed experience itself) and exercise little control? And if we accept Osis' findings, then we must reject the conclusion that a close encounter with death is necessary to have such an experience. Either way, something important has been lost for the advocacy of the NDE as proof of survival. The problem is increased by the fact that some people are able to achieve autoscopic experiences simply by being invited to and being given some helpful suggestions by way of guided imagery.[33]

Understandably, we tend to be impressed by what a person returned from the near-dead has to tell us. The drama of the situation can even threaten to overwhelm logic. However, if similar or identical experiences are related by people who have not come close to death, then the power of the near-death situation over our minds diminishes considerably.

Let us ask another question. Who should be more likely to have an NDE – the person who objectively is very close to death, or the person who is in less extreme jeopardy of his life? By definition and usage, the closer to death, the more impressive the NDE. One study has addressed this question specifically. Greyson[8] found that the survivors' subjective sense of being close to death was not related to the depth or completeness of their NDEs. Furthermore people who objectively had been in a less perilous situation were more likely to report NDEs in the first place! In effect, this study distinguished between Near and Very Near Death Experiences – and the results indicate that fewer memories are reported the closer the individual actually has been to death. This single study should not be taken as definitive. Nevertheless, the survival hypothesis is certainly not strengthened by results which show that people who are very close to death have fewer experiences to report.

HOLD THAT PARADE! THE WAR HAS NOT BEEN WON!

There are additional problems with the NDE approach to survival. Take, for example, a methodological issue that could hardly be more obvious: *NDEs are reported only by people who complete the round-trip to the borderlands of death and back.* This is an undisputed fact. And this undisputed fact by itself undermines the claim that NDEs provide evidence for survival of death. We have absolutely no basis for assuming that the experience at the time of actual death – final, irrevocable death – is similar to the reports that have faithfully collected by Moody, Ring and many others. A person who is willing to make such an unsupportable assumption must also be adept at counting fairies at the bottom of the garden.

Ten thousand cases of vivid NDEs tell us nothing dependable about what experience, if any, a person has when death 'lives up' to its reputation for finality. Nowhere in all the reports and all the statistics on NDEs is there one scrap of evidence that the experiences of those who returned from a supposed NDE are the same as those – the great majority – who died and stayed dead. Researchers would be wasting their time in the hope that more cases, more numbers will change this situation. This is a fundamental flaw in NDE research – namely that we learn only from the returnees – and no viable alternative has been suggested.

Actually, few researchers are still trying to prove that NDEs provide evidence of survival. Most studies reported in past several years have dealt only with secondary aspects of NDE reports that do not attempt to test the survival hypothesis. Read for yourself the *Journal of Near-Death Experiences* and you will find that most contributors simply assume that the central question has already been settled. This attitude is akin to declaring a great military victory after holding a rally, a parade, and firing a few random shots into the darkness. It is pretty ridiculous to continue to spin stories about stories instead of facing up to the daunting methodological challenges that remain for those who would establish NDEs as proof of survival by accepted scientific and logical criteria.

Consider, for example, another obvious problem that the NDE fanciers persist in ignoring: all those who have reported NDEs did, in fact, have viable physical bodies remaining to them. No reports have come from people whose bodies were absolutely destroyed by, say, explosion, avalanche or fire. The expression of mind has invariably depended on a relatively intact, if jeopardized, body. Were the 'spiritual body' really as free as some believe then this strict dependence on an intact physical body should not be necessary. Advocates may enthuse about holograms until the cows come home, but they will still be expecting real cows who will give real milk on the morrow. They would feel cheated if they were told to content themselves with a phantom herd, even if this herd could moo about the most remarkable experiences.

Are you ready to believe that there are merely dead people and really dead people! The merely dead would be those who return to their bodies – they had just been visiting The Great Beyond. The merely dead would, occasionally, have stories for us, and, occasionally, these stories would be pleasant. The really dead, however, would be those who have neither stories nor bodies. These are the ones whose NDEs would be of most interest – but then we would already be in the next chapter, playing tag with ghosts. I for one am not ready to distinguish between the merely and the really dead. People who have NDE reports to share with us are people whose bodies were still intact and capable of life.

Here now is a problem that is not quite so obvious. In fact, it seems to have escaped all the researchers and advocates of NDEs as evidence of survival. No NDE study has pinned down *precisely when* the experience actually occurred. Most studies think they have – but what they have settled for is only the period of time when the person's life was in greatest jeopardy. This will not do. It cannot be assumed that the time of prime jeopardy is equivalent to the time at which the individual had a NDE.

What little we actually know about the NDE comes to us as a form of memory – and much is known about memory in its biological and psychosocial aspects. Memory is not a simple, automatic, and passive process. The act of remembering calls upon a set of complex processes.[34] It is not at all like plunking a coin into a vending machine, selecting a memory-item, and having that item tumble down to us. It is a lot closer to the truth to think of the brain as a salesperson who rummages through the available stock of information and impressions, hoping to come up with something that we will buy. The brain searches its data bank rapidly and creatively. Many possible memory-fragments are evaluated and combined in various ways. If we do not accept the first memory that pops into mind, then the brain must go back to constructing another memory. "You didn't like that one? All right, give me a minute and I'll come up with one that you will like better!"

Remembering is not only an active and constructive but also a purposeful activity. "I want to recall that song title so I can win the prize on this quiz show!" "I want a childhood memory that will make me feel good about my parents." "I want a memory that will explain what happened to me because it's a terrible feeling to go through something so powerful and not know what it was."

Remembering, and forgetting, are functions we carry out in the midst of our lives and are subject to many influences. Our memories may go through several phases before reaching a more or less permanent form. Moreover, a memory may be attributed to a different time or place. The person may have a firm grasp of certain aspects of the memory – what somebody's face looked like, how the music sounded, etc. but not place it accurately within its original context. There is a distinction, in other words, between memory content and what might be called the 'memory frame', the time and place in which the individual locates it. Making errors in which we attribute otherwise accurate memories to the wrong time or place (or even person) is not unusual in daily life. Making such misattributions is much more likely under the exceptional circumstances experienced by survivors of near-death.

MORSE'S DUAL NERVOUS SYSTEM THEORY

Morse's neurophysiological theory proposes that we have dual nervous systems. This is an imaginative and provocative theory that deserves further study. Let us suppose for the moment that this theory is substantially correct. Our everyday memories, then, would be processed chiefly by the left temporal lobe and its connections with the hippocampus and other midbrain structures. There is ample evidence that this traditional memory system can make plenty of mistakes, and that these mistakes become increasingly common when we function under pressure and stress. These errors usually involve the ordinary facts of our lives, things we should be expected to recall easily and accurately.

Now let's step into the twilight zone. The alternate nervous system, mediated by the right temporal lobe, comes into dominance under the exceptional stress of a life-threatening situation. Some time afterward (when, of course, we do not know), the survivor has a memory. Is this memory accurate? Is it easier to organize and articulate a memory when, under great stress, we are using a mechanism that has seldom been called upon and which has had no practice in processing everday experiences? Should we accept the *content* or *text* of this memory as a reliable report of *any* reality external to the 'silent' brain's wired-in response?

There is a far more reasonable interpretation. In Morse's own theory, as well as the suggestions of some other investigators, the NDE is viewed

23

as a coping strategy. When this coping strategy is working effectively we feel good instead of terrified. The brain releases good-feeling opiate-type substances, and we return with memories of extraordinary visual and auditory experiences. Furthermore, there is nothing implausible about the possibility that such an experience might lead to a personal transformation. But: back to the *content*. What we have here are not facts that have been reality-checked, but the swirling, entertaining, fascinating stuff of dreams. The snail-like hippocampus and its midbrain neighbors as well as the temporal lobes are in the business of processing dreams as well as waking perceptions. Morse knows this to be true, and includes this fact in developing his theory. It is quite consistent with Morse's own dual nervous system theory to say that the "silent brain" may become a private theater of heavenly light, comforting sounds, and healing-feelings when we are in a life-threatening situation. It is also consistent with this theory to say that this theatrical experience does not provide reality-checked information from either inner or outer sources. The content of the NDE does not provide evidence for any reality. It does not even provide evidence for itself.

The advocate may protest that information linking the memory directly to the near-death episode is too difficult to obtain. The difficulty of obtaining evidence, however, is no reason to accept the relationship without evidence. One might, for example, try to obtain direct descriptions of what is taking place at the very moment when a person is in a life-threatened situation. The electrical brain-stimulation technique pioneered by Wilder Penfield suggests one way of doing this, but there may well be other, less obtrusive, techniques, such as the magnetic resonance devices that have been coming into widespread medical usage. Naturally, I am not recommending doing anything further to imperil or discomfort people who are hovering between life and death. Perhaps , though, we can find a way of enabling them to share their thoughts and feelings as they occur. High-tech communication geniuses – where are you?

NDEs ARE CONSTRUCTED ON THE WAY BACK

Until such time as positive evidence is produced to pinpoint the time of the NDE I will offer the following alternative explanation. The memory is not created in anything like its final form while the person is in the midst of his or her physical crisis. Instead, the memory starts to develop on the way back. The worst of the stress and disorganization is over. Intense feelings and images have been generated, but these do not add up to an integrated memory. The central nervous system starts to work on these residual feelings, trying to reduce the tension associated with them. Sometimes this can best be accomplished by elaborating a kind of 'story' in which all the parts more or less fit. At a more remote point in time, the survivor will then be equipped with what seems to be a mental record of specific experiences that occurred at a specific time. Actually, what the survivor has is the elaboration of an integrated memory-story by higher levels within the nervous system. This elaboration uses various 'raw materials' that include, but are not necessarily limited to, what was experienced during the crisis itself. The memory conforms, then, to the general principles of mental organization. It may be of great interest for a number of reasons. But it does not necessarily correspond to what the person experienced during the peak of the crisis.

Anaesthesiologists sometimes observe that a woman appears by all signs to be in pain and discomfort during the last stages of her labour. Soon after the delivery, she may speak about her pain and fatigue. Over a period of hours and days, however, the first and observed response to the demands of labour vanishes. It is replaced by a memory of 'how wonderful' it had been. This is only one pattern observed during and after labour, but it is instructive. At present we really do not know the relationship between what comes forth as the NDE and what was actually experienced when the person was nearest to death. The 'memory-story' explanation is just as good, if not better in some ways, than the assumption that the experience actually occurred at the moment closest to death.

I SAW ME DEAD

One more problem now. This one by itself is sufficient to sink the NDE as a proof of survival. The only difficulty in understanding this truly critical problem is that it is so simple. Perhaps this is why it has eluded the attention of so many.

Listen again to the NDE, to almost any example. The late Sheldon Ruderman,[35] himself a psychologist, underwent two NDEs several years before Moody's book brought such experiences to general awareness. Ruderman's encounters were extremely vivid. On one occasion he was told that a minor procedure would be carried out to drain fluid from his chest. His surgeon reassured him that the procedure was so trivial that anaesthesia was not necessary. The situation became rather alarming even before the NDE took place.

> *Since this was a teaching hospital, the event would be attended by about twenty five trainees who would stand around the table. For teaching purposes the surgeon would explain each move before he made it. 'What he was explaining ... sounded very much like chest surgery to me. That was obviously impossible; chest surgery requires the patient to be unconscious.'*

Impossible or not, chest surgery it was, preceded by only a shot of novocaine. Ruderman was soon in torment and terror from the very painful surgery that followed. Trying to distract himself from this unbearable experience, Ruderman visualized himself as being somehow above the operating-room scene, lying on an imaginary board extending from the wall.

> *No sooner had I imagined this scene than I found myself watching from that very point in the room, somewhere near the top. It felt perfectly normal ... Yet all of me was not there, since I could still feel cutting and pounding in my body. It was as if I was only half out of my body. I still experienced pain but it seemed muffled. It was as if someone had wrapped a hammer in some padding and hit me with it. That feels differently than being hit with a bare hammer. The image is not accidental: my ribs were being broken. The surgery continued for three hours ... I could see all the people in the room clearly ... The outline of my body was fuzzy...The wound itself was a total blank. It was as if I knew I was not brave enough to look into my own body.*

The horror of the scene is obvious. Also obvious is the split between observer and observed. Ruderman was down there, and Ruderman was also up here. The observing self is present as narrator, as experiencer even when his attention turns away from the body. It is possible to have the observing self without the observed, but not vice versa. And that is the point. In some NDEs the observer-reporter recognizes that the body is in trouble, but not dead (as in this episode), in other instances, the body seems to be devoid of life. In all cases, however, some 'body' or some something is obviously still alive: the observing self.

We would never know that a person saw himself as dead unless his observing – and therefore, not-dead – self had been on the scene. It is possible for any of us to observe another body and say, 'dead'. We cannot do so for ourselves, however, because of the very act of observation. There is activity of mind and this 'falsifies' or contaminates the report of deadness. To put it another way, 'aliveness' has taken refuge more or less completely in the observing self. A person returns to tell us, "I was dead." This is a compelling statement. Nevertheless, it is not an accurate statement The "I" was and is alive, even if there was an element of deadness in the total situation.

On logical and on evidential grounds, then, the NDE tells us nothing at all about death, and, what's more, it probably never will. The NDE is worth our attention as an exceptional human experience, but it has no bearing on the survival question.

THE CORE NDE IS A DEPERSONALIZED RESPONSE TO DANGER

Psychiatrist Russell Noyes and his colleagues[10-16] have contributed a series of studies and observations that place the NDE within its situational context. Like other investigators, they have collected cases of people whose lives were in extreme danger through illness or accident. Unlike most investigators, however, the Noyes group has carefully examined the psychodynamics of the individual's experience within the context of extreme jeopardy to life. In other words, they have not become so caught up in the NDE report itself as to forget what was happening around the individual at the time and how one might respond to overwhelming peril.

Using a statistical technique known as factor analysis, which enables investigators to discover the central commonalities within a large and complex pool of information, Noyes sorted through many individual NDE reports. He discovered three main factors. A *mystical* factor involved experiences of joy, revelation and harmony or unity with the universe. *Hyperalertness,* another distinct factor, referred to unusual speed of thought processes, sharpened vision or hearing, and an altered sense of time's passage. The person's attention was acutely and sharply focused on the dangers being faced, aroused to a heightened sense of vigilance and awareness. The third factor was entirely different. *Depersonalization* was a calm state, curiously without emotional arousal even though the individual was quite aware of the jeopardy faced. It often included the sense of being a detached observer whose only role was to observe what was happening around him and to him, not participating at all. As we will see in a moment, the interaction between the hyperalertness and depersonalization responses is of special interest.

What is most important for us here is the explanation that emerged from these findings. Whenever we become extremely anxious – no matter the cause – we are likely to interpret ourselves as being in danger for our lives. Anxiety arouses fear of death. And the dynamics work just as effectively in the opposite direction: when we are in fact threatened by death we tend to become extremely anxious. The outcome may be the same whether it is anxiety stimulating death fear, or death fear stimulating anxiety. What is one to do?

An important clue has come from another area of human experience in which the individual undergoes both physical and psychological events of unusual force. Roth and Harper[36] studied people afflicted with epilepsy centred in the temporal lobes of the brain. They suggested the existence of a neural or brain mechanism that helps the individual to cope with the psychophysiological stress involved in epileptic seizures and possibly in other situations as well. According to Roth and Harper, when one is faced with a dangerous circumstance a mechanism enables us to become either unusually vigilant or unusually distant ('dissociated' is the technical psychiatric term). Most useful of all is the response which makes someone both highly vigilant and also emotionally distant. This represents "an adaptive mechanism that combines opposing reaction tendencies, the one serving to intensify alertness and the other to dampen potentially disorganizing emotion."[36] Let us now follow some of the main steps in

Noyes' integration of results from Roth and Harper's work and from his own:

- Depersonalization, the process of treating one's own body and self as though a foreign object, may be the key element in the adaptive mechanism to life-threatening danger.
- Psychologically, depersonalization is a defence against the threat of death. "The depersonalized state is one that mimics death. In it a person experiences himself as empty, lifeless and unfamiliar. In a sense he creates psychologically the very situation that environmental circumstances threaten to impose."[16]
- The psychological outcome of this manoeuvre can be highly successful: "In so doing he escapes death, for what has already happened cannot happen again; he cannot die, because he is already dead."

The findings of Noyes' studies supported the depersonalization interpretation. The respondents often described themselves as feeling calm in situations that otherwise would have frightened them enormously. They felt more like observers than participants, remote from what was happening to their bodies. This interpretation is also consistent with a large and diverse set of observations made of animals as well as humans. Many creatures have the knack of engaging in thanatomimetic (death-feigning) behaviour when faced with the prospect of actual death. This can take the form of arranging one's body to look as though one is dead, or, in the case of humans, arranging one's thoughts and feelings for the same effect.

Notice that the depersonalization explanation is well rooted in established fields of research and clinical experience. When approached from this standpoint, the NDE does not hover in mid-air as a unique and exotic specimen. Instead, it is seen in relationship to the stress response of both humans and animals, and its key elements have already been identified in other areas of research. No need for us to fumble around in the dark for weirdly glowing explanations left over from the age of ignorance!

We see that the NDE has a purpose to serve: it helps life-endangered people to remove themselves psychologically from situations that would otherwise make them unbearably anxious. Additionally, the sense of calm that accompanies depersonalization enables them to observe what is happening more accurately than if drowning in waves of terror.

Let us also be as clear as possible about the very specific function of depersonalization in the guise of the NDE. As Noyes puts it, "the elusive 'I', or observer of the self, remains one step away from destruction … in the face of death, it seems prepared to sacrifice the entire self in a futile attempt to master the unmasterable." In other words: the ego or 'I' might be compared with a fox whose leg is caught in a trap. When desperate enough, he will try to chew off his own leg, sacrificing that member in the effort to escape. Similarly, 'I' will try to escape by sacrificing 'me' (that body lying motionless on the road or the operating table). This is an understandable manoeuvre in an untenable situation. However, we should not mistake this desperate act of depersonalization for an authentic trip – and round trip at that! – to the realm of the dead.

The work of Noyes, Roth, and Harper preceded the studies and theories of Morse. Nevertheless, they identify an important dimension to Morse's view of the NDE as a protective strategy when under extreme stress. The escape from the experience of trauma and loss is achieved at the cost of the individual's connection to the world and to his/her own self. It is a kind of self-abandonment, a dissociation. In ordinary waking life this would be a pathological response. Whether or not one finds (or is found by) God as part of the NDE, it is clear that one is in danger of losing one's self.

The observing self is homeless. As a dissociated, depersonalized wisp, it no longer belongs to the down to earth world of human interaction. Neither is it an enfranchised citizen of some supernatural realm. A lost, wandering soul it is, mercifully liberated from pain, but without domicile, purpose, or substantiality. This is not so wonderful a picture as the one usually given by NDE advocates.

Doesn't this make you think again of angels? It should. Remember those deathbed escorts? There was the dying person – looking up. There was the angel – looking down. Dying person. Angel. Looking up. Looking down. Same person. So much for deathbed escorts. So much for depersonalized, dissociated observing selves bathed in the light of eternity. The NDE is a split-self phenomenon and, as such, represents an authentic altered state of being but no evidence at all for survival of death.

THE CORE NDE IS PRODUCED BY BIOCHEMICAL EVENTS WITHIN OUR BRAIN

Neuropsychologist Ronald Siegel[31] has observed human response to brain stimulation on the surgeon's table and to a variety of mind-affecting drugs, including those with hallucinogenic effects. He sees a 'strong resemblance' between NDEs from several sources and drug-induced hallucinations and is quite specific about the nature of the resemblance. Hearing voices, for example, is characteristic of surgical patients recovering from anaesthesia as well as of split-off selves on their NDE journeys. Bright, radiant light, so common a feature of the core NDE, is also found in many types of mental imagery and is the result of stimulation of the central nervous system that mimics the effects of light on the retina. It can also occur when the electrical activity in the brain is altered in such a way that the threshold for perception of phosphenes (electrical activity in the visual system) is lowered and bright lights are seen in otherwise dark surroundings. Furthermore, Siegel notes that Lilly[37] has found that similar experiences of bright light also occur when the person is in a situation of sensory isolation.

Siegel finds that several characteristics of the core NDE occur in the presence of hallucinogenic drugs, anaesthesia, sensory deprivation and other types of altered mental state. These include the popular out-of-the-body or autoscopic experience, meeting 'spirit guides' and beholding cities of light or other vivid geometric patterns. All such experiences have been documented as occurring in situations in which death was not in prospect. Take, for example, the phenomenon of meeting dead relatives or famous religious personages. Siegel reminds us that "neither the fact that such relatives may be dead now nor the fact that such religious figures may never have existed proves that they are alive and well in the hereafter." What, then, do these experiences mean? "Rather, [they] support the argument that deathbed visions are retrieved memory images (or fantasy images) that were alive and well when originally stored." [31] There is no occasion and certainly no firm evidence or logical connection for assuming that the hallucinating person actually met what might be called 'real spirits'.

Siegel draws on research into the nervous system that dates back to the mid-nineteenth century. Winters,[38] for example, found that excitation and arousal of the central nervous system led to temporary disorganization of the brain's ability to regulate incoming stimuli – with hallucinations as the outcome. What happens is that the experiencer mistakes internal sensations and imagery within his brain for external stimuli. It is easy to be 'fooled' in this way, because the normal balance of internal and external stimuli has been upset. One responds to internal stimuli as though they were 'out there' in the world.

Many aspects of the dying or near-death situation can produce this type of functional disorganization. Fever, anaesthetics, depletion and fatigue, and sensory isolation often occur. We might also add that the individual's sense of his or her basic relationship to the body is likely to be changed under these circumstances, increasing susceptibility to altered states of consciousness. With little opportunity or ability to act upon his actual physical environment, the person close to death may shift over to private thoughts. This increasing subjectivity contributes to the imbalance between internal and external stimuli, once again increasing the likelihood of mental wanderings, including the now famous NDEs.

The hallucinogenic basis of NDEs centers, then, on electrical activity in the central nervous system, but also takes close account of transactions between the individual and his or her environment. The depersonalization theory is not at all inconsistent with this approach. In fact, Siegel cites studies of drug and anaesthesia effects which indicate that dissociation and depersonalization can be produced through biochemical means. Users of PCP (Angel Dust), a very dangerous 'recreational drug', have reported experiences of serenity amidst images of death and nothingness.[39] The individual who finds himself in a situation of high stress and danger might resort to depersonalization on the basis of both psychological and biochemical factors.

Siegel may have overstated his case, however. There is evidence that hallucinatory experiences that occur during some types of drug-induced conditions are different in significant respects from the classic NDE. Morse and others have made this case, and it is one that should be taken seriously. Memories that have some important features in common with NDEs do occur under some biochemical conditions in which one's life is not in danger. Whether or not the classic NDE is a totally different experience or just a variant of our hallucinatory response capabilities is a question that has not yet been firmly answered.

THE CORE NDE IS THE SURFACING OF CULTURAL AND RACIAL FANTASIES

Very early in life we absorb attitudes, expectations and fantasies from those around us from our immediate family, but also from our culture at large. This process continues through the years, but we are most susceptible to influence at two points in the life-span: when we are quite young and therefore have little ability to compare and criticize what is presented to us; and during adolescence when we are forging our grown-up selves and considering the shape of our futures. From this point onwards we travel with a set of images, dispositions and expectations that are always ready to insert themselves into our conscious lives.

Episodes of stress, fatigue and danger invite these images to break through, perhaps even to seize command. The NDE can be understood as a release of cultural and racial fantasies, just as much as it can be a release of individual perceptions and memories. At the deeper levels of mind we carry images and tendencies that seldom present themselves to our conscious awareness. Some of these images go beyond our own personalities, representing an unconscious heritage that has been passed along down the ages through our culture.

The stress and danger of a life-threatening situation require the most powerful response the individual can develop. Ordinary conscious thought and action may not be sufficient, and have often been impaired or interrupted. In seeking a deeper response, the imperilled human organism reaches into its store of both personal and universal images and symbols. These provide a subjective sense of coherence and meaning amidst the objective crisis.

The NDE is a powerful surfacing-into-awareness of residual

symbols, images and fantasies. The particular form these fantasies take will differ somewhat depending on the individual's specific cultural background and personal experiences. However, there will be much in common among NDEs because, in the depths of our minds and in the connections of our central nervous system, we are all made pretty much the same way.

Still another powerful source of imagery streams into the stressed and vulnerable mind. C.G. Jung[40] has made a strong case for the existence of a deep layer of mental/nervous system processes that reaches beyond the experiences and personality of the particular individual. The 'collective unconscious' brings forward some ways of thinking that have been the common heritage of humankind across many generations into the distant past. We all have certain basic 'racial memories', carried chiefly in the form of imagery rather than verbal concepts.

Historians, anthropologists and archaeologists as well as psychoanalysts have uncovered intriguing similarities among people living at various times and in various places that appear to support Jung's view. Whether or not Jung is correct in all respects, there is abundant reason to believe that we all share some mental characteristics of the human species at large, as well as those acquired from our particular cultural heritage or shaped from our own individual life experiences.

Researchers are only now starting to examine the contribution of cultural and racial (or 'panhuman') images to the core NDE. Lundahl[41] finds that the social organization of the afterlife in Mormon NDEs closely reflects their views about the way life should be on this earth. The following summary illustrates how much the NDE owes to the guiding images, expectations or fantasies that a particular group has made its own:

> The social system of the other world is very organized and based on a moral order. The basic societal unit is the family. The other world has a system of social stratification and its most important desirable is morality. Social control processes are also evident in the other world ... [which] is vast and located near the earth. It contains buildings that are better constructed than the buildings on earth and landscape and vegetation indescribably beautiful.

Mormon NDEs have characteristics of their own. More recent observations suggest that Buddhists and other cultures also have culturally-specific NDEs.[42, 43] The existence of culture-specific NDEs supports the interpretation of image and fantasy release, rather than a universal reality that the split-off 'I' encounters regardless of his or her upbringing. Under extreme stress, with our lives and our sanity in jeopardy, we welcome the rush of stored-up imagery from our individual, cultural and racial roots.

THE CORE NDE PROMOTES EITHER SURVIVAL OR A PLEASANT EXIT FANTASY

The various explanations offered all converge on one central point: the NDE is an adaptive psychobiological function. We have such experiences because they are in some way helpful to us when we are in special jeopardy. Here is how we might integrate the basic points of these explanations and also take account of some other important findings:

- We have two ways of responding to a situation we recognize to be dangerous: we do something about the danger; or we alter our own psychophysiological condition. If we see that our car might be struck by another vehicle, for example, we engage immediately in some kind of instrumental behaviour, some action intended to master the situation. In this situation we do not go off into fantasy trips. NDEs are reported only in situations of the second type: in which we have come to the conclusion, often very quickly, that there is nothing we can do to change the situation itself. We are helpless, ineffectual from the standpoint of practical action.
- In the second type of situation ("I can't do anything to get out of this") we switch to an alternative way of functioning. Although it appears to be a passive approach, or even a form of surrender, the truth is that we are still acting in our own interest, in the interest of our survival.
- For our internal adaptive system to work properly, we must reduce the outpouring of energy. We must not waste precious resources in useless struggle and arousal. Instead, we must attain a psycho-physiological state that is ideally conducive to healing. We must give our bodies a chance to recover.
- This is accomplished by activating those brain substances that exercise a powerful soothing effect on our nervous system. The so-called 'brain opiates' comprise part of our own private chemical factory. Endorphins and related peptides emerge to bathe our troubled body and mind. We enjoy a state of profound relaxation. Subjectively, this produces the often pleasant or even ecstatic tone of NDE reports. It amounts to a very successful 'drug high' – but the drug in this case is our own, designed especially for such occasions.
- We recover and perhaps become survivors with NDEs to share. This happens if our bodies have sufficient self-healing potential and the stress and damage do not continue too long. Or we die. Despite activation of the internal adaptive system, the circumstances of our illness or injury are too massive, too excessive for recovery. Even when death is the outcome, however, the brain hormones still perform a valuable function. They comfort. They lull. They throw open, for the last time, the gates that hold back our reservoir of

33

individual, cultural and racial fantasies. Out come these images, arranging themselves to please. Arranging themselves to tell us one final bedtime story.

This explanation is far superior, far more grounded at many points in established fact, than the naive conclusion that NDEs involve an actual round trip from death. Knowledge supporting this explanation is continuing to accumulate. We have had important research findings on endorphins and opiate receptor areas in the brain for several years now. There are also promising efforts to relate brain hormone action to the NDE.

Finally, let's take one last, quick trip through that legendary tunnel. Several plausible explanations have been offered of the tunnel experience on psychophysiological facts. We recommend in particular the work of Susan Blackmore.[44, 45] She has created computer simulations of the tunnel experience as well as examined the psychophysiological aspects. Blackmore notes that people do have a real experience of a tunnel, but not a real tunnel. The brain constructs its version of reality from the available stimuli or signals. Specifically, the perception of random movements on the periphery of the visual field is interpreted by the brain as outward movements. From this interpretation the brain then infers that it has also moved. What presents itself to the brain as an apparently enlarging patch of flickering white life is then interpreted as a tunnel through which the person is moving.

We all have fantasies enough, lodged smugly in our neurons waiting for the opportunity to express themselves. However, this does not mean that we must willingly surrender our appreciation of reality and our own command of logic and common sense to unleash these fantasies before their time. The core NDE is a fascinating episode involving physiology, psychodynamics and cultural heritage, all in the service of helping us to survive a threat to life or to end our existence with a comforting dream. If you insist on making more than this of the NDE, then you are insisting on fantasy.

2

SAFE CONDUCT: ANGEL ESCORTS ACROSS THE BORDER?

ANGELS OF THE FIRE DREAM

One way to study the experiences of dying people and their families is to review a series of consecutive patients who were under the care of a hospital or a hospice program. Although there are limitations in this method, it has the advantage of being a naturally-occurring sample. The dying people are not selected by either the hospice or the researcher on the basis of any pre-existing theories. By simply including all clients from one point in time to another we avoid the temptation of focusing on the especially dramatic case or selecting people because of one or another special feature. My colleagues and I have done several studies of this type over the years. In these studies we were not looking for strange, otherworldly happenings, we were just trying to improve our knowledge of what dying people experience, how they cope with their crises, and how we might provide better care and comfort for them.

It was during a recent study of this type[1] that I came across the experiences of a person we will call Mrs Woodward. Her breast cancer had not been discovered in time. When it became clear that she had only a few months to live, Mrs Woodward and her husband called on the services of a local hospice organization. She was in great pain. The hospice immediately instituted a pain-control regime, but it did not bring relief. This was unusual. Dosage was increased and increased again – still no relief. The hospice continued its efforts, exploring all the techniques it had available. In addition to medications, the hospice staff tried guided imagery, hypnosis, and relaxation procedures. Mrs Woodward remained in agony. The hospice staff was almost as devastated as Mrs Woodward and her husband. These were skilled and dedicated care-givers who had successfully controlled the pain of many other terminally ill people. Why couldn't they help her?

There was another disturbing element. Mrs Woodward seemed to be not only in agony but also in terror. There was something about her sense of dread and near-panic that seemed to go beyond physical suffering.

SAFE CONDUCT: ANGEL ESCORTS ACROSS THE BORDER?

The home situation did not seem to be at fault. Until the cancer was discovered, this had been the best time of her life. She had been the abused child of an alcoholic father and the wife of a man who also mistreated her. Her strong Catholic faith had been a source of strength through the troubled years. Now she had a devoted husband with whom she had served as foster parents for an abused child. During her illness, Mr Woodward willingly took time from his business activities to be with her. Her life should have continued to be rewarding, but first there was the cancer, and now the unremitting agony and terror. Astonishingly, she lived in this misery for a full year, an unusually long period of preterminal suffering.

And then came the dreams. Actually, it was the same dream, night after night, with only small variations. The dream was so alarming that Mrs Woodward often screamed aloud. When she would awake it would be in a state of exhausted terror. "There was a fire", she would tell her husband. "A terrible fire, and I was running, running away, but I couldn't get away!" At times she would describe the nightmares as "like the fires of hell. I will be punished. I am being punished."

It was during this intensified ordeal that Mrs Woodward had one or more visits from a clergyman (whose identity was not known to the hospice staff). She not only told him of her dreams, but also revealed that there had been a real fire incident in her childhood and somebody in the neighborhood had died, but that was not the hellish fire of her dreams. Mrs Woodward told the pastor she was now convinced that her dreams represented the flames of retribution and that she must have been an evil person from childhood on. The clergyman told her that her dreams would improve.

One night soon after, she did experience a different kind of dream. Three angels appeared at her bedside. She knew they were angels even though they were wearing ordinary clothes. The first angel called her by name. "It's going to be OK," he told her. The second angel added, "You're going to see somebody soon." The third angel smiled gently and said, "You're not going to have anymore pain. You're not going to need anymore pain medication."

The next morning she woke up relaxed and refreshed. Where was the pain? It was gone, completely gone, so, too, was the terror. Her husband brought the medications. She refused them. "You need them," he insisted. "Not anymore." It became clear to her husband that she really was free of pain. "The pain is over," she told him, "I'm going to have a great day."

As it turned out, the Woodwards had two good days together. She was serene and relaxed for the first time in more than a year; this made is possible for her husband to relax as well. A hospice nurse who was with Mrs Woodward at the moment of her death reports that, "After all that pain, she had one of the most peaceful deaths."

I have summarized this sequence of events without interpretation.

SAFE CONDUCT: ANGEL ESCORTS ACROSS THE BORDER?

Do angels or other spiritual beings provide a safe conduct from life to death? Or are there simpler explanations that do not require such a leap of faith? The debate in this chapter might contribute to your own interpretation.

FROM NEAR-DEATH EXPERIENCES TO ESCORTS

There is a point of connection between near-death experiences and deathbed escorts. Consider the following pair of typical NDE reports:

> The light dazzled me so, I really couldn't see who it was, even whether it was a man or woman. But the voice was my mother's. She told me to go back. And so I did.
>
> An old man was standing there at the end of the tunnel. No, I can't say it was the end of the tunnel because I didn't get all the way to the end. He was ahead some distance from me, though, standing perfectly still. I didn't know him, yet I knew him, if that makes any sense. From the look on his face, I knew that everything would be all right and I wanted to keep going toward him, away from life but somehow not away. He was stern and welcoming at the same time.

Encounters with a person or supernatural being have often been reported as part of a NDE. What must be added now is the fact that such encounters seem to occur at the point of actual death as well. People who do not return from their life-and-death crisis have been observed to interact with a 'somebody' visible only to themselves. Observations of this kind have been made for many years, well preceding the current interest in NDEs. We now explore the phenomenon of escorts across the life/death border. What are these experiences? What do they mean? Do they provide evidence for survival of death?

Through the centuries there has been a persistent belief that life and death share a common boundary. Perhaps the most famous example is the River Styx. In Greek mythology the souls of the dead had to cross this dark and melancholy river to reach the underworld. Charon, an aged but vigorous ferryman stood ready to receive passengers into his boat, providing they had the fee in hand. The dynastic Egyptians and other people of antiquity also believed that after death the soul journeys to the land of death, and is in need of a knowledgeable guide. One does not have to be an ancient Greek or Egyptian to feel that, in Shakespeare's words, death is "the unknown country", yet a country that is just across the border from life.

THE ADVOCATE'S CASE

One of the arguments pushed most vigorously against NDEs was that the person did not actually die and stay dead, and therefore the report is of a return, not a one-way trip. This argument cannot apply here. We will speak only of situations in which the person did pass from life. The observations made here are important in their own right and also lend further support to the NDEs.

SPONTANEOUS OBSERVATIONS

The most fascinating human experiences seldom occur under the artificial conditions of the experimental laboratory. Events happen when and where they will. We will first sample some of the many spontaneous observations that have been made and then turn to findings from systematic research. We begin with one of the classical episodes, that of the *grey lady*.

Patients dying in a London hospital were attended by a 'grey lady' wearing a nurse's uniform from earlier times.[2] She was described by the patients as a woman of middle years who approached them with a compassionate and comforting manner. These reports surfaced from time to time and so often did this mysterious visitor appear that the 'grey lady' was felt to be almost a permanent part of the staff. Physician Paul Turner investigated this legend in the 1950s and discovered that new instances were still occurring. Nurses told of patients who asked the name of 'that other nurse' who was standing by their side – when the attending nurse was alone, as far as she could see. Dying patients insisted that the 'grey lady' visited them frequently, and even filled their water jugs. The reports were always of a grey uniform – yet the staff nurses actually wore blue. This is interesting because grey uniforms had been worn years before. Turner's analysis of the incidents indicated that the patients died within a day or two of their visitations and that none previously knew about the *grey lady*.

Other examples were collected and carefully evaluated by Sir William Barrett,[3] one of the leading physicists of his time. More than half a century later, his book, *Death-bed Visions*, remains a classic for its demonstration of astute scientific reasoning applied to a phenomenon that some would regard as beyond empirical investigation. Barrett found that dying people sometimes had visitors 'from the other side'. Usually it was only the dying person who could see and hear the visitor, but there were also instances in which other people bore witness to the mysterious guest.

Here is an excerpt from one such example given by Barrett. The report comes from Mrs Joy Snell, a hospital volunteer. A friend of hers, "a sweet girl of seventeen," was dying of consumption (tuberculosis).

> *She suffered no pain, but the weariness that comes from extreme weakness and debility was heavy upon her and she yearned for rest.*
>
> *A short time before she expired I became aware that two spirit forms were standing by the bedside, one on either side of it. I did not see them*

enter the room ... but I could see them as distinctly as I could any of the human occupants of the room. I recognized their faces as those of two girls who had been the closest friends of the girl who was dying. They had passed away a year before and were then about her own age Just before they appeared the dying girl exclaimed, 'It has grown suddenly dark; I cannot see anything!' But she recognized them immediately. A smile, beautiful to see, lit up her face. She stretched forth her hands and in joyous tones exclaimed, 'Oh, you have come to take me away! I am glad, for I am very tired!'

Mrs. Snell saw the dying girl stretch forth her arms and also saw one angel grasp her right hand, the other her left hand.

Their faces were illuminated by a smile more radiantly beautiful even than that of the face of the girl who was so soon to find the rest for which she longed. She did not speak again, but for nearly a minute her hands remained outstretched, grasped by the hands of the angels, and she continued to gaze at them with the glad light in her eyes ...

The parents entered the room, weeping over the impending loss of their daughter. The angels relaxed their grasp of the girl's hands, which then fell back on the bed.

And in another moment she was what the world calls dead. But that sweet smile with which she had first recognized the angels was still stamped on her features.

After a short interval, the angels rose and left the room. Two angels had entered. Three angels departed (pp. 109-111).

Mrs Snell, like Mrs Woodward in her final dream, had no hestitation in identifying the visitors as angels. It is interesting to be reminded that the current surge of interest in angels[4, 5] does not represent so much a new turn of thought, but a return to the appreciation of spirit beings that had been for a time cast aside by our materialistic society. And, of course, there was a critical difference between these two accounts. Mrs. Woodward's angels revealed themselves in the privacy of her dreams; the dying girl's angels could be seen not only by her but by the hospital volunteer as well.

In his survey of *Death-Bed Visions,* Barrett raised and answered several important questions:

Q What was the mental status of the dying person when the visitor appeared?
A Clear and rational.
Q Why had the visitor come?
A To escort the dying soul from this life to the next.
Q How did the dying person respond to the visitor?
A With serenity or exaltation.
Q Was there anything unusual about the visitor?

A Yes. Sometimes, as in a case witnessed by Lady Barrett, herself a physician. A woman lay dying after delivering a healthy baby. She saw a "lovely brightness", then spoke to her deceased father as though he were standing right before her, and also her sister, Vida. The sight of Vida at her bedside puzzled her because she knew that, unlike her father, Vida was still alive. In fact, however, Vida had died three weeks previously but the news had been kept from the ailing pregnant woman. This is an example of objective information (the unknown death of her sister) showing up as part of a deathbed vision.

SYSTEMATIC RESEARCH

Certainly, there have been enough reports to arouse curiosity. And we are fortunate that qualified researchers have been among the curious. Karlis Osis and Erlundur Haraldsson's careful and systematic study[6] supports what Turner, Barrett and many others have suggested. The angelic dead do seem to return to the dying.

Osis first conducted a pilot study through the New York Parapsychological Association in 1977. Observations made on approximately 35,000 dying persons were reported by 640 physicians and nurses. The promising leads discovered in this study were followed up by a second project that included studies made in India as well as the United States. This produced data on more than 50,000 additional deathbed observations by another 1000 physicians and nurses in the USA. The study in northern India was conducted to gain information on cultural similarities or differences in the experience of visitations on the deathbed. About 700 medical personnel filled out the research questionnaires.

What did Osis and Haraldsson find? Here are some of their more important results, culled from both the original and the follow-up study. Within each study there were further follow-ups on positive cases, that is, instances in which a physician or nurse reported that the dying patient seemed to be interacting with a 'visitor' or 'apparition'. The question-and-answer format will be useful here as well.

Q Isn't it possible that the patients' minds were wandering? That they were confused, perhaps heavily drugged, and hallucinating?

A This does happen. However, such cases were excluded from the analysis. Experienced physicians and nurses as well can tell the difference between the ramblings and distortions of a mind compromised by illness, and the kind of experience the project was designed to study.

Q Were 'visitations' experienced by people with clear consciousness?

A Yes.

Q And without fever? And who hadn't been given drugs? And in India as well as the United States?

A Three more yesses!

Q Did people who were not thought to be very sick sometimes have deathbed visions – and then die?

A That was also found. A young girl in India, for example, seemed to be in good health but suddenly started to cry out that "God is calling me and I am going to die." The family brought her to a hospital, but no illness could be discovered. And yet she died, of circulatory collapse that had no apparent cause.

Q Did people's attitudes towards their illness change after the 'visitations'?

A There were cases in which a person thought he was going to recover, but after the visitation became convinced that he would die; and did die.

Q Do dying people always welcome these 'visitors' or 'apparitions'?

A Not always. Some people do not seem ready to leave this life, and they feel that the 'visitor' has come to take them away. Yet other people relax and accept their situation; they seem to have been put at ease by their 'visitor'.

Q Does the person lose contact with the real world, the immediate situation, when the 'visitor' comes?

A Sometimes yes; sometimes no. Often the patient responds to the 'visitor' while at the same time speaking to actual people in the room and otherwise dealing realistically with the world. In what are called 'total hallucinations', however, the person is tuned in only to their 'visitation' and the spiritual world it seems to have opened up for them.

Q Who were these 'visitors'? Somebody the dying patient had known, or the angel of death?

A Both kinds of 'visitors' were reported. Some dying people saw the 'apparition' of one of their parents, for example, while others saw what they took to be a messenger of God – or God Himself. There were some instances in which the patient was visited at the same time by both a deceased loved one and a vision of God. The Indian equivalent to the angel of death is a Yamdoot, that is, a messenger from Yama, the mythological god of death. Yamdoots came to some dying people in northern India to discharge their historic function of escorting the soul to the land of the dead.

Q Did the observers – doctors or nurses – ever see or hear anything themselves, or was it all in the dying person's mind?

A There are reports that indicate something was going on beyond what the patients themselves experienced. Here is a good example involving a man in his 40s whom the nurse had known well for years:

He was unsedated, fully conscious and had a low temperature. He was a rather religious person and believed in life after death. We expected him to die and he probably did too as he was asking us to pray for him.

SAFE CONDUCT: ANGEL ESCORTS ACROSS THE BORDER?

In the room where he was lying, there was a staircase leading to the second floor. Suddenly he exclaimed: 'See, the angels are coming down the stairs. The glass has fallen and broken.' All of us in the room looked toward the staircase where a drinking glass had been placed on one of the steps. As we looked, we saw the glass break into a thousand pieces without any apparent cause. It did not fall; it simply exploded. The angels, of course, we did not see. A happy and peaceful expression came over the patient's face and the next moment he expired. Even after his death the serene, peaceful expression remained on his face. [6]

These are some of the questions that have been answered by systematic research. A few additional points should be made. The most typical finding was that "dying patients see persons whom others around them cannot see." [6] The researchers considered only those instances in which the dying person was coherent and in which he was not simply reliving memories of earlier experiences. In other words, what the patients saw and experienced could not be dismissed as the distortions of a disturbed mind. This fact needs to be faced squarely.

We have quite a bias against hallucinations in our society. Not all societies share this bias. Native-Americans and many other peoples believe that knowledge and insights can come to us through hallucinations – which they honor with the more positive term, *visions*. It is true enough that some hallucinations do represent mental disturbances – the terrifying sights that appear to a person suffering delirium tremens, for example, the 'voices' that issue commands to a psychotic, or even the distorted perceptions that can accompany severe sleep deprivation. Osis and Haraldsson were well aware of such varieties of hallucination and did not include these among the cases selected for final analysis.

Careful follow-up investigation made it clear that the true deathbed visions differed from hallucinations of a negative and disorientated type. The typical deathbed vision involved visitation from a deceased person who came expressly to take the dying person away. By contrast, most ordinary hallucinations involve the sense of contact with a living person – and it was only the deceased person or messenger of God who came to take the dying person away. Furthermore, the usual response was serenity and acceptance, rather than discomfort, confusion or terror. Deathbed visions, then, were set apart from the type of hallucinations that give hallucinations a bad name. In both India and the USA, for both children and adults, men and women, the 'visitor' was usually experienced as an escort or guide to assist the dying person in making the transition from this realm of existence to another.

There is another side to the deathbed escort phenomenon: the *crisis apparition*. Some people at the time of their death have spirit visitors – but they may themselves become apparitions to others. Many such cases were reported in the pioneering study of apparitions conducted by the British Society for Psychic Research a century ago. Haraldsson[7] collected 350 new reports from Icelanders who had experienced apparitions of the dead. About 1 in 7 of these reports involved encountering the spirit of a person within 12 hours of that person's death: "Even more startling is the finding that in 84% of these cases the person who had the encounter did not know that the person he or she was perceiving had died or was dying." We will be discussing apparitions or ghosts in detail later in this book. The point for now is that deathbed visions may well be only part of the total story of spirit interaction around the time of death.

DEATHBED VISIONS PROVE SURVIVAL OF DEATH

We might doubt the significance of deathbed visions if there were other, more commonplace explanations available. One by one, however, such explanations have been tested and found unsatisfactory.

Some physiological conditions can lead to hallucinations. This explanation, however, does not hold up to the evidence compiled by Osis and Haraldsson. Many of the dying patients had received no sedation (especially in the Indian sample), and others received very little. Overall, deathbed visions could not be explained away as an effect produced by drugs. Furthermore, why would drugs administered to a person near death result in a different kind of hallucination than usual? It was found that only one per cent of patients with 'visitations' had received enough medication to have a substantial effect on their thought and perceptions, and only another eight per cent had received enough for even a moderate effect. High fever, another possible explanation, also applied to only a small number of cases (about eight per cent).

Furthermore, their nurses and physicians reported most of the patients with deathbed visions to have been in a "normal, wakeful state of consciousness". The diseases and physical problems most likely to produce hallucinations were also present in only about 11 per cent of cases (e.g. uremic poisoning from kidney dysfunction, or brain injury). Osis and Haraldsson constructed an 'hallucinogenic index' incorporating all the possible physiological effects. The index was weighted towards physiological explanation – but, again, it proved inadequate to account for the great majority of deathbed visions. In fact, whenever physiological factors that could induce hallucinations were present they tended to disrupt all kinds of communication, with those physically present as well as with potential escorts. No, the physiological explanation just will not do!

It might also be easier to explain away deathbed visions if they were limited to people of a particular age or sex. But the analysis demonstrated that escorts appeared to people of either sex and any age.

'Wish-fulfillment' could be another easy explanation. Perhaps dying people simply imagine that comforting figures come to them because they are so in need of comfort. Perhaps the desire to reduce an overwhelming fear of death creates visions of an escort to the afterlife. Perhaps, perhaps, perhaps. The facts, however, indicate that the apparitions often have purposes of their own. They do not necessarily represent the dying person's own thoughts and desires. Observers have witnessed the dying person attempting to negotiate with the 'visitor', or responding as though something unexpected had been said. At times the visitor's intention to escort the dying person away is in direct opposition to the patient's own expectations and wishes. There are cases in which the patient had been expressing confidence in his ability to recover. In such instances there may at first be alarm when the escort appears with the unexpected and unwelcome call to come away. This is not at all what one would expect from a wish-fulfiling fantasy!

Sometimes the dying person does accept the summons before the vision is over and achieves a state of serenity. Whether the person dies serenely or in agitation, however, the encounter with an independent purpose – the escort's summons – tells us that wish-fulfilment fails as an explanation.

There is one explanation that does not fail: we do survive death, and are often escorted by compassionate spirits.

THE CRITIC'S VIEW

We have been told another set of interesting stories whose entertainment value is not to be doubted. 'grey ladies', Yamdoots, deceased relatives! Really! The serious business of dying and facing the prospect of extinction is trivialized by the insistence that deathbed visions have a basis in objective reality.

Let us begin by granting – just for a moment – a very large assumption. Let us put our good common sense aside and assume that not only are the observations themselves accurate, but that those responding to the survey actually saw and heard what they said they saw and heard. In other words, we will suppose that the descriptive information we have been given is substantially accurate. What conclusions can be drawn?

DEATHBED VISIONS DO REPRESENT WISH-FULFILMENT FANTASIES IN THE FORM OF VISUAL OR AUDITORY HALLUCINATIONS

This possibility has troubled those who believe deathbed hallucinations involve actual contact with deceased or spiritual beings. And well it might! Psychology and psychiatry have long been aware of 'need-determined perceptions'. Everything that comes to us through our senses must also pass through a sort of mental and emotional filter. Out of all that we might take in of the world, we tend to select what seems most relevant to our needs. The stronger our motivational state at the moment, the more our perception is influenced. The starving person is hypersensitive to food, the thirsting person to drink. Reality often cooperates. Driven by intense needs or heightened sensitivity, we pick out selected bits and pieces of what the world presents to our senses. These may then become exaggerated, elaborated and subtly blended with both our past experiences and our hopes for the future. The fragments of actual reality, then, form a nucleus that attracts memories and fantasies.

The result may be likened to the product of creative artists who use aspects of ordinary reality but transforms them in accordance with their artistic vision. For the artist, the product may be a painting, sculpture, novel or poem. For the person who is driven by strong emotional needs, the product may be an hallucinatory experience. This experience may indeed have some of the qualities associated with artistic products, including beauty and dramatic confrontation. Similarly one can also admire or be touched by need-driven visions.

Error marches in, however, when we mistake the hallucinatory transformation of experience for the objective truth. It is one thing to be fascinated by a work of creative fiction or by a deathbed vision. It is quite another thing to accept these mental products as discoveries or confirmations of the real nature of the world. This is why we have both science and art!

Osis and Haraldsson's data remain the best available source of information on deathbed visions. Furthermore, there is no reason to doubt either their integrity or their craftsmanship. Unfortunately, few others have taken up the task of studying these phenomena systematically. Osis and Haraldsson did not intend that research should end with their efforts. Believers, though, are content to believe – why continue to check their beliefs against reality? Until other findings of at least equal scope and quality come along, both advocates and critics we must continue to rely on these data. And when we look at some of the reports we do indeed find a clear wish-fulfiling or need-driven quality. Here is one such example:

> The condition of one man, suffering from a heart attack, had been serious for the last few days. Suddenly he gained consciousness. He looked better and cheerful. He talked nicely to his relatives and requested them to go home. He also said, 'I shall go to my home. Angels have come to take me.' He looked relieved and cheerful.[7]

Suffering and the prospect of death were replaced here by an optimistic outlook. This can be counted as a highly successful transformation of unpleasant reality through the wish-fulfilment mechanism. There were many other similar cases.

Osis and Haraldsson reject the wish-fulfilment interpretation chiefly because not all hallucinations had this quality. It would be more prudent to begin by accepting the wish-fulfilment interpretation where it does apply! An explanation may fit some cases and not others. It is not reasonable to toss away an explanation that does fit many cases simply because it does not seem to explain all. This point is strengthened by the fact that the phenomenon of need-determined perception is well established in psychiatry, psychology and the social sciences. We do not have to introduce Yamdoots or angels when there is a well researched and demonstrated phenomenon that fits many of the cases. Need-determined perception cannot be set aside in favour of vague and exotic speculation when it fits the data so well. At the very least, then, the possibility that deathbed visions are a type of wish-fulfiling fantasy does rank as the best available explanation of cases in which wishes are fulfiled.

And that's not all! The other deathbed visions reported are also consistent with need-determined perception. We need only move beyond the most superficial layer of interpretation. Wish-fulfilment does not always come in a simple and direct form. This is one of the lessons that have been learned from intensive psychotherapy, case studies and dream analysis. One alternative form of wish-fulfilment is especially relevant here. To understand how this psychological mechanism works we must first enter more fully into the mind of the dying person. Indeed, the failure to do so has limited and distorted much of the campaign to 'prove' survival of death.

Few people go through life with their own death firmly in mind. We engage in a variety of strategies to avoid, trivialize or deny our mortality.[8-10] This general tendency to evade acceptance of personal mortality is a well-established fact. Serious illness challenges our defence system, however. We experience ourselves becoming weaker; we feel our vulnerability. This is especially true in long-term illnesses. A person may die suddenly, as in a massive heart attack or an automobile accident, and never have the time to reflect on mortality. More and more of us now end our lives after a lingering illness – and it is also the more extended type of dying process that produces most deathbed visions, according to Osis and Haraldsson.

Perhaps you can already see what I am driving at. It is hard for many of us to accept the reality of impending death because we had previously excluded death from our conception of self. Day after day, sometimes hour after hour, however, we are barraged by signals that the end is approaching. Many of these signals come from internal changes, what is happening inside our bodies. Other signals come from the way people have started to treat us (e.g. standing further away, not meeting our eyes, behaving uncomfortably). The time may come when we can no longer ignore these signals. And yet we have become so accustomed to supposing that we will live forever. Something has to give.

Something has to develop as well: the sense of being a whole person on the verge of our death. That long-silent voice within us must find a way to be heard, to tell us that there is an end and it is near. How are we to make ourselves listen to our own truth? By projection. This psychological strategy or defence mechanism is very well known to those who work with the mentally ill. We encounter projection in an extreme form with the paranoid schizophrenic who hears voices that tell him such terrible or grandiose things. "You are the world's greatest sinner!", the voice roars that only he can hear. This voice and its message are projections from the paranoid's own troubled mind. He has, at least for the moment, lost his struggle to keep highly disturbing thoughts under control. Even so, he cannot bear to say these things himself as himself. The voices provide an external source of expression, daring to say what he could not say while remaining within his own identity. The mechanism of projection takes many forms, varies in extent and intensity, and is not limited to mental illness as such. You and I may ourselves use this mechanism – just a bit – every now and again.

The dying person who has never really accepted the fact of death before may also use the mechanism of projection. One part of his self communicates with another part through the deathbed hallucination. This is a way of breaking through internal barriers within his personality. The message has come from a previously suppressed or repressed part of his own mind and the escort is likewise a creation, an extension, a projection of the same mind.

This can be a creative solution to the problem we have recognized, the problem of accepting the truth of impending death in a personality that has previously lived as though immortal. It should be understood that this is seldom if ever a conscious or deliberate action. The 'visitor' and his or her message are created largely by those aspects of the personality that lie beyond the narrow band of conscious awareness. Furthermore, this action enables one to create precisely the best, the most appropriate, type of visitor, "I might not believe myself...but how can I doubt an angel?"

It is not at all surprising, then, to learn that some of the 'visitors' told the patients things they had not expected or wanted to hear. That is precisely why the 'visitors' were created in the first place! This type of deathbed vision satisfies the need to balance reality ("I will soon die") with desire ("It's all right to die").

There is no reason to burden ourselves further with extravagant speculations: deathbed visions originate in some form of wish-fulfilment.

There is reason, however, to recognize that our susceptibility to wish-fulfiling visions can itself be life-threatening. Here is an instructive example. An ardent hiker had noticed but dismissed a sign that warned of a dangerous bull on top of the steep hill he was ascending. A bull on the top of this high hill? Not bloody likely! But the bull was there, as advertised, as big as all outdoors and as malevolent looking as any

47

mythological monster. The hiker decided without delay that he had seen enough of that particular hill. As he rushed down, he fell. Something very bad had happened to his leg. It was much too painful to go on. He would have to stay where he was. The image of the enraged and outsized bull was a great motivator, however. He was obviously of two minds: stay, rest, and minimize the pain, or drag himself forward in agony.

Two minds! Let us sample how these two mindsets in the same person interacted during the crisis. He had encountered a broad stream in his escape path.

> *Several times I felt my consciousness ebbing and feared I would faint and drown in the stream; and I ordered myself to hold on, with strong language and threats.*
>
> *'Hold on, you fool! Hold on for dear life! I'll kill you if you let go – and don't you forget it!'*[11]

He made it to the other side of the stream, "shuddering with cold, and pain and shock."

> *Then, somehow my exhaustion became a sort of tiredness, an extraordinarily comfortable, delicious languor.*
>
> *'How nice it is here,' I thought to myself. 'Why not a little rest – a nap maybe?'*

Oliver Sacks' next reaction probably saved his life. The noted physician and author recognized this "soft, insinuating inner voice" for what it was.

> *'No,' I said fiercely to myself. 'This is Death speaking – and in its sweetest, deadliest Siren-voice. Don't listen to it now! Don't listen to it ever! You can't rest here, you can't rest anywhere. You must find a pace you can keep up, and go on steadily.'*

Sacks recognized this firm, dissenting voice as his "life voice". He also recognized that he would probably die of cold and shock if he did not find shelter. He silenced the death voice. He went on. He survived.

In stressful situations we are especially susceptible to the mindset that could ease our way to death. Why bear the burden of pain, doubt, and uncertainty? Why not just float out blissfully with the ebbing tide?

The deathbed vision may comfort some of us – all too well. If we were a little less comforted – and a little more chastised by the voice of life – we might have a better chance of getting out of that bed!

PHYSIOLOGICAL FACTORS DO PLAY A ROLE

Those who prefer to believe in survival of death again betray their eagerness by passing too swiftly over another important explanation of deathbed visions. It has been claimed that most of the reports collected by Osis and Haraldsson involved patients who had little or no medication that could affect mental functioning. Experts in pharmacology effects would hesitate to draw this conclusion. It is naive to assume that only a few drugs affect the mind. What we call the mind is a partner of the body or perhaps, as many have argued, a function of the body. Biochemical substances taken into the body (including food) can influence our ability to attend, perceive, concentrate, persist with mental tasks, remember and make decisions. Furthermore, the interaction among various biochemical substances can introduce further alterations in mood and thought. Dosage is also crucial. A 'small' dosage might prove to have strong effects in a body that is in an unusually vulnerable condition (such as terminal illness). While some drugs have especially obvious and predictable effects on mental functioning, it cannot be lightly maintained that these and only these drugs have any effect at all. More is learned every year about drug effects and about interactions that have effects well beyond their physiological targets. It is much too early to rule out drug-related physiological effects as part of the background of deathbed visions.

The dismissal of physiological effects appears even more premature since the discovery of chemical substances produced by the brain itself under special circumstances. We manufacture our own opiate-like substances that lead to experiences of well-being, serenity, time-space distortions, and so forth. The effects of endorphins and other self-generated substance we were offered as a possible explanation for the near-death experiences that have already discussed. They are also a possible explanation for the emotional state that accompanies many deathbed visions. The absence of prescribed medication does not at all rule out the possibility – the probability, in fact – that we create our own soothing medicine when suffering and facing the prospect of imminent death.

NOT EVERYBODY HAS AN ESCORT

In Chapter 1 we wondered why everybody who survived a close call with death did not report a NDE. The fact that many have returned without such a report casts doubt on the relevance of the near-death experience to the question of actual survival of death. There is a similar problem here. Only a minority of the observations collected by Osis and Haraldsson – who were looking for deathbed visions – fit into this category. If we do survive death, and escorts do come to take us away, why not everybody? On the other hand, if deathbed visions emerge from wish-fulfilment needs and specific physiological states (and specific situations), then many individual differences can be expected and the results are not puzzling at all.

QUESTIONABLE DATA

So far we have courteously accepted the basic data offered by Osis and Haraldsson (although we cannot quite extend this courtesy to 'grey ladies' and other scattered reports from hither and thither and, especially, yon). But how exactly trustworthy are these data?

Osis and Haraldsson are reputable and competent researchers. I accept what they have done with the reports they collected, but the value of these data in the first place must be questioned. Here are some of the problems:

- The data were retrospective (remembered from the past) rather than directly observed by Osis and Haraldsson.
- The people who made these observations were not trained to collect and record these data with an acceptable degree of scientific accuracy.
- Some of the remembrances went back many years prior to the time when the observers were asked to report them, thereby increasing the reliance on long-term memory. Such reports would not stand up very well in court or any other form of critical review.
- The observers were often highly involved in the situation themselves and therefore not in a position to make objective observations.
- Witnesses often give conflicting testimony and healthcare professionals often disagree in their descriptions and interpretations.

Let us take that last point a little further. It requires many years of training before nurses and physicians are able to make reliable assessments of conditions in which they specialize. What they reported to Osis and Haraldsson, however, dealt with phenomena for which they have had no systematic training. Obtaining reliable descriptions and interpretations from different people is recognized as a significant problem. It is not taken for granted. We are expecting too much from these reports of deathbed visions, then, if we treat them as objective and accurate descriptions. The caution I am urging – and which almost any social scientist or lawyer would urge – does not mean that the nurses and physicians were making up stories. It means simply that the quality of the data does not support firm conclusions, no matter how competently the investigators manage to put the obtained information through its paces.

Lovely stories! But they 'prove' survival of death only to those who already have embraced that conclusion, and who will continue to do so, evidence or no evidence.

ANOTHER WORD FROM THE ADVOCATE

Our critic has told some lovely stories of his own. Consider for example, the point that seems most to excite him.

SAFE CONDUCT: ANGEL ESCORTS ACROSS THE BORDER?

The dying person is accused. Of what? Of having motives, of having wishes, of being involved in his own life and death! It would be an unusual person indeed who did not have wishes and desires at the moment when life and death seem to merge. This is taken by the critic to signify that the dying person is too involved and therefore his experiences must be disqualified. Are we to live and die without desires? Is it only the ideal objectivist whose word is to be trusted, a person who does not care one way or the other? What strange reasoning!

The critic cleverly reminds us that hungry people are sensitive to the availability of food, and thirsting people to drink. Well, of course! This is no whim or accident of nature. Heightened sensitivity helps us to meet our needs! Super-alertness increases our ability to relieve our needs or fulfill our desires. The hungry or thirsty person is more likely to discover unsuspected sources of nourishment. The same is true for the many other types of needs and desires familiar to us.

It is apparent that the critic is offended by the very process that leads to deathbed visions. A heightened need state is brought about by the proximity of death. This, in turn, produces heightened sensitivity, a super-alertness or receptivity that attempts to reduce the need state or to fulfil desire. *And this heightened alertness and receptivity does in fact make it easier for contact to occur between the dying person and his or her escort.* We have to meet our escorts half-way, or, at least, be receptive enough to open the door when they knock. The critic spins round in fury and disdain because dying people may have strong needs. He completely misses the point that this is an adaptive process: it leads to relief and fulfilment because it opens the way to contact with the compassionate escort.

It is certainly true that our minds conduct an inner dialogue. We may be of two – or more minds – about many things. How useful it is to have that voice of caution speak up when we are too quickly enthused about a doubtful project. And how useful it is to have that forceful "voice of life" urge us onward when we feel weak and vulnerable. This inner dialogue, however, by no means excludes angels and other spiritual beings. The inner dialogue itself partakes of spirituality. If there are, as many of us believe, spiritual forces and intelligences in the world, why should they not be attracted by our inner dialogues? Our waking thoughts and sleeping images invite the attention of angelic beings. Although themselves free from human conflicts and passions they are aware of our circumstances and sympathetic. Guardian angels may guide us in subtle ways through life. Many intelligent and competent people believe this to be so. Why, then, should they abandon us in our most critical moments?

Inner dialogue? Yes, of course. Endorphin-mediated serenity? Very well could be. But when the conflicting voices merge into one affirmation of faith and joy, and when endorphins are released at this very moment, would it not be gracious to thank our angels as well? It is time to free ourselves from the materialistic assumption that we have fully explained something when we have identified a physical correlate. We can have our inner dialogues and our endorphins and our angels, too.

The current revival of interest in angels indicates that people are less intimidated by the dominant materialistic ethos. Experiences with angels are recognized for what they are, and without apology. The new wave of reports is consistent with what people have experienced with angels through the centuries. For our purposes here, perhaps the most significant characteristics of these encounters are what Sophy Burnham[4] identifies as the first and second marks of an angel.

The first mark of an angel is that "It brings a calm and peaceful serenity that descends sweetly over you, and this is true even when the angel is not seen." The second mark is their invariable message: "Fear not! ... Things are working out perfectly. You're going to like this. Wait." Burnham adds that "Never once do you hear of an angel trumpeting bad news, and when we think about dying, well, that's what we want to hear from the Angel of Death: peace and joy and light."

Sad to say, the critic turns his back on revelations and transformational experience. His credo seems to be: if it cannot be reproduced under controlled conditions by a team of well-funded scientists, then it just doesn't exist. Science and critical theory are asked to perform more than the useful and honorable tasks for which they are well equipped. This overdependence on one approach to reality leaves its believers in an impoverished world. There is little to nourish the spirit and the imagination – worse, there is no faith in the intrinsic value of human life. Sad for the critic, sadder if we choose to emulate this narrow and nihilistic approach.

AND ANOTHER WORD FROM THE CRITIC

The advocate has now told us that need-driven perception provides impeccable evidence because it helps to create its own reality. He would have us ignore the difference between a hungry man finding bread – a substance we all have tasted – and a dying man believing that he has been found by the insubstantiality that is called an angel. It is absurd to think that one has proven the reality of angelic visitors – and therefore survival of death) because these hallucinatory figures have been produced by need-driven perceptions. He is playing an unscrupulous game in which one unproven assumption is taken as proof of another.

It is time to retire the whole retinue of angels, Yamdoots and deceased personages and concentrate instead on the actual situation of the dying person. We will all have that hour in which the living flesh loses its glow, and we will then stand in need of compassionate companionship. We may hope that such companionship is available to us when that time comes, and we may endeavor to prepare ourselves to offer our companionship to others when it is their time to depart this life. The story of spiritual escorts across the border is one of humankind's more charming inventions – but let us emulate the angels as best we can and not stake everything on the rustle of their hallucinatory wings.

3

DO THE DEAD STAY IN TOUCH? AND DO THEY DO IT WITH MIRRORS?

Many people believe that near-death experiences provide evidence for survival. Although reports of deathbed escorts have not received very much attention in recent years, there are people who also accept these experiences as indicative of survival. We have moved, then, from episodes in which a person had a close brush with death to those in which the person actually died, but not before seemingly having an interaction with a spirit-visitor. We now take another step toward the outermost edge of human experience.

— Beyond the near-death experience and beyond the deathbed scene is the person who has been certified as dead and whose body has been placed in the ground or reduced to ashes. Is it possible for the dead stay in touch with the living? Through the centuries there have been many reports of interactions between the living and the dead. If we find these reports – even just a few of them – credible, then we have still another foundation for belief in survival.

But are these reports – even just a few of them – really credible? Since we are already survivors (of the NDE and deathbed escort chapters), we should be forewarned that this question will prompt bitterly oppositional arguments from the advocate and the critic. And they have something new and provocative to dispute over: reports of the mirrored dead as part of the ongoing studies of one of the key contributors to the current dialogue about survival of death. We will come to Raymond Moody's *psychomanteum* reports after the advocate and critic have had the opportunity to cross swords on some of the classic issues regarding possible living-dead interactions.

THE ADVOCATE'S CASE

We know death is survived for a very simple yet decisive reason: the dead have repeatedly communicated with the living. There can be no doubt in the minds of those who have had such an experience. It no longer becomes a matter of speculation or belief. They know! Nor are such experiences very rare. We will see that many people have had visitations from the dead, and that some instances are remarkably well documented. There is so much evidence, in fact, that to begin with we will concentrate on just one type of situation: the newly deceased person finding a way to contact the living. This seems to be the most common circumstance.

A FEW ILLUSTRATIVE CASES

These contacts have been occurring throughout the centuries – perhaps since the first death. Our ancestors throughout the world, whether in nomadic tribes or bustling cities took it for granted that the dead were still interested in the affairs of the living and could intervene in various ways. The living and the dead were known to be on different levels of existence, but capable of interaction under appropriate circumstances.

It is only since the centralization of political power and the smoggy dawn of the industrial era that the dead have been systematically segregated from the living.[1] And it's been lonely ever since – both for the living and the dead! Reports of contacts between the living and the dead became somewhat heretical or, as we tend to put it today, 'politically incorrect'. It is hard to keep the dead in their places, however, especially when they are more accurately described as survivors of death. Yet such experiences continued to occur even though they did not accord with the rules of legalistic and mechanistic modern societies.

It was a little more than a century ago when the people who dared to take a responsible interest in living-dead interaction also had the inspiration to use the techniques of science to evaluate reports that seemed at variance with the expectations of science. We will look at a few examples and then see how rigorously this material was evaluated before being accepted as evidence.

My little son, Arthur, who was then five years old, and the pet of his grandpa, was playing on the floor, when I entered the house at a quarter to seven o'clock, Friday evening, July 11th, 1879. I was very tired, having been receiving and paying for staves all day, and it being an exceedingly sultry evening, I lay down by Artie on the regard to my parents. Artie, as usually was the case, came and lay down with his little head upon my left arm, when all at once he exclaimed, 'Papa! PAPA! Grandpa!' I cast my eyes towards the ceiling, or opened my eyes, I am not sure which, when, between me and the joists (it was an old-fashioned log cabin), I saw the face of my father as plainly as ever I saw him in my life. He appeared to me to be very pale, and looked sad, as I had seen him upon my last visit to him three months previous. I immediately spoke to my wife, who was sitting within a few feet of me, and said, 'Clara, there is something wrong at home; my father is either dead or very sick.' She tried to persuade me that it was my imagination, but I could not help feeling that something was wrong. Being very tired, we soon after retired, and about ten o'clock Artie woke me up in determination to go at once to Indianapolis. My wife made light of it and overpersuaded me, and I did not go until Monday morning, and upon arriving at home (my father's), I found that he had been buried the day before, Sunday, July 13th.[2]

The narrator, a decorator and house-painter, later told his mother and brother of this experience. They reported that his father, a Methodist minister, arose early on what was to be the day of his death. He announced that he felt unusually well and ate a hearty breakfast. After spending much of the day with the Bible, he also enjoyed a hearty dinner "and went to the front gate, and, looking up and down the street, remarked that he could not, or at least would not be disappointed, someone was surely coming. During the afternoon and evening he seemed restless, and went to the gate, looking down the street, frequently." He then mentioned the name of his son (the narrator) and expressed his conviction that God would in "His own good time" set his son on the right path in life. After supper, the minister moved his chair closer to the door and started again to converse about the son who had not yet set his feet securely on the right path. "The last words were about me, and were spoken, by the mother's clock, 14 minutes of 7. He did not fall, but just quit talking and was dead."

The narrator's wife subsequently prepared and certified her own account of the occurrence, which agreed what her husband had reported. This was also the one and only time in this man's life that he had such an experience.

You will have noticed that this report is full of detail and has corroboration from those who actually witnessed the father's death. It is also clear that the minister had a special motive for contacting his son: fatherly concern that he put aside youthful foibles and meet the expectations established for him. If an experience of this kind happened in your own life, how could you not acknowledge its authenticity?

Here is another example: Captain Ayre was staying with a friend named Hunt at a small farmhouse one summer. One evening the two men heard a noise at the side of the house and went to the window to investigate.

The captain distinctly saw a man walking outside, but Hunt could see nothing there, though he had heard the tramp of feet as well as the captain. Being astonished that Hunt could not see the man, Captain Ayre proceeded to describe him. He was a man of short stature, with a stoop, and wore knee breeches, a red-fronted waistcoat with sleeves, and a little black hat. Hunt instantly identified the description as answering exactly to his own father.[2]

The captain had never seen his friend's father. Late that night both men again heard a noise

> as if the end of the bedstead had been wrenched, which continued until midnight, when Hunt's brother arrived on horseback from Gilberdyke with the news of their father's death, which occurred about three hours earlier that evening. The noises then ceased.[2]

This remarkable instance, like the first, involved not one but two people who made spontaneous and simultaneous observations, although, strangely enough, it was the captain rather than Hunt himself who experienced a visual as well as an auditory contact. This 'strangeness' is hardly something that one would invent.

And still another example: Mrs J. Bennett and her daughter Annie had been drinking tea with two other women and discussing their brother, Preston Moore, who was so ill that he was not expected to recover. Returning home, the mother and daughter met Preston. Indeed,

> he passed so near us that we shrank aside to make way for him. As soon as we got to Mrs Newbold's she exclaimed, 'So, Preston Moore is dead!' when we both answered in a breath, 'Oh, no, we have just seen him!'
>
> We found, in fact, that he had died about half an hour before he appeared to us.

Follow-up investigation indicated that,

> neither doubted at the time that what they saw was Preston Moore in the flesh … he was a peculiar looking man, very plain, and with an eye chronically inflamed; wore habitually a white hat on one side of his head, a loose shabby long coat, open down the front, and carried a long, hooked, heavy stick … They took no particular interest in him, just knew him.

Yet the odd-looking Mr Moore had previously taken some interest in Mrs Bennett, for "once he brought her pansies, stolen from a neighbouring gentleman's garden, and another time cauliflowers – equally illegitimately acquired."

The investigation also indicated that,

> Preston Moore was the last person whom the percipients would at that moment have expected to meet out of doors; and they were, therefore, very unlikely to assume that the figure was he, without looking at him attentively.

It would have been virtually impossible to mistake anyone else for Preston, nor was there any reason for the women to have either expected or desired to see him at that time (or, probably, at any other time). Here, then, are three detailed and persuasive examples, a minuscule sampling of all those that have come to light.

PHANTASMS OF THE LIVING: A CLASSIC STUDY

Do not be misled by the fact that all these examples are about a century old and limited to the British. Contacts between the dead and the living have occurred in many other times and places, including our own. These particular cases are cited here because they come from the first major rigorous investigation of such phenomena. The story of this investigation is worth telling. It will help us to appreciate the keen critical judgment and integrity of the investigators, people who were not inclined to be taken in by faulty information. Furthermore, we will draw repeatedly from other findings and observations made by this group of pioneers.

The Society for Psychical Research (SPR) was established in 1882 by an exceptional set of British scholars and scientists, among the most learned and accomplished savants anywhere in the world. Not a naive or moonstruck person among them! Some had already taken part in other groups interested in spiritualistic phenomena. There was at the time an upsurge of interest in contacts between the living and the dead and in what is now called extrasensory perception, precognition, psychokinesis and the like: all topics that are still being studied by modern parapsychologists. Although many people were convinced that the deceased do communicate with the living, some required more rigorous evidence. They raised question after question, which did not increase their popularity among the convinced, and soon broke away to form their own working group, the SPR.

Traditional religious beliefs had been assaulted by a series of scientific advances, including Darwin's theory of evolution. At the same time, new industrial technologies were bringing about many changes in life-style. The prospect of a better life on earth seemed to be at hand. The emerging 'modernity' promised unprecedented material comforts and amenities, along with more opportunity for individualism. Those who cherished traditional religious views started to find themselves on the defensive. Some SPR leaders believed or hoped that fundamental religious values could be rescued from this onslaught – and would perhaps even be confirmed rather than undermined by the scientific method.

This motivation could arouse suspicion that they would merely find what they sought, whether it was there or not. But there was a strong counterbalancing motivation – the need to meet high standards of evidence. As scholars and scientists they had reputations at risk. Weak-mindedness or bias in evaluating data on survival would have destroyed their credibility and self-respect. From the outset, the likes of Sir William Barrett, Henry Sidgwick, Frank Podmore, Edmund Gurney and Frederick W.H. Myers were resolved to exercise unstinting critical judgment.

The first major SPR project was an attempt to collect testimony on psychic phenomena experienced by the public at large – spontaneous events that had suddenly intruded into the lives of people who had no training, expectations or involvement in spiritualism. Thousands and thousands of contacts were made by correspondence and personal interview. The method and results were described in a massive two-volume work, *Phantasms of the Living,* from which our examples were selected.

The Gurney-Myers-Podmore team winnowed out many reports that did not meet their criteria. No matter how fascinating an experience might have been, if it was deficient from the evidential standpoint, out it went! For example, second-hand reports, were almost always excluded. Testimony had to be received from at least one of the people who had actually had the experience. Exceptions were made in some cases when they were sure that the percipient (the individual having the experience) had described the event before any objective confirmatory knowledge was obtained. If I told you on Monday that a mutual acquaintance suddenly appeared to me where I would not have expected to see him, and we both learned on Tuesday that this acquaintance had died at about the time of the reported experience, this might be an accepted case. But if I told you about this incident on Tuesday, after having learned of our friend's death, the case would be discarded. Using this criterion, the SPR project committee almost certainly excluded many instances in which there actually was contact between the dead and the living.

Reports suspected of being fraudulent were, of course, quickly rejected as well. Still other cases were set aside because the experiences could be explained more simply as coincidences. There had to be something in the report – and the follow-up inquiry – that went beyond the limits of ordinary coincidence. The investigators therefore looked for multiple details. While perhaps any one or two points in the report might be explained as coincidence, the existence of many confirmable details seemed to require a different conclusion. When the percipient's experience and the objective event (e.g. death of a friend) were more than 12 hours apart the case was usually rejected as well. This was one of the ways in which the margins of coincidence could be reduced. There were still other criteria for dismissing reports. For example, the case would be discarded if the independent testimonies of several percipients or witnesses differed in significant ways.

The more promising cases were checked against all the objective information that could be found. If the objective facts were inconsistent with the percipient's report, this case, too, was rejected. Nor was this all! *The most dramatic reports were often rejected precisely because they were so dramatic.* The investigators distrusted reports that showed the marks of embellishment, where the original experience had perhaps been elaborated and 'improved' to make a better story. The more startling or picturesque the report, the more thorough and critical the evaluation.

Similarly, experiences that occurred when the percipient was in a disturbed or unusual mental state were also examined with special care and were often rejected. This procedure again probably had the effect of losing true experiences that were genuinely dramatic. However, the investigators were willing to lose many possible 'positives' in order to avoid accepting even a few 'doubtfuls'.

The authors of *Phantasms of the Living* were not push-overs. They accepted only a fraction of the reports that came their way. Our doubts about the value of ordinary anecdotes do not apply here. Survival of death was demonstrated only by those reports that managed to survive a rigorous process of investigation and evaluation.

FROM ONE MIND TO ANOTHER

Many explanations were considered for the valid cases. The investigators were as careful in drawing conclusions as they were in evaluating the actual reports. Acting on behalf of the research group, Gurney reached the conclusion that agreed best with their evidence, and which was at the same time consistent with studies of telepathy or thought transference. Early experiments on telepathy seemed to have demonstrated the reality of telepathy. Taking these findings into account, Gurney suggested that *a crisis in the mind of one person might lead to an impression being formed in the mind of another*. Dying, he reasoned, is a powerful crisis and may therefore generate a strong flow of communication between two or more minds.

This is a conservative interpretation. There was a tempting alternative: *the dead person himself actually appears* in some form to people miles away from his physical body. This alternative explanation would have accorded well with some of the reports. In accepting the telepathic hypothesis instead, Gurney was not necessarily rejecting the bolder conclusion. Instead he was deliberately limiting himself to the most conservative interpretation that could account for the facts. We will see later that other kinds of evidence do indeed support the alternative hypothesis. Sticking with the material collected and analysed in this first SPR project, however, we might as well go along with Gurney's admirable caution: telepathy demonstrated, direct contact possible.

And this conservative interpretation is itself powerful enough to confirm survival of death! *What does it matter how the dead contact the living?* Telepathic communication is effective enough, at least on occasion, to bring the dead person into the mind of the living. Sometimes the communication is limited, passing Preston Moore on the street for instance; but, then, sometimes communication among the living is limited too. In other instances specific facts are communicated and, perhaps more important, the percipient develops an emotional impression that is right on target. Those who have just crossed over not only have keen motivation for reaching us, but also the ability to do so.

EXAMPLES FROM OUR OWN TIME

Many episodes with the ring of authenticity have been occurring in our own time. Here is one that was the subject of an investigation by Arthur Berger[3], who has conducted a number of open-minded inquiries into evidence for survival:

> *James L. Chaffin, a North Carolina farmer, made a will leaving his farm to one son and nothing at all to his wife or other three sons. Fourteen years later he tried to rectify matters by making a new will. After he wrote it out and signed it (legal in North Carolina), he inserted it into an old Bible. For his own reasons, he never told anyone about it.*

The original version of the will became operative when Chaffin died. Years passed. And then

> *one of the sons left out of the first will saw his father dressed in an overcoat at his bedside. The father told him that he would find the new will in the father's overcoat pocket. The overcoat was found along with a note ... (that) contained a reference to the chapter of the old Bible where the second will could be found. It (the revised will) was probated in court. The lawyer who investigated the case could not, despite all his skill, find any reason to suspect the honesty and sincerity of the parties involved.*

There are two especially interesting features of this case: firstly that the apparition of the dead person did not appear promptly after his death, as usually happens, but seemed to have waited for some unknown reason; and secondly there was a palpable physical outcome – discovery of the revised will whose existence no one had suspected.

We do not want to give the impression that all reports of living-dead contact involve visual perception. Often the communication is auditory and, sometimes, tactile or olfactory. Several of these modalities may be involved in the same episode. Here is one of the incidents collected recently by the distinguished parapsychologist Erlendur Haraldsson.[4]

> *The night after my husband died I could not sleep. I was at home in my bed and very lonely. Suddenly I sensed him standing by my bed. He seemed to be covered in something like mist. I **saw** him and **felt** his hand as he stroked my head and he **recited** part of a well-known poem that was about how good it was to rest and then wake up one day surrounded with eternal joy. I felt quite differently after this.*

This newly-widowed woman had visual, auditory, and tactile contact with her dead husband – all of which changed her feelings from depression and loneliness to "eternal joy".

The mention of olfactory contact might sound odd. "What does a spirit smell like?" It is not necessarily the spirit that smells, as another of Haraldsson's cases demonstrates:

I lived in Sandgerdi where we had just bought a house two months ago. I was alone in the house.

My husband was out working. Suddenly I see that a man enters through the front door and goes to the kitchen. This happened suddenly and was over.

I then felt a strong smell of liquor. I never use alcohol. Well, then my husband comes home, and he says: 'Who has been here?' Nobody I tell him.

'Oh, there is such a strong smell of liquor.' Yes, I say, but nobody has been here ... The next day my husband comes home for supper and says: 'No wonder there was a liquor smell here yesterday ...'

... Erlingur from whom we bought the house was missing in Siglufjord yesterday. He had been quite drunk and it was feared that he had fallen into the harbour and drowned. Two weeks later his body was found floating in the harbour. When this incident occurred we had no idea about what had happened.

In another example, a widower was getting out of bed when he "smelled a particular perfume that my wife always used." As he explained it: "My wife was making me aware of her to comfort me."

Whether the experiences occurred a century ago or just last night, and whether the communication was by sight, sound, touch, or odor, there is no doubt that the dead are at least sometimes with the living. And this, of course, means that there is some form of meaningful survival of death.

THE CRITIC'S RESPONSE

We have been offered a cunningly constructed web that is spun of the same material that fashioned the emperor's new clothes. The spinner impresses and delights us with many a gesture. It is all to no purpose, however. The material is without substance; the web is fabricated out of moonbeams for those who are content with illusion. Let us now move out of the web of moonlight and shadows into the bright light of reason

TELEPATHY: AN EXPLANATION IN NEED OF EXPLANATION

The advocate spoke admiringly of Gurney's "conservative interpretation". A conservative interpretation indeed! I saw a winged unicorn in my garden this morning – but, never mind, it was only a small unicorn! Reduce the size of an error and what remains is error none the less. The 'conservative' interpretation requires us to accept a proposition that has not earned acceptance.

Mental telepathy is an hypothesis. It is not a proven fact. This was true a century ago and it is true today. Furthermore, the 'conservative' interpretation places extra weight on this shaky hypothesis. Telepathic communication between two or more living people is questionable enough. Asserting that telepathic communication between the living and the dead exists is an exercise in speculation. There is not much harm in it as idle speculation. We are being misled, however, when telepathy between the living and the dead is grafted on to the basic telepathy hypothesis as though fact. 'Grafted' is an appropriate word: it is as though a fabulous new fruit were attached to a non-existent tree while nobody was looking. We are given no positive evidence for telepathy between the living and the dead, no evidence for the existence of such a process. The 'SuperESP' hypothesis, as it is sometimes called, is itself unauthenticated and cannot serve as explanation for anything else.

Problems with the living-dead telepathy hypothesis can be seen even more clearly when we remind ourselves of the persistent difficulties that parapsychologists have had in trying to establish the less presumptuous hypothesis of 'ordinary' extrasensory perception (ESP). Consider the following problems.

Research on telepathy has suffered from many flaws. The studies that impressed Gurney and his colleagues were among the first of their kind, and their limitations would eventually become apparent. Even the later studies often have reveal serious flaws. Apply high standards of evidence and we find a high casualty rate among studies that seem to show ESP effects.[5,6] (We use 'telepathy' and 'ESP' interchangeably here.) Some people remain impressed by the sheer number of studies, however, and continue to accept findings that have been discredited. There is not nearly as much presentable evidence as many would like to believe.

Only the positive findings are reported. A few studies with negative results have found publication because of the insistence of the more responsible parapsychologists. Nevertheless, the major body of research reports on ESP is biased in favour of positive results. Here is another factor, then, that generates the impression that telepathic communication has been well documented: studies that fail to show such effects lie unpublished and forgotten.

Some studies have been fudged. Those who know this field of research well do not contest this sad fact. Honest researchers are embarrassed and distressed by evidence of data-tampering on the part of some of their colleagues. Investigators who may have been honest to start with have sometimes 'improved' their findings or ignored deceit on the part of their respondents.[7] This is easy enough to do if one is already convinced that ESP is real – and therefore a little fudging of the facts is thought not to matter. It does matter, of course. Nobody knows how many studies that purport to show ESP are tainted.

The 'mechanisms' of telepathy remain obscure. How telepathy works and what rules it follows remain obscure after all these years. This is not for lack of attention and ingenuity. Interesting research and theories continue to come forth.[8] There are still no hard facts, however, nor established laws. After more than a century of investigation and speculation, we still have little to go on. The case for telepathy will never be firmly established until the conditions and principles of its operations are identified and confirmed.

Telepathy cannot be produced on demand. This is crucial. In all the sciences we require that a finding or a phenomenon be replicable. An occurrence here and there only arouses curiosity. For a phenomenon to be established it must be observed repeatedly under carefully specified conditions. To the constant frustration of parapsychologists, this is precisely what ESP refuses to do. ESP seems to happen when it feels like it, often enough under conditions that make definitive study impossible. Friends of telepathy offer many excuses for its elusive nature. We are left, however, with scattered experiences that are a long way from meeting the criteria for scientific verification.

The case for 'ordinary' telepathy has not been proven. Furthermore, explanations for this unproven phenomenon have not been convincing. Something that requires as much explanation (and faith!) as telepathy cannot be used to prove something else – especially when that something else happens to be survival of death.

CRISIS TELEPATHY WOULD NOT PROVE SURVIVAL, ANYHOW!

What has already been said is enough to bury the telepathy-survival hypothesis. But let us pretend for a moment that telepathy does exist. Would cases culled from *Phantasms of the Living* and other sources then prove survival? Not at all!

First of all, many of the crisis-telepathy experiences seemed to occur before the 'transmitter' died. Examine all the cases and you find that often the investigators could not establish the precise moment of death. Frequently they settled on the day of burial, an objective fact that can be more easily ascertained. In some instances it was clear that the transmitting person was still alive at the moment the communication occurred. All cases of this type should obviously be set aside so far as the survival hypothesis is concerned. At the most, they would only indicate that a person in the midst of a crisis can sometimes communicate with somebody else through the process we call 'telepathy' or 'ESP', for want of solid knowledge. This would be a fascinating fact, if established, but would not bear on the survival question.

This leaves other cases in which the precise relationship between time of death and time of communication is uncertain. When in doubt it is always advisable to take the simpler and more conservative position. In other words, the doubtful cases probably belong with those in which the transmitting person was still alive when the percipient had his experience. We are now reduced to the relatively few cases in which there was firm evidence that the percipient received his or her impression after rather than before the sender's death. Remember, also, that the original pool of possible cases was in the thousands. Apparent evidence for telepathic communication between the dead and the living has a way of evaporating, as holds true also for ordinary telepathy as well.

A few good cases, though – isn't that enough? Possibly: yes. Theoretically: yes. Practically: no. They would have to be very good cases, and these are not to be found even in the extensive Gurney-Myers-Podmore collection. Furthermore, the explanation that the dead have spoken or somehow impressed themselves on the living can be accepted only if simpler and more straightforward explanations prove inadequate. This is not the case. Here is a much simpler hypothesis of events:

The sequence begins as Mr A realizes he is dying. At this critical moment in his life he has an intense desire to communicate with his close friend, Mr. B. Unfortunately, Mr B is miles away at the time. (Let us suppose that for some reason telephone communication is not feasible. Mr A starts to generate a telepathic signal. Nobody really knows the nature of this signal nor how it is transmitted; nevertheless we will assume for now that this phenomenon does exist. At this point one of the following things happens:

- Mr B fails to pick up this signal at first. Perhaps the signal is weak, has become obscured through 'noise', or has gone astray. Or perhaps Mr B is either a marginal receiver of telepathic signals or is not in a mode that allows him to be receptive at this moment.

- The signal is received without delay, but translation takes a while. Ordinary information received through our senses must go through a complex process of registration, classification and screening before it reaches consciousness. Extraordinary information received through unusual means might take some processing too.

- The signal is transmitted and received in a manner that cannot be understood by use of our conventional time-frames. The rate of time's passage and such markers as minutes, hours and days may falsify what is actually taking place. Even the categories of *before* and *after* may not apply. In dreams, for example, the time markers and categories we use in ordinary waking life are replaced by a totally different set of rules and processes. It may be that objective time as measured by clocks and calendars is external and irrelevant to telepathic communications. When we apply ordinary time categories to telepathic communications, then, we may be distorting and misunderstanding the process of thought transfer. Perhaps we know so little about ESP because it follows different rules from those that govern communication in the objective time-space manifold.

Suppose Mr A dies at 7 a.m. What is 7 a.m. to the inner world of the psyche? Who can specify the speed of thought transmission? Who can even say that the concept of speed or of simultaneity even applies to this realm? *The fact that modern society is so relentlessly time-conscious does not prove that objective time also reigns over our dreams, our paranormal communications, or our innermost minds.*

Mr B has the awareness of telepathic communication after the death of Mr A. Nevertheless, the communication was initiated while Mr A was still alive. It took a little while (in objective or clock time) for Mr B to respond. Telepathic communication is not necessarily instantaneous. And why should it be? So little is known about the specifics of telepathic communication (still assuming for the moment that it does exist) that it would be arbitrary to insist that transmission and reception of the message is instantaneous; there is certainly nothing that resembles evidence for this proposition.

I have made more assumptions than I would prefer in sketching this alternative explanation. Even the fanciest alternative however, requires fewer and less radical assumptions than does the contention that the dead touch the living. It is far more reasonable to conclude that the dying might on occasion be able to generate a signal or impulse that the living eventually pick up. This is a big assumption in itself, but it stops short of assuming survival. Extraordinary communication between living people is a much different proposition than communication between the living and the dead.

HOW GOOD WERE THE DATA TO BEGIN WITH?

The work of Gurney and his associates has been praised to the rafters by the advocate. This is supposed to soften us up to accept the data and, therefore, the conclusions. And in truth their work is praiseworthy. They were intelligent and honourable people. What's more, they probably did as thorough and diligent a job as the situation permitted. I doubt that anybody else could have carried out this work better at the time. All this zeal and competence, however, cannot elevate flawed and incomplete information into quality data. To put this in a more bucolic way: even a skilled craftsman cannot turn the sow's ear of unreliable data into the silk purse of survival. Gurney and his colleagues recognized many of the limitations themselves. Many reports were eliminated because they failed to meet the criteria. That was a good start. They should have kept going and eliminated all the reports! There is an almost apologetic tone in *Phantasms of the Living* that suggests they had serious misgivings about even the best cases. Again and again they point out limitations in the reports and in their method of inquiry. The reports, for example, sometimes involved incidents that had occurred years ago. "If the percipient does not record his experience at the time of its occurrence, even a week's interval may destroy the possibility of making sure what its exact date was." This poses serious difficulties when the event is recollected over an interval not of a week but of years. It is all too likely that "the percipient may assume too readily that his own experience fell on the critical day; and as time goes on, his certainty is likely to increase rather than diminish."

The information collected by Osis and Haraldsson had to be criticized because it was retrospective and second-hand: essentially a collection of stories told to the researchers. The same problem exists here. It is a more serious problem because we are also separated from the researchers themselves by an entire century. The best available study of deathbed visions and the pioneering study of 'phantasms' are both crippled by their reliance on incidents reconstructed from the memory of very fallible humans. There would be problems enough in a direct observational study; here, however, the problems are simply overwhelming.

There is no point in criticizing the SPR project committee for doing what it could and coming up short. However, I am sure the advocate would want you to know that *the investigators themselves soon realized that these data could not be put forth as proving survival of death.* They make this point repeatedly:

- "Here no voice can speak with absolute authority." [2]
- "The game (of understanding the world) is one in which it will never be safe to bet far ahead; and it is one which will certainly never end." (Volume 1, p.3)
- "The experimental investigations must be greatly extended, the spontaneous phenomena must be far more intelligently watched for and recorded, before the place of telepathy in scientific psychology can be absolutely assured." (Volume 2, p.xiii)

Although encouraged by some of their findings, Gurney, Podmore and Myers cautioned that much more and better data needed to be collected and evaluated just to establish the telepathic communication thesis on a firm basis. And, as we have already seen, it is still a long step from telepathy between the living and contact between the living and the dead. The advocate would do well to heed the good advice of his forebearers and tone down his assertions.

The more recent examples presented by the advocate are not great improvements over the reports collected by Gurney and his colleagues a century ago. This pioneering team might well have rejected the farmer's overcoat saga in which one person claimed to have seen the deceased gentleman after many years had passed. The convenient discovery (or creation) of the revised will could have preceded the fortuitous postmortem visit. The authenticity of this incident seems to hinge on the conclusion reached by a lawyer who found no reason to suspect "the honesty and sincerity of the parties involved". The parties involved were in a situation in which they might have been quite honest and sincere ... in their desire to have the original will overturned. The lawyer, who did not himself view the apparition, nevertheless might have had the vision of an envelope stuffed with money passed under the table for his certification of the revised will. By all means, let's investigate the pockets of old overcoats, but let's not take such tales as proof of survival.

It was useful for the advocate to mention cases in which the reported mode of contact was auditory, tactile, or olfactory. Visual experiences tend to be more dramatic, but many reports are based on what people hear or feel. As a matter of fact, it is relatively common to have a general 'sense of presence' of a loved one who has recently died. The person who has such an experience may be convinced that this was an authentic contact with a deceased person. Hearing or just 'sensing' can be almost as persuasive as seeing. The individual's sense of authenticity, however, does not itself confirm authenticity. You may recall Morse's right temporal lobe hypothesis[9] as discussed in the near-death experience chapter. Memory, dreams, and paranormal or altered states of consciousness all seem to be subject to stimulation within the same region of the midbrain. Stress, fatigue, depression, and other intense need-states can increase the sensitivity of this area or, even more likely, reduce the usual inhibiting effects of the rational-coping functions of the nervous system. In consequence, one tends to lose the boundaries between 'perception'. 'memory', and 'fantasy/dream'. Whether we accept Morse's neurophysiological hypothesis or any of its leading competitors, we see that the brain/mind is now credited with the ability to generate its own perceptions when the going gets rough.

And perhaps this is why the advocate has been so productive in generating his own perceptions of the survival question: the going is still very, very rough for this fantasy.

THE ADVOCATE'S RESPONSE

What the critic has labored and labored to say will not trouble those who have actually experienced communication with the dead. In addition, it does not come close to disproving either of the two survival explanations: direct appearance of the deceased person to the living, or, more conservatively, telepathic communication. He merely suggests other explanations for these experiences and quibbles about methodology. One can always suggest other explanations ... one can always quibble.

Let us be clear about something. The experiences carefully reviewed by Gurney and his colleagues are entirely consistent with communication between the living and the dead. More specifically, communication between the newly deceased and the living may be especially common. The fact that other explanations can be invented does not require us to withdraw the original conclusion. And the reports we have been considering are only a small part of the total evidence available. Would you like more proof? Coming right up!

THE PSYCHOMANTEUM: MIRRORING THE SOUL

The name of Raymond A. Moody, Jr. was prominently featured in our discussion of NDEs. It was Dr. Moody who first recognized the significance of this close encounter with death. He has remained a respected leader in the exploration of NDEs ever since. And now this same man has brought another astonishing phenomenon to our attention. Like the NDE, this phenomenon has an ancient history but can also be experienced today. And again, like the NDE, this phenomenon could have been identified and explored by a great many people, yet required the curiosity and open-mindedness of Dr Moody. Unlike NDEs, though, visionary encounters with deceased loved ones take place in relaxed, none-life-threatening circumstances in the comfort of a pleasant room. A room equipped with a mirror. He calls this place a *psychomanteum*, and he also calls it an apparition chamber.

One of the most famous of all mirrors is the one through which Alice passed *en route* to Wonderland. Long before this famous literary adventure, however, people had been gazing into reflective surfaces and having extraordinary experiences as a result. Because Moody's current work draws from ancient sources, it will be useful to review the historical background.

THE ORACLE OF THE DEAD AND THE
MIRRORED SOUL

One of ancient history's most fascinating sites is seldom visited. In a remote mountainous area of Greece, "My wife and I were alone on the spot immortalized by Odysseus and Orpheus and visited by thousands of people in their quest to see lost loved ones".[10] Moody is referring to the temple of the Oracle of the Dead (or *Psychomanteum*) located on a hill top near what had been the city of Ephyra. A Roman army razed the city and the temple, but the legends emanating from this source have fed the world's imagination for centuries. The living and the dead were thought to meet at this sacred location through the mediation of the priests (known as *psychopomps*) who summoned the apparitions.

> *The roof of the structure is gone, leaving exposed the maze of corridors and rooms that apparition seekers wandered through while waiting to venture into the apparition chamber. All of the portions of the oracle are still visible ... Leaving the priest's quarters and winding through*

the maze of corridors, I tried to imagine what this place would have been like two thousand years ago when it was as dark as a cave and filled with a kind of eerie anticipation.

What did people do for the weeks they were in here? What did they think about and talk about? Even though I like to be alone, my mind boggled at the thought of such lengthy and total sensory deprivation. (p. 62)

Once in the temple's largest chamber – the apparition room – Moody imagined

what a rush to the senses it would be to enter this room after nearly a month in semidarkness. In this majestic chamber torches would be flickering against the walls as robed priests guided apparition seekers to the polished metal cauldron that dominated the room. At the rim of the cauldron they would be told to gaze into the shimmering metal and behold the vision that they came to see.

And, reportedly, they did see visions, visions of the departed.

So have many other people in many other times and places. Moody identified numerous examples throughout history. It became clear that the dead could appear to the living under certain conditions. But what, precisely, were these conditions? Visual concentration on a reflecting surface seemed to be the basic requirement. Other factors might improve the chances. Expectation and a preceding period of sensory deprivation were noted as possible enhancing factors by Moody in his readings and personal inspection of the Oracle of the Dead. Rituals also seemed to contribute to the experience. In Madagascar there was a time when elaborate group ceremonies helped to evoke the spirits of the dead. The rituals would begin with the priests' attempts to contact spirits through the use of mirrors.

Moody pursued the theme of visionary encounters with the dead in mythology, literature, history, anthropology, and other related fields. He attempted to identify the most salient and universal element in the visionary experience. Moody noticed that many details could vary, but the indispensable element seemed to be the practice of gazing at or into a reflective surface. He also identified a scholar who had investigated the powers of the psychomanteum more than four hundred years ago. John Dee, born in 1527, was a confidant of Queen Elizabeth who was renowned for his contributions to navigational techniques and mathematics. He also served the Queen as a secret agent. Dee came across a divination mirror that had been used by the Aztecs. To his surprise, Dee could see visions in the mirror, and the Queen visited his house to see this wonder for herself.

Dee made his home into a consciousness research center. As one of the leading scientists of his time, Dee did not see himself as dabbling in games or mysticism but, rather, investigating the communicational potentials of the mind. Mirror-gazing was not his only line of investigation, but it was an important component. When Moody recently established his own consciousness research center in Alabama, he dubbed it The Dr John Dee Memorial Theater of the Mind.

MODERN PSYCHOMANTEUM EXPERIENCES

Moody's own explorations of the psychomanteum experience have yielded fascinating observations even though this work is in its early stages. He converted the upstairs of his old gristmill into a psychomanteum or apparition chamber. A mirror four feet tall and three and a half feet wide was mounted on the wall. A comfortable chair was modified to achieve the best viewing angle and placed about three feet from the mirror. With this arrangement, there was a clear depth view of the mirror, but viewers could not see their own reflections. "The result was a crystal-clear pool of darkness."

For his first set of explorations, Moody recruited mature, emotionally stable people who were capable of describing their experiences in an articulate manner. He wondered if they would see apparitions of their deceased loved ones in his modern day version of the ancient Greek temple. They did.

Here is an excerpt from a typical report.[10] The experiencer is a woman in her 40's whose father was deceased. At first she saw colors and clouds and then glimpses of a passing scene. For example:

… a little village that looked like it would be in England or maybe France, but old. This was very old. I had the feeling I was peering back in time …

After several glimpses of other scenes that had no apparent relation to her own life and times, she saw her father:

He just came up suddenly and I was looking right into his face. He talked to me, yes he did. He was funny like he always was. He asked me, why in the world are you trying to talk to me, girl? Or something like that. I can't say I heard a voice like I'm hearing you talk, but it was stronger than thoughts. I can't say we needed words. I just could tell what he was trying to say.

This was not a fleeting experience. The woman was in the psychomanteum for about an hour, and estimated that nearly half of that time was spent in conversation with her father.

The last thing he said to me was, 'Now you go on and enjoy your life.' I felt so good when he said that. There was a flood of relief and good feelings came rushing in. I don't believe I've felt so good since he died.

When he said that it was like something just closed off and it was over. Then there was just the mirror.

But I thought, well, if I need to talk to him or anybody else who died, I know I'll be able to do it now.

A young man in the psychomanteum was "sitting in there and all of a sudden it seemed that three people stepped right into the room around me. It looked like they stepped out of the mirror but I felt like that couldn't be, so I was shocked. I didn't know what was going on." The apparitions were his sister and grandfather, and a friend. "All of them looked very alive, just looking at me. I didn't hear any voices or really communicate with them. It happened so fast ... They seemed very happy. This was completely real ... It was just like they were there in the room with me."

In report after report the experiencers affirmed the reality of their contact with deceased loved ones. Their relatives or friends were *really* there. Sometimes there were long conversations; sometimes not a word was exchanged, but there was always that sense of actual presence. There were even experiences of direct contact, as with this woman who had been devastated by the death of her grandfather:

I was in tears, and I knew it was him. Then before I knew it he was hugging me and wiping away my tears. I felt him just like when he was alive.

Her profound response to this experience was also typical of those who have seen visions of the deceased in Moody's old grist-mill:

As long as I live I will remember this day at the Theater of the Mind. Thank you for making a place where people can come and be healed.

Please bear in mind that these people were emotionally stable adults. They were not under the influence of mind-altering substances. They were not exposed to the prolonged period of sensory deprivation and temple rituals that were part of the process at the original Oracle of the Dead. They were just responsible people walking into Moody's grist-mill from their everyday activities and responsibilities.

Has Moody himself tried his psychomanteum?

... at the time I honestly believed I could do so without compromising my objectivity. For, frankly, the most unsettling feature of the stories I was hearing from subjects coming out of the apparition room was that they were convinced that their visionary reunions were real and were not fantasies.

Moody had expected that if his "very grounded, reasonable" subjects did see apparitions they would conclude that there was no way of telling whether or not their experiences had been 'real'. Although surprised at his subjects' belief in the reality of their contact with deceased loved ones, Moody was confident that he wouldn't be fooled, should he also happen to see somebody in the mirror.

He hoped to see his maternal grandmother with whom he had been very close. Instead, to his astonishment, he had a brief but significant visit from his *paternal* grandmother. In Moody's childhood he had not much cared for this unpleasant person who frequently warned him that he would go to Hell if he disobeyed any of God's many strictures. Now, however, she was a younger-looking and much more positive person than the grandmother he remembered from his childhood. Death – or what comes after death – had somehow improved her.

The meeting itself was "completely natural ... In fact ... this was the most normal, non-crazy, satisfying interaction I had ever had with her, even while she was alive." Throughout this interaction Moody was amazed that he was with a deceased person, but the interaction itself seemed both real and positive. Moody's response to the experience was similar to those of his subjects. It also had a profound effect on his beliefs:

> *What took place between my departed grandmother and me that day resulted, I am happy to say, in a complete healing of our relationship, as well as leaving me with an abiding certainty that what we call death is not the end of life.*

No doubt much more will be learned at The Dr John Dee Memorial Theater of the Mind. Furthermore, the path has been cleared for other investigators to follow.

In the meantime we have evidence that the dead do stay in touch when given a reasonable opportunity to do so. This fact, once known to a great many people, was obscured for many years in materialistic societies and their rigid, blinkered ideologies. Now we can rediscover the consoling truth that not only do we survive death, but, as Moody noted, death at least sometimes can "do us a world of good".

FIDDLE-DEE-DEE! IT IS OUR HOPES THAT ARE MIRRORED

Dr John Dee was a remarkable person, and the same may be said for Dr Raymond A. Moody, Jr. Both were endowed with curiosity and courage; both have challenged their compatriots with mind-teasing ideas and observations.

In his latest adventures on the fringes of the mind, Moody may well have reinvigorated a valuable technique for helping grief-stricken survivors to help themselves. We have already seen that it is not unusual for recently bereaved people to sense the presence of the dead. These experiences are sometimes followed by a sense of consolation and relief. The psychomanteum experience could be a powerful and accessible way of working through feelings of grief:

● The 'sense of presence' now has a place to call its own.
● It has its build-up of expectancies.

- It has its legitimization, through Moody's prestige and his evocation of the ancient lineage.
- The mirror seems to focus, externalize, and therefore intensify the experience.

This is all well and good. The psychomanteum experience might prove to be a useful modality for people who are almost ready to resolve grief-related problems but who need some help in doing so. It is their own hopes and needs that are mirrored, and their own minds that serve as agents of healing and transformation. Should favorable reports continue – and disturbing experiences not occur – then there will be reason to give thanks to Moody, Dee, and the ancient priests of Ephyra.

None of this, however, constitutes credible evidence for survival of death. We all know that our minds can play tricks on us. The psychomanteum experience demonstrates how good these tricks can be. This is not necessarily a matter of deliberate self-deception or of naiveté. Visual imagery is especially susceptible to systematic error. Our eyes are wholly owned subsidiaries of our brains, as you can confirm by studying the anatomical and functional connections. A lot of information processing must occur before we have an integrated visual experience. As this processing takes place there is competition between information from external and internal sources. Internal sources include dreams, wishes, memories, expectancies and the like. The relationship between *Image and Brain*[11] is as complex as it is fascinating.

Let no one underestimate the ability of the brain to generate images, project these images, and then suppose itself to be viewing external reality! Our other sensory modalities are also quite capable of joining in the fun.

What is the psychomanteum experience, then? It is a meeting of ourselves and, perhaps, a healing of ourselves through this encounter. If these experiences continue and remain consistently positive, then there is wonder enough! But have these reports given us a single shred of credible new evidence for survival? Sorry – not a shred. Moody was right on target when he decided to call his old grist-mill a theater of the mind!

4

THE SPIRIT SURVIVES:
CASE HISTORIES

O good and innocent dead, hear us.
Hear us, you guiding, all-knowing ancestors.
You are neither blind nor deaf to this life we live:
You did yourselves once share it.
Help us therefore for the sake of our devotion, and for our good.

(a prayer from the Mende of Sierra Leone[1])

Nothing save mind is conceivable.
Mind, when uninhibited, conceives all that comes into existence.
That which comes into existence is like the wave of an ocean ...
Mind is beyond nature, but is experienced in bodily forms.
The realization of the One Mind constitutes the
All-Deliverance.
Although sentient beings are of the Buddha-essence
itself, not until they realize this can they attain Nirvana.
Seek, therefore, thine own Wisdom within thee.
It is the vast Deep.

(from *The Tibetan Book of the Great Liberation*[2])

WE ARE NOT ALONE IN THE WORLD

The body is not the spirit. People have known this since ancient times.
To this day many are convinced that their ancestors not only continue
to exist as spirits but are capable of taking a loving and protective
interest in their lives. The assumption that we are alone in the world
would have surprised most of the people who inhabited the earth before
our time. Unlike us, they had not been exposed to the alienating
influences of centralized power, bureaucracy, and technology. Mostly,
like the Mende of Sierra Leone, they lived within a sacred and coherent
world. Bodies changed and eventually perished, of course, but the spirit
moved on to its next phase of existence. The living and the spirits of the

deceased had their own agendas and concerns, but still cared about each other.

As the great world religions and philosophical systems came into being, this basic insight was expressed in diverse ways. The sophisticated dialogues of Plato affirmed the reality and persistence of spirit. Buddhism offered the beautiful vision of a state of spiritual being that transcends both life and death, a 'vast deep' that includes all the universe, yet is within us. Whether in an ancient tribal prayer or a sophisticated philosophical analysis, the reality of spirit survival has been affirmed repeatedly.

The rise of industrialization and technology led to doubts, fears, and confusions regarding all previous beliefs. The roar of the locomotive, the heat of the blast furnace, the numbing monotony of the assembly-line, and the impersonal face of corporate and governmental bureaucracy – all had the effect of isolating the individual.

Today, however, science is no longer the slave of narrow, mechanistic thinking. The universe that presents itself to physicists, neuroscientists, and other sophisticated researchers is consistent with the reality of spirit survival.[1,2] We turn now to a sampling of cases that demonstrate spirit survival. After a few such examples – some from the past, some from our own times – we will reflect on the place of spirit survival in our overall view of life.

AN OLD FARM HOUSE IN NEW JERSEY: A VERIFIED HAUNTING

We begin with a recent example that has had the advantage of sophisticated investigation. The researchers were Karlis Osis and Donna McCormick,[3] who describe their work in the *Journal of the American Society for Psychical Research*.

The events took place in an old farmhouse in southern New Jersey. Built in the years immediately preceding the War of American Independence, it survived at least one fire, and was reconstructed and enlarged several times. Descendants of the original family owned and resided in the house for about 200 years. By American standards, then, this house had experienced much history, much continuity – and there is something about continuous family occupancy that seems to encourage spirit manifestations from the deceased. The family graveyard (with burials from 1787 to 1856) remains undisturbed on the property, though not in direct view from the house. Its current owners converted the house into a gift shop. This could be regarded as both an intrusion and a disruption from its long history.

Unusual happenings were observed for a decade after the new family moved in. In fact, they were still being observed when Osis and McCormick read the proofs of their article. These observations were not been limited to the building's present owners, nor to these researchers. *At least 24 people have observed some of these phenomena!* On some occasions several witnesses were present. Here, then, is not a case one must dust off from the shelf, nor is it a sketchy report from some inaccessible place. The spirit manifestations have been repeated over the years, and have been repeatedly observed by many people as well as checked by experienced investigators.

And just what has been happening? Objects have resisted staying where they belong. A table has repeatedly moved itself from its new location in the master bedroom back to the spot it enjoyed in another room for many years. Tools have scattered themselves in the few minutes it took a repairman to return from his truck to the empty house. A piece of tile slid down from the fireplace and attacked a man's head from a most unlikely angle. This assault seemed almost impossible – how could a piece of tile hit him from that angle even if it wanted to? But it happened nevertheless. A filing cabinet drawer stuffed with heavy catalogues was known and cursed for its tendency to stick. Yet this heavy and reluctant drawer has repeatedly rolled out by itself – as though in defiance.

Let's not forget the old grandfather clock. Not having been wound up for a year, it had no business to tick. But it has repeatedly started ticking – and chiming – of its own accord. This behaviour (or misbehaviour) continued for almost a year, until it was removed from the building. These events exemplify the physical phenomena.

Another set of odd and unexplained behaviour has emanated from electrical appliances and systems. On numerous occasions electrical equipment – including a sewing-machine, an adding-machine and the ceiling lights – has inexplicably started or stopped without identifiable cause. A television surveillance camera in the old master bedroom misbehaves frequently, although no problems have ever occurred with other cameras in the same security system. Interestingly, the music system (a commercial installation) has repeatedly turned itself on just before somebody was about to do so. Several people have observed these apparent anticipations of an employee's action on a number of occasions. Did 'whoever' somehow know what a person had in mind, and decide to do it for him? There is certainly the impression of intentionality.

Especially thorough attention has been given to the burglar alarm system, which has not only been repaired, but was even replaced three times and finally converted to the most advanced model available. Nevertheless, it continues to issue false alarms that have resisted both explanation and elimination by the experts.

And there have been disturbing and unexplained sounds as well! Consider this example: the malfunctioning alarm system had been shut down. It should therefore have been as silent as a stone. The alarm did sound anyhow – at about midnight – and aroused both a police officer and an electrician from the alarm company, a Mr Warren Nelson.

When they arrived at the unoccupied house they found no signs of forced entry but, according to Mr Nelson, they "heard all kinds of noises coming from the chimney" in the Crystal Room. These were soft, "flapping" noises that lasted for 10 to 15 seconds. At first they thought that birds were stuck in the chimney, but found that the chimney had been sealed with concrete. They then searched for an intruder in the attic, but there was no opening which could serve as a passage for birds or anything else. We were only able to interview Mr Nelson, but he told us that both he and the police officer heard the flapping noises – which made the latter reluctant to search the attic. He did so only after Mr Nelson's prodding: "You have the gun, you go first!"

Flapping sounds were heard again by another person, whose search likewise failed to find any trace of a bird or animal, or any place where one might have entered the house. We focus here only on occurrences that have defied ordinary explanations, and these instances are clearly set aside from other unexplained sounds heard from time to time which the investigators believe might be explained by normal settling movements of the house itself. Alternative explanations for all the phenomena were considered carefully before being rejected, e.g., the possibility of a power surge that might have affected the electrical systems in the manner described.

Before describing the odd happenings themselves any further we should dispose of the complaint that the reports might have been distorted by psychological factors such as suggestion or the desire to tell a good story. These possibilities must always be considered, and the investigators did not fail to do so. Some of the witnesses contacted were reluctant to talk about their experiences, while others were so upset by them that they steadfastly declined to add their observations. One woman, for example, a former employee of the gift shop, declared that what she saw and heard went completely against her religious beliefs: it was all just too disturbing to talk about. Furthermore, many of the observations were made well before the house developed any reputation for strange goings-on. The investigators were thus able to establish that there was no history of 'hauntings' and thus no basis for expectations that might lead people to imagine or misinterpret the events.

Some of the phenomena have been extremely curious. A "gathering of people" was heard by two employees. It sounded "like both sexes, everybody talking at the same time ... It did not sound like a party – I did not hear people laughing or anything like that. It sounded like people talking about a more serious matter ... it was more like a ritual." On another occasion an equally non-existent person seemed to be whistling an old tune. Footsteps were often heard coming from the oldest part of the house when it was known to be unoccupied. (There have been reports of these footsteps from 12 people.) The investigators classified these occurrences as "retrocognitive awareness of past events" – in other words hearing voices and actions of the past. The house has no known history of murder or other violent and dramatic events, nor has there been anything threatening about the sounds themselves, apart from the question of their source.

Have any spirit manifestations been visible as well as audible? Yes. One day two of the gift store clerks heard voices when nobody else was present. After the voices stopped, Connie Cleese went about her business, in this instance, vacuuming the floor. She looked up at the doorway to the second room. "There I saw a black shadow or figure go across the doorway. I became petrified. I closed up and left...I didn't believe in ghosts before: I do now." Her partner, Danta Kiburis, saw a white, indistinct figure glide across the field near the old family cemetery one evening. The apparition simply passed by and made no effort to approach her. (She was not disappointed!)

A woman who had owned the house for six years often mentioned seeing similar apparitions and became very uncomfortable about staying alone. One morning an apparition was standing at the foot of the bed when she woke. Unfortunately for research, her experiences so unnerved her that she declined to be interviewed, although she had reported the sightings to her employees on a number of occasions. There were also many instances when observers felt the presence of a Somebody Else, a vivid, tactile sensation as though actually being touched or brushed against.

On several occasions people living or working in the house have played with the spirits, calling on them and asking them to do things. These attempted interactions did not begin until after the manifestations had occurred many times. Did the spirits respond? Well, somebody or something responded, although not frequently. Sometimes disturbances either started or stopped when a person challenged or made demands on the whoever. "That's enough!" and the footsteps stop. "Performance please!" and rapping sounds come from the ceiling. The 'performances' were almost always gentle and non-destructive, whether spontaneous or apparently in response to a request (even the flying tile did not strike its victim with punishing force). However, some of the happenings did seem intended to attract attention or give vent to anger.

What is to be made of these phenomena? That they must be taken seriously is clear enough: the occurrences have been varied and numerous, have been observed by groups of people as well as individuals, and cannot be convincingly explained by ordinary psychological or physical mechanisms. The witnesses have had little or nothing to gain by sharing these accounts, and many were reluctant to face their experiences again. Furthermore, all physical explanations were investigated until they were found to be inapplicable.

There is one possibility other than the manifestation of deceased spirits. Perhaps these phenomena belong to the realm of the para-normal, to what is popularly called ESP. In other words, might the sights, the sounds and the spontaneous movement of physical objects have somehow been produced by living people through unusual means? It has never been easy to distinguish paranormal events from spirit manifestations. Fortunately, Osis is one of the most experienced researchers in this difficult area, and he did consider the possibility that the 'agent' of all these happenings might be a living person.

Parapsychologists have studied a class of phenomena known as psychokinesis (PK) for many years. PK involves physical action produced by mental or psychological forces. The sticking file drawer opening as though of its own accord and the piece of tile sliding and hurtling at an odd angle are types of action that have been interpreted as PK in other settings. A person may have PK and other paranormal abilities without realizing it. Was a PK agent present? No case could be built for this possibility. The 'hauntings' occurred over a period of more than five years in front of a shifting cast of witnesses. No one (living) person was consistently part of the happenings. Many of the disturbances occurred when nobody was at home. Furthermore, there was no evidence that the witnesses included people with unusual paranormal abilities, or that the phenomena were observed under any specific set of emotional conditions (e.g. they were as likely to happen when people were relaxed as when they were tense).

The evidence suggests instead that the disturbances were created by one or more deceased persons. *Spirits*. The best candidate is Hester, one of the former residents. Her personality and life-style seem to be well represented in the pattern of manifestations, and in life she had been closely attached to the house. It was only after a careful analysis that Osis and McCormick finally concluded that "our investigation of the various explanations for the individual events and our analysis of the data obtained in interviews with witnesses *failed to reveal any living poltergeist agent*. But the data do seem to suggest – though they do not definitely identify – a deceased agent."

Osis and other investigators associated with the American Society for Psychical Research have developed a systematic approach to studying possible spirit manifestations such as the case just described. There is nothing amateurish about their procedures: the techniques are up to date and carefully specified, and the observations well documented. The scientific method must always adapt itself to the particular problems and circumstances involved. The specifics of the research plan must differ if one is studying complex interactions in real life or in laboratory conditions that allow a larger measure of control and manipulation. Yet the quality of the research can be high in either situation. Sophisticated and determined scientists can do better work in 'ghost-hunting' than naive or careless researchers in the laboratory. Osis and others have demonstrated that the scientific method can indeed be applied to the investigation of 'hauntings'. In other words, it can be both reasonable and proper to inquire into the possible manifestation of spirits, and the scientific answer will at times be affirmative. This was certainly true of the old farm house in New Jersey. We now look at some classic examples from the past.

SOME HAUNTING EXAMPLES

The success of contemporary investigations lends further support to classic investigations performed earlier this century. These studies employed the best available methodologies, and, indeed, their own rigour and innovation often exceeded existing standards.

Professor Charles Richet,[4] a distinguished French scientist, excelled in debunking false claims of spiritistic phenomena. He was well aware that unscrupulous people had attempted to enrich themselves through fraudulent and deceptive practices, and he was one of many who helped to expose those who simulated spirit apparitions and other such phenomena for profit. Like many other people of high reputation and learning, Riochet was reluctant to associate himself with a field that had gained an unsavoury reputation because of the invasion of some unprincipled individuals. Nevertheless the scientist in Richet forced him to consider the phenomena themselves, opinion and misrepresentations aside.

While condemning the "scoundrels and wretches who are the worst enemies of spiritualism", Richet devoted himself to rigorous investigation of the phenomena themselves. His studies were "prolonged and exhaustive", the better to uncover any possible fraud. Richet's work encompassed many types of unusual phenomena, and his classic book, *Thirty Years of Psychical Research*, remains a testament to scientific objectivity and courage in exploring the unknown.

What did he conclude? "It has been proved that a whole world of powers, sometimes accessible, vibrates around us. We cannot even suspect the nature of those powers; we only see their effects. These effects are, however, so clear that we can assert the reality of the forces." This was not a conclusion reached lightly. Richet, like many other scientists, persistently sought the simplest, least remarkable explanation for the phenomena in question. It was only when the simpler and more obvious explanations failed that he would even consider a spiritistic view. This failure occurred in his analysis of hauntings as well as of other survival-related phenomena.

HAUNTINGS AUTHENTICATED BY RICHET

These are some of the episodes that were reviewed by Richet and found to be authentic.

● Sir William Barrett, another distinguished scientist of the time, spent several nights in a house at Derrygonnelly (Ireland) reputed to be haunted. A series of loud noises that could not be attributed to any of those present was heard banging on the walls, the doors and the bedsteads. Hammer blows were also heard and at one point a large shovel fell on the bed. Sir William not only verified that these phenomena were authentic, but also conducted a little mental experiment as the events occurred. He asked whoever – in his mind, not aloud – to express the number that he had selected. Four times Sir William picked out a particular number between one and ten. Each time the correct number was expressed in a series of bangs or blows. The probability that the correct answer would be given four successive times under these conditions was only one in ten thousand. Sir William had to conclude that a perceptive intelligence was guiding the manifestations.

- At the home of a government official in Niedelsdorf, Switzerland, a series of disturbing events occurred over a six-week period, often in full daylight. Chairs and tables were turned over; objects were removed from the walls; latches were broken off; the house was shaken by heavy blows. Singing was heard, as well as such varied noises as splitting wood and winding a watch. These sights and sounds occurred in the absence of any likely source and even after precautions had been taken. For example, stones were thrown from all sides although the house was locked and bolted. In one particularly unnerving type of occurrence pictures reversed themselves on the walls while the family watched in alarm and disbelief. These phenomena were confirmed and described by a professor from the University of Berne.

- In Count de Larmandie's chateau at Sudrie, France, a piece of wood was lying quietly in the corner of the room, just as one would expect of it. Suddenly, this inanimate object rose and struck the ceiling, then fell at the feet of the Count and his sister. As though to demonstrate its talents further, it bounded around the room several times, striking at the door, the floor and the walls. All this happened in full daylight. When the Count or his sisters entered certain rooms subsequently there was a hail of little stones.

- A château in Normandy already had a reputation of being haunted when Monsieur de X inherited it. Abnormal events occurred over three months, witnessed at times by as many as 12 people. In fact, as the disturbances continued, all the occupants of the house preferred to gather together in their common fright. The alarming sounds were often loudest and most violent when everyone was in the same room. They were not limited to a single location. They might be heard, for example, in the room where everybody had gathered, but then just a second later they would emanate from another part of the house. Monsieur de X and his wife did not take kindly to these intrusions. They instituted careful search and control procedures, including letting two formidable watch-dogs loose every night. Just to be sure, the much put-upon Monsieur de X kept a loaded revolver handy and let it be known that he would not hesitate to use it. Visual phenomena also occurred. One day Madame de X came out to investigate yet another noise. As she approached the door, she saw the key turn quickly in the lock, then move towards her and strike her left hand. This bizarre occurrence was witnessed by the Abbé Z, tutor to her young son. Here is an excerpt from Monsieur de X's diary reporting one of the many incidents experienced:

One o'clock. Twelve blows followed by a long drumming, then thirty rapid single knocks, one would have thought that the house was shaken; we were rocked in our beds on every storey...then a long rush of feet; the whole lasting only five minutes. A minute later the whole house was shaken again from top to bottom; ten tremendous blows on the door of the green room. Twelve cries outside, three bellowings, followed by furious outcries. Very loud drumming in the vestibule, rhythmical, up to fifty knocks. 1.30 a.m. The house shaken twenty times; strokes so quick that they could not be counted. Walls and furniture alike quivered; nine heavy blows on the door of the green room, a drumming accompanied by heavy blows. At this moment bellowings like those of a bull were heard, followed by wild non-human cries in the corridor. We rang up all the servants and when all were up we again heard two bellowings and one cry.

CHARACTERISTICS OF AUTHENTIC HAUNTINGS

These are typical examples of what some people call 'hauntings' and others 'poltergeist' activity. The term poltergeist (literally 'noisy ghost') is merely descriptive and by no means explains away the phenomena. As Richet (and Barrett) have pointed out, those poltergeist cases that stand up to investigation usually have several characteristics in common:

● They cannot be dismissed on the basis of fraud or hallucination.(Some cases are dismissed for these reasons: not necessarily fraud or hallucination established, but fraud or hallucination still in contention as a possible explanation).
● The physical effects (noises, movements of objects) seem to be associated with an invisible intelligence which, although odd or imperfect, has some resemblance to human intelligence.
● The phenomena are usually associated with a particular place.
● The phenomena are sporadic and temporary. They occur over a period of a few days or a few months, and often both begin and cease without any known cause.

These characteristics can be found in both recent and 'classic' cases of haunting or poltergeist, in those that have been investigated with modern techniques, and in those observed several generations ago.

Particularly interesting are those episodes in which there is a clear *intentionality*, episodes in which we can glimpse the likely purpose behind the manifestations. One such example is recounted by John Mulholland.[5] When he was fourteen he lived on a farm in Massachusetts. One morning he rode to town on a wagon filled with grain, accompanied by the farmer's twenty-seven-year-old son.

> *On the way to town we had to pass a graveyard. The farmer's son was in a grouchy mood and very talkative. His particular complaint was about an 'old skinflint' who had died several years previously. The man had been, the son said, both shrewd and crooked and had amassed a fortune by tricking the farmers. 'And what did he do with the money?' Said the farmer's son: 'Built himself a fancy tomb – that's what. There it is there. I wish it would fall apart and his coffin fall to pieces.' We had just come to the cemetery and as he expressed his hopes he pointed at the tomb. The moment he pointed the huge metal door began slowly to swing open. He was so amazed that automatically he pulled on the reins and stopped the team. We both sat watching the slowly opening door. We were badly frightened and speechless. Finally the door was wide open and stopped moving. That instant there was heard a dull boom and a cloud of dust came out of the door and hid the tomb from our sight. Slowly the dust settled and everything was as before except that the door was still open.*

Mulholland and his companion were consumed with curiosity but at the same time too frightened to approach. After about five minutes they did tie the horses and move towards the tomb where

> *we discovered that the coffin, which had been on trestles, had just fallen apart. We could see no reason for the door to have swung open but decided that the fresh air had caused the coffin to fall apart. The trestles still stood and a part of the bottom of the coffin was on them. The body was on those boards and a part of the top of the coffin was flat on the chest of the body. We had seen enough and were happy to leave the tomb. Once we were outside we swung the heavy door closed and braced it with a large stone.*

There is something interesting not only about the experience but also about the person who recounted it. *Mulholland was a sceptic who earned a living by poking fun at psychic phenomena and exposing fraud and credulity.* Yet Mulholland himself as well as many of his respected friends had their share of hard-to-explain experiences. Could it be that the need to criticize such phenomena arose from his frightening experience that summer day? Sceptics and 'debunkers' have their motives too!

The admixture of amusement and fear is not unusual. In fact people often use an amused attitude to protect themselves from the more unsettling aspects of such experiences. Consider what happened to a young university student of my acquaintance. She had been very close to her grandmother, who lived for many years with her family. They all missed the old woman after she died, but Veronica was left with the uncanny sense that Grandmother was somehow still there. She felt Grandmother's presence so keenly that she would sometimes talk to her ("so she wouldn't feel lonely and left out"). Veronica also thought that Grandmother was occasionally moving small objects around the house as though to confirm that she was still with them in some way. Being a vivacious and open person, Veronica often shared her little "adventures with Grandmother" with her family and friends. It became an amusing on-going story. "What's new with Grandmother?" her parents or friends would ask from time to time.

After a while, however, a darker tone intruded. Veronica felt that all was not right. Grandmother was restless and was after her in some way. Veronica was still perfectly confident that Grandmother or her spirit had lingered, but she was increasingly anxious about the way Granny was behaving. When a book dropped out of the shelf of its own accord one evening Veronica was prepared to believe that Grandmother was responsible. The book Grandmother selected was a popular work on health maintenance to which Veronica had not paid much attention before. Feeling a little foolish about it and teased by her family – Veronica decided to see a doctor. She had never been much concerned about her health, and in fact was noted for her vigour and beauty.

The examination revealed a cervical growth – a cancerous condition of recent origin, prompt detection of which led to quick and effective treatment. Veronica prefers not to think about what might have happened without Grandmother's intervention.

This incident also illustrates the special relationship between living people and the spirits of the deceased. The affection and intimacy Grandmother and Veronica had shared for many years seemed to come to the fore when they were most needed. Incidentally (or not so incidentally) Grandmother's manifestations gently faded away after the diagnosis and treatment.

SEEING GHOSTS

None of the incidents reported here involved seeing ghosts. Rather, they seem to bear out Richet's conclusion that some kind of 'exterior energy' has come into play, leading to effects we cannot help but perceive, although not vouchsafing us direct access to the cause. But people do see ghosts. Or what shall we call them? Apparitions? Phantoms? Spirits? Ectoplasmic manifestations? The word we choose hardly matters: it is the reality we must respect. On the principle that a short and common word is to be preferred whenever it does the job, we will stay with 'ghosts'. We will use this term when referring to the spontaneous visual appearance of 'whatevers' under ordinary circumstances, i.e., not

near-death experiences or deathbed visions, but encounters witnessed by people of sound health and mind in the middle of everyday life.
Here are a few examples of seeing ghosts.

THE WOUNDED GHOST

The hour was high noon, and the sun was shining cheerfully into my room. While busily smoking a cigar and writing out my orders, I suddenly became conscious that someone was sitting on my left, with one arm resting on the table. Quick as a flash I turned and distinctly saw the form of my dead sister, and for a brief second or so looked her squarely in the face; and so sure was I that it was she, that I sprang forward in delight, calling her by name, and, as I did so, the apparition instantly vanished. Naturally I was startled and dumbfounded, almost doubting my senses; but with the cigar in my mouth and pen in hand, with the ink still moist on my letter, I satisfied myself I had not been dreaming and was wide awake. I was near enough to touch her, had it been a physical possibility, and noted her features, expression, and details of dress, etc. She appeared as if alive. Her eyes looked kindly and perfectly natural into mine. Her skin was so life-like that I could see the glow of moisture on its surface, and, on the whole, there was no change in her appearance, otherwise than when alive.[6]

So impressed was this English businessman that he took the next train home and told his parents and friends what had happened.

My father, a man of rare good sense and very practical, was inclined to ridicule me, as he saw how earnestly I believed what I stated; but he, too, was amazed when later on I told them of a bright red line or scratch on the right-hand side of my sister's face, which I distinctly had seen. When I mentioned this my mother rose trembling to her feet and nearly fainted away, and as soon as she sufficiently recovered her self-possession with tears streaming down her face, she exclaimed that I had indeed seen my sister, as no living mortal but herself was aware of that scratch, which she had accidentally made while doing some little act of kindness after my sister's death. She said she well remembered how pained she was to think she should have, unintentionally, marred the features of her dead daughter, and that unknown to all, she had carefully obliterated all traces of the slight scratch with the aid of powder, and that she had never mentioned it to a human being from that day to this. In proof, neither my father nor any of our family had detected it, and positively were unaware of the incident, yet I saw the scratch as bright as if just made. So strangely impressed was my mother, that even after she had retired to rest she got up and dressed, came to me and told me she knew I had seen my sister. A few weeks later my mother died, happy in her belief she would rejoin her favourite daughter in a better world.

Confirmatory statements from the father and a brother were subsequently obtained. It is worth noting that the sister appeared not as a corpse "but as a blooming girl, and the scratch showed as it would have shown as if made during life."

THE FAITHFUL SECOND TENOR

The church choirmaster was at home upstairs, busy looking over some music. He had just selected a *Te Deum* for the morning service, and discovered he would be needing a second tenor. He wondered where he could find this additional singer and, deciding to substitute a different piece of music, rose and went to the door. There, "he saw Mr Russell, a man who regularly sings bass in his choir. Mr Russell stood with one hand on his brow and with his other held forth a sheet of music. The choirmaster advanced, extended his hand, and was going to speak, when the figure vanished."[7]

The choirmaster collapsed in shock and terror at Mr Russell's sudden appearance and his even more sudden disappearance. He had no way of knowing that Mr Russell, a well-known businessman who as far as anybody knew had been in excellent health, had died of a stroke just three hours previously. The rector, one of several witnesses to the choirmaster's experience (having seen him pale, prostrated and very shaken) was convinced that Mr Russell was a man of the utmost regularity and faithfulness in fulfilling his duties. He had sung for us without pay for many years. His first thought (or one of the first), after his stroke of apoplexy, must have been: "How shall I get word to the choirmaster that I cannot go to rehearsal tomorrow night?" In an hour he died, without ever having recovered consciousness. My notion is that in some way he was enabled to make himself appear to the choirmaster. If you refer to the attitude in which he appeared, you will see that it answers to my supposition. It indicates his illness (a pain in the head), and his desire to give up his duty as singer.

It is worth bearing in mind that the choirmaster was a complete sceptic on the subject of spiritualism – at least until this experience!

WHITE BONNET, BLACK SATIN DRESS

A mother and her two daughters were doing needlework and chatting quietly about ordinary topics one afternoon in their West Philadelphia home. At the same moment the mother and the elder daughter suddenly observed a woman's figure advancing toward them. The 'visitor' wore a white bonnet and a black satin dress with a white muslin handkerchief crossed on the breast. She carried a white silk band whose string was wrapped around her wrist. The younger daughter first saw the startled expressions on the faces of her companions, then turned and saw the ghost herself. The visitor continued to approach slowly until it stood near a portrait of the husband and father.

After gazing at the portrait for perhaps half a minute, the figure turned and moved slowly to the door where it had first been seen. The door did not open, but the figure, coming close up to it, disappeared suddenly while the woman and her two daughters were looking at it. In moving through the room and returning, the figure passed so close to the elder daughter that its dress almost touched hers. Yet there was no echo of a footstep, nor the least rustle of the dress, nor any sound whatever while the figure moved. Only this silence, and the disappearance of the apparition without opening the door, caused the appearance to seem other than an ordinary and material one. To the sight it was as distinct and palpable as any human visitor..."It was Grandmamma!" the elder daughter exclaimed, as soon as she was able to find her voice.

The house was searched thoroughly. Nothing was amiss; there were not even any footprints in the recent fall of snow outside. Two children had been playing on the front veranda the whole time, but they saw no one enter or leave. The three women's perceptions of their visitor agreed completely. Sociologist and psychic researcher Hornell Hart later learned that shortly before her death 'Grandmamma' had promised to return from the other world to visit her son if she could. She had also advised her son to buy a house in the neighbourhood (which he did: this was the house). Hart adds:

> On the very day, and at the very hour when his wife and daughters witnessed the apparition of his mother, the deeds by which Dr R. became the legal proprietor of the house in which she appeared were delivered to him by its former owner. On his return in the evening, to their surprise, he threw down on the table the deeds which completed the purchase.

ORDINARY PEOPLE, EXTRAORDINARY EXPERIENCES

You will recall that many NDEs went unreported until Moody's book, and subsequent interest among other researchers, made the topic seem legitimate and that people had been reluctant to share their experiences for fear of misunderstanding and ridicule. At the moment ghost-sightings are in a similar phase of anxious suppression. People who are quite 'normal', 'ordinary' and 'respectable' continue to have such experiences, but often prefer to keep them to themselves. In independent studies, Richard Kalish[8] and myself[9] found that almost half the everyday people we interviewed had experienced at least one inexplicable encounter, an encounter that could be interpreted as contact with a deceased person. Some of these reports included the visual appearance of a deceased person or other spirit-being.

Interestingly, not only were many of the respondents slow to share these experiences, they often also commented that they had tried to keep them out of their minds because they just did not fit their basic, practical view of life. They had little motivation for sharing these experiences. The preference for keeping quiet as well as the fact that the experiences themselves were fairly common among ordinary people argues against the possible interpretation that the incidents were concocted in order to make a good story.

THAT YELLOW DRESS ...

In my clinical work I have learned to slip in a quiet little question about possible experiences with deceased persons when the situation justifies it. The first time I asked such a question it was only a matter of intuition. The 82-year-old man had been in a chronic care hospital for several years, and I had become fairly well acquainted with him. Mr D. was an irascible independent New Englander – a 'Yankee' in the traditional sense. He had often expressed contempt for the 'bunk' and 'nonsense' that 'weak-minded' people let themselves believe. Mr D. felt that he had experienced life's rough edges so long and thoroughly that he could not believe in much of anything. Instead, he enjoy looking contemptuously at those who, unable to take things as they are, surrendered to fantasies.

One afternoon I learned that Mr D's health had taken a turn for the worse. He was flat on his back, his eyes sunken and his body looking frail and ravaged. Usually, despite his chronic ailments, he seemed appreciably younger than his years and conveyed an impression of vigour. That day he looked old, sick and exhausted. Despite his deteriorated health, Mr D. insisted on sitting up and displaying as much independence as possible. During our conversation he acknowledged matter-of-factly that this latest episode had taken a lot out of him and that he might not be around much longer. I could not help but notice his sense of serenity as he acknowledged the possibility of his demise.

I had seen Mr D. in many moods before – but serenity? Never! Somehow – I don't know precisely why – this prompted me to ask if he had ever experienced any contacts 'from those who have gone before'. Under ordinary circumstances such a question would undoubtedly have resulted in a derisive snort and a lecture on my mush-minded stupidity. This day, however, Mr D. turned his head aside for a moment, as though considering whether or not to share his thoughts, and then looked me straight in the eye and told me quietly of the following incident.

A few years before, he had been in a rehabilitation hospital, concerned about his wife's health as well as his own. It had almost been a toss-up as to which one of them should receive hospital care first. Mrs D. died rather suddenly, and he could not leave the hospital to attend the funeral. A few weeks later, though, he was on his feet again, if precariously. It was time to attend to some legal details, although he really didn't have the heart for it. Mr D. made an appointment with the family lawyer in a nearby town. He arrived early and decided to pass the time over a cup of coffee. After a while he realized that he was the only person sitting in the little café. There were no other customers and the waitress had gone into the back room. "And everything was so quiet. It wasn't just that there wasn't any noise, any sounds from any place. It was more than that. It was positively quiet."

And then he saw Elsie.

"She was right there. I knew she was there before I saw her, though I can't tell you why." Mr D. gave me a probing look. "Do you think this is crazy?" He answered the question himself. "I should have thought it was crazy! But it wasn't. It seemed as natural as anything. Elsie was wearing that yellow dress I liked her in so much, and she knew that of course." Mr D. had waited for his wife to say something, but "she just floated there a little off the floor, as peaceful as an angel." Mr D. added quickly, "And I don't believe in angels, never have!"

Had he been surprised or alarmed to see his deceased wife floating near him in a deserted café? "Surprised? Yes, but alarmed, no. And after a moment, not even surprised. I should have been surprised, though, shouldn't I?" This experience left Mr D. with a sense of comfort, although he couldn't begin to explain it, "Except that maybe she had come back to let me know that things were OK. That's the only way I could figure it."

There was a second visitation. A few evenings later he was sitting in front of the fireplace in their old home, soon to be sold.

I was wide awake mind you, just sitting and taking it all in, this place we lived in half our lives And then there was Elsie again She was floating up near the fireplace, still wearing that yellow dress, too. I knew right away that she wanted to tell me something, and this time I was more ready. I told her, I mean I told her inside my mind, that I was listening and she should just go ahead and say what she wanted to.

And Elsie did say a few words ("in her usual voice"). She let her husband know that she was all right and that "there was nothing to worry about. I didn't have to worry about her and I didn't have to worry about myself. Elsie said there'd be a place for me when the time came, but that it would be a while." And then Elsie was gone. The sense of comfort and serenity these visitations induced remained with Mr D., however, ready to be called upon when his time did arrive.

But did Mr D. really believe in his experience? How could he reconcile these visitations with his practical, no-nonsense view of the world? "I don't know what to make of it," he admitted. "If that had been you telling me, I'd probably say you're off your trolley. But how can I say it didn't happen when it did? I can't explain it, but I can't let go of it either."

Some ghost-visitations subsequently shared with me by others have also been related by hard-headed people who would not have believed such things could happen and who had kept the incidents to themselves for fear of being ridiculed or thought crazy. You do not have to be a clinician or researcher to obtain first-hand accounts of ghost-visitations from normal and intelligent people. All you have to do is ask, or, often enough, just allow a conversation among mutually respecting people to drift to the subject of true but hard-to-explain experiences.

A LITTLE GIRL ABOUT HER OWN AGE

This is what happened one evening at a restaurant in Toronto where an editorial conference was continuing over dinner. One of the editors participating was a very bright and very businesslike young woman whose responsibilities required analytic and tough-minded decision-making. We will call her Ms Y. She was not a person who could afford to be taken in by fantasy or illusion. Somehow the conversation gradually shifted from business to an odd experience another person at the table had once had. The others showed an open-minded interest in this experience (which was a possible episode of ESP rather than survival), but Ms Y. remained silent.

We were astonished a few minutes later to notice her trembling, tears forming in her eyes. The conversation had recalled to mind a childhood experience she had tried to forget because it absolutely did not fit in with the realistic, rationalist view that dominated her adult life. We were fascinated not only by the experience itself but by the physical transformation in Ms Y. as she relived the episode. Before our eyes, she seemed to discard her everyday shell as a highly organized and businesslike person and emerged as a vivid, expressive and emotionally powerful individual. One of the other people present, herself an editor and a friend of Ms Y., was especially amazed to see this transformation in a person she thought she knew well.

The incident itself occurred one evening when, as a child, Ms Y. went to bed in the attic of her grandparents' home. This was the normal procedure, and she felt entirely secure. Not quite ready for sleep, she was lying awake when she noticed two other people in the room. One was a rather sad-looking man in work clothes. The other was a little girl, about her own age. The girl was sitting in the chair, the man wandering around with a lost and searching look in his eyes. Ms Y. did everything she could to make sure she was still awake and not dreaming. She opened and closed her eyes, pinched herself, rapped her knuckles against the bed, etc. She was wide awake, and her companions remained.

Both ghosts looked like ordinary people rather than bizarre apparitions. They took no interest in each other; in fact, neither behaved as though the other was there. The man also took no apparent interest in her. The little girl, though, looked at her from time to time, and then slowly approached the bed. She came close enough to touch, stood there for quite a while, then moved away again.

Ms Y. was not frightened by these inexplicable companions. Instead she felt sorry for them. It was as though something terrible had happened to these people that they couldn't get over. She didn't want to disturb them, but wanted to let her family in on the event. Going downstairs, she described what she saw. Her grandparents took her report in a matter-of-fact manner that did not surprise her at the time, but which she later regarded as curious. They said some comforting things and accompanied her upstairs again. The visions were gone. Did she want to sleep downstairs? No, she felt perfectly comfortable staying in the attic. Her grandparents tucked her in again and returned downstairs. A few minutes later the man and the little girl were quite suddenly back in place. Ms Y. felt she had nothing to fear from them, and was mostly upset at how sad the little girl looked. Neither visitor was doing anything in particular, and so eventually she fell asleep. It was only some years later that Ms Y. learned that one of the previous occupants of the old house had lost a little girl to a high fever, and that she had not been the first person to experience such a visitation. The man had been seen before as well, although his identity could not even be guessed at.

Like Mr D. and many others, Ms Y. is not a person who thinks much about the afterlife, nor someone who is attracted to odd or sensational reports. But what are you to think when ghosts have strayed into your own life – or you have strayed into theirs?

THE GOODNESS OF GHOSTS

When ordinary people get up the nerve to share their extraordinary experiences there is often a remarkable characteristic that should not pass without notice. This characteristic was included in Ms Y.'s recollections of her visitation. She had not been frightened. Instead, she had actually felt sorry for her sad-looking visitors. The reputation of ghosts as menacing intruders comes mostly from fictional portrayals. The mass media has perpetuated and elaborated on the scary-ghost theme, as in the special effects dear to the hearts of film producers. In real life, though, children as well as adults are more likely to feel curious or compassionate than to be chilled to the marrow. In this regard, we must separate the surprise and anxiety that may accompany the first signs of ghostly presence (as in a poltergeisted house) from the observer's dawning awareness that these spirit-beings mean no harm.

The realization that ghosts are mostly "good folk" appears in many contemporary accounts. Here are a few typical examples.[10]

"HI, GUS!"

A young woman's father-in-law was eagerly anticipating the birth of her first child and his latest grandchild. Unfortunately, he died before the birth.

Late in October I awoke suddenly in the middle of the night for no apparent reason. As I sat up in bed, I saw smoke in the doorway. It was just a tall, thin pillar of smoke. (My father-in-law was more than six feet tall.)

At first I was quite alarmed because I suspected a fire. Almost as quickly as I panicked, however, I felt a strange calm come over me and absolutely no need to move or check the baby.

The smoke-figure lingered in the doorway for a moment, then turned and entered the baby's room. Next, it entered their room, paused at the foot of the couple's bed, then bent over her husband's head as though to kiss his cheek. The figure then vanished.

Two years later a baby girl was born to the couple. At that time the boy was fond of repeating everything he heard. He was distracting his mother by saying, "Hi, Gus" over and over again. This name had no meaning to his mother.

When my husband came home, our son ran to the door yelling, 'Hi, Gus.' My husband's face went white and he asked, 'Where did he get that from?' I said we hadn't been out of the house all day and I had no idea, but it was driving me nuts. By then the child had said it at least a thousand times.

My husband said, 'Maybe my father has visited us. He used to call me that when I was little, but no one else ever did.' I had never heard this story before, but I wasn't surprised.

Over the next two decades the father-in-law's ghost made repeat nocturnal visits to his sleeping grandchildren. A teenage babysitter, who knew nothing about the history of these incidents, reported that she had seen a ghost enter each child's bedroom. This was a startling experience for her because it was so unusual and unexpected; nevertheless, she had not felt threatened or frightened. The visitations ended when the children had grown into young adults and moved out of the family home. "I miss him," the mother admits.

And one day she had a visit from her own father, dead for several years. She was washing the after dinner dishes when she felt hands on her shoulders.

Thinking it was my new husband, I turned but found no one there. When I went back to the dishes, I felt the hands again. Dad had done that occasionally when I did dishes at home. This time I stood still and enjoyed the feeling.

On another occasions the empty rocking chair started to rock. The rocking stopped when she looked at it. She glanced away, and the rocking started again. This sequence happened three times.

> *Finally I went to the side of the chair, placing my left arm around the back and right arm across the chair arms as if to hug the person in the chair. I said aloud, 'Whoever is sitting in my chair, I love you.' The chair never rocked again.*

"HI, HANK!"

A twelve-year-old girl was with her family at their summer cottage. She was infatuated with a handsome neighbor who served as an art critic for her crayon pictures. She looked up from her in-progress drawing of sunflowers to see him,

> *as handsome as ever in his 'Great Gatsby' three-piece suit with real gold buttons. His suit, because it was white, stood out in the greenness of the afternoon.*
>   *He smiled and reached into his pocket for his horn-rimmed glasses. I reached into my coloring box for another yellow, intending to ask Hank which would be the best color. When I looked up he was gone.*

Her cousin asked where Hank had gone as she worked on her own drawing. Suddenly the girl realized that she had forgotten to remember one very important and very sad fact: Hank was dead. Her parents had gone to his funeral and had suggested that she not mention his death to her eight-year-old cousin. In reply to the younger girl's question, she said she wasn't sure where Hank had gone.

> *I knew that I couldn't tell my cousin who still believed in Santa Claus and the tooth fairy that she had seen a ghost.*

Years later she made a special trip to the cottage that her family no longer owned. She sat on the old porch and looked toward the vacant red-brick house at the other end of the hollow. Standing up, she yelled, "Hank! ... Hank, where are you?" Now it was time to take leave of this scene of so many childhood memories. She settled into the driver's seat of her car and adjusted her seat belt. Then she glanced into the rear-view mirror.

> *For an instant I saw the reflection of the white suit, the gold buttons, and the smile. I turned to look. He was gone.*

AN EMPTY KITCHEN AND A COLD TOASTER

A young couple moved into a New England barn-style house that they had been admiring for months.

The house was charming, with high ceilings, lots of mysterious alcoves, and a huge yard. It had had only one previous renter since the owners had passed away there, and we promised the former owner's son that we would treat the house with as much respect as if we owned it personally, which we hoped some day to do.

Soon after moving in, both of them realized that "someone else lived there, too." It took a while before they felt comfortable in sharing their awareness of the sound of footsteps in the night and Christmas carols from an invisible radio, as well as the smell of bread toasting in the morning. Occasionally their bedroom door would open and close. They wondered: "Did it – or they – come in or go out?"

One day the wife was at work when her sister, their house guest, called her in a trembling voice. She wondered how long the wife had been at work. Why? Because somebody had asked her if she'd like toast for breakfast. Sleepily, she had mumbled that would be very nice. She then smelled the bread toasting and wandered downstairs to the empty kitchen and the cold toaster.

When the landlord's family learned of these happenings, they came to visit and were

astounded when they found that I had decorated the kitchen in strawberries, as their grandmother had done, and that my newly purchased dining-room set was identical to hers. The list went on.

Up to this point the young couple's experience with their unseen companion had been entirely congenial. However,

one evening I was hemming a new pair of slacks and, after trimming off the excess and laying them across the bed as I threaded a needle, I picked them back up to find there was blood dripping from each leg.

She thought at first that one of their dogs had had an accident or a virus. She plunged the slacks into cold water and sponged up a large quantity of blood from the hardwood floor. A veterinarian examined the blood and said that it could not have been tossed up by a dog. The next day she scraped up some particles of blood from the floor and brought them to a laboratory at the University of California at Davis. The scientists confirmed that the substance was blood, but could not determine the type.

When she related this incident to the landlord's family she was told that Mr Foster, the previous owner had died in that bedroom of emphysema – and, just prior to his death, had hemorrhaged in that very spot.

She went to bed early that night, while her sister went out to visit some friends. At midnight she was awakened by the sound of laughter downstairs. It was obviously a man and a woman speaking to each other excitedly.

Both of the dogs jumped up at the same time and started downstairs with their tails wagging. However, they stopped at the landing and would not descend the stairs. The woman was annoyed with what she took to be rude behaviour on the part of her sister and her friend. She made a few loud comments to that effect, and the voices finally stopped. Just then she received a phone call from her sister telling her that she was going to spend the night with her friends because the hour had grown so late.

I realized then that I had been a witness to Mr. Foster's return. He had finally come to take his wife, who had been waiting for him for years ... I knew that they would never come back.

The woman felt privileged that she had experienced these events. Although she was pleased for the Fosters' reunion:

The house was never the same after that; the warmth was gone. It's hard to describe what it was like to sit at the top of the stairs and hear the laughter, listen to the music, and smell the toast, especially when you're talking about ghosts, but I swear that every last word of this account is true.

Notice that all three of these accounts involved more than one experiencer/witness. And notice that in the case of the Fosters' reunion, there had been no previous relationship between the experiencers and the ghosts.

Ghosts not only exist, but warmth and compassion can also exist between the living and the spirit visitors. The goodness of most ghosts is one of the most reassuring of facts.

THE EVIL OF GHOSTS

Unfortunately, the goodness of ghosts is not the entire story, nor are the horror tales entirely without foundation. Most of the malicious spirits who have come to my attention are the survivors of people whose deaths occurred under tragic or dishonorable circumstances. These troubled deaths produce troubled spirits, and troubled spirits may sometimes retaliate against the living.

Some Native-American peoples have a tradition of being fearful about reprisals from the disaffected dead. Navajo, for example, generally avoid even using the word 'death,' and are appalled at the prospect of seeing or touching a human corpse. *Skinwalkers* are especially feared. These malicious spirits have sometimes been described as the Native-American equivalent of the werewolf, but this comparison is not entirely accurate. They are roving spirits in quasi-human form who have the intent to do mischief or serious harm. A human services professional who is a sophisticated participant in mainstream American life has told me of his several sightings of skinwalkers on Navajo lands in Arizona. He just could not deny their reality.

An anthropologist working with another Native-American population reports that there is great anxiety about the increasing number of violent deaths among young people.[11] High unemployment and other adverse circumstances are contributing to high rates of suicide, homicide, and accidental deaths, many of these associated also with alcohol and drug use. The community is not only concerned about the tragedy of these deaths as such, but also with their product: unsettled and, therefore, dangerous spirits. How to enable these ghosts to ease their way into a more positive afterlife is one of the major problems that the tribe is attempting to resolve.

Dangerous ghosts are especially prominent in traditional Chinese culture.[12] In China the Hungry Ghost Festival is held throughout the entire seventh lunar month in order to satisfy the ghosts needs and reduce the likelihood of their molesting the living. As with Native-Americans, it is only the mistreated or disturbed spirits who must be placated and avoided. It is a pretty good bet that a spirit will be angry and restless if it has died without having worshipping descendants. Victims of violent death are also common among the dangerous sort of ghost. Another cause of misery among ghosts is the misfortune of having died far from home. Living relatives may show their consideration by helping to guide the spirit safely to home, e.g. by placing floating lamps on streams. Funerals may attract the wrong kind of ghost, so people have been known to ignite great displays of fireworks to chase them off.

The preceding observations pertain to traditional Chinese beliefs and practices. Have ghost-visitations ceased as social change, technology, and globalization have left their impact upon traditional Chinese culture? I am pleased to report that ghosts are alive and well. Charles and Chee Emmons[10] found that young, well-educated people in Hong Kong have had many experiences that affirm the existence of ghosts. It is not, then, the past-embedded 'superstitious' person who remains the core believer, but, "just as in the United States, educated youth among Hong Kong Chinese are the most vigorous consumers of popular culture and the most open to change." And these are the people who provided the Emmons with many of their reports of current visitations.

Although the Emmons found both good and bad ghosts, they concluded that there was more malevolence than one finds with Western ghosts. For example, people reported being chased by a ghost in a dream, then awakening to feel pressed down by a ghost to the extent that they couldn't even move a finger. This experience of being squeezed by a ghost or devil can endure for half an hour or longer. Not pleasant. A typical experience:

One night, I couldn't sleep. I sensed some light in front of me. I wanted to open my eyes and look but there was something pressing on my eyes. I couldn't open them. At the same time, I felt someone sitting on my body. I got scared and wanted to jump up, but no matter how I struggled I couldn't get up … Because of my weight and height, I can usually push a person away if he is sitting on me, but not this one. This is really strange.

"I was very afraid and closed my eyes" said another experiencer who had seen "a blurry grey figure standing next to the bed" and then felt a heavy weight on her.

Cultural differences in the attitudes and behaviors of ghosts should not entirely surprise us. These spirits once were living participants in the culture and took with them some of their characteristic needs, expectations, and habits. On a metaphysical level there is almost certainly some basic commonality among ghosts. Their particularities, however, may well be shaped by the distinctive lives that they once led.

THROUGH THE CAMERA'S EYE AND THE RECORDER'S EAR

If people much like you and me can at times see ghosts, might not a camera do likewise? If at times we can hear poltergeist activity or disembodied voices, can these sounds be registered on a recording device? The answer is yes, and yes again.

A PHYSICIST AND HIS CAMERA

The distinguished British physicist Sir William Crookes decided that all this 'humbug' about spirits should and could be laid to rest through scientific investigation. However, what he eventually laid to rest were his own doubts. He found that several types of observation supported the spiritistic hypothesis. Perhaps most convincing was a series of photographs he himself took. A young woman by the name of Florence Cook had revealed exceptional abilities as a medium. Over a period of time, Crookes observed and tested her abilities including the most spectacular of all: the visual materialization of a ghost whom Florence Cook considered to be her spirit guide. The physicist employed his camera as one of his tools of investigation.

On several occasions he was able to record the photographic image of 'Katie King', the spirit guide. Her form would sometimes appear in a lighted room while Cook had permitted herself to be tied to a chair in a curtained off corner (known then as a 'cabinet'). The photographs are clear enough to show the main features of the materialized form, although not usually quite as sharp as contemporary pictures taken of living subjects. Some of Crookes' photographic observations involved as many as five cameras, arranged to show the spirit materialization from multiple angles. Other photographs show Crookes and Katie King together, walking arm in arm. Crookes also managed to take one picture of Cook and King together, but the spirit guide was partially in front of the young woman so that both faces could not be fully seen.

To quell doubts that Katie might really be Florence, Crookes enlisted the help of a well-known specialist in electrical phenomena, Cromwell Varley, distinguished for his work on the Atlantic cable. Varley established an electrical circuit around the cabinet in which Florence Cook remained while the spirit form of Katie King materialized elsewhere in the room. A powerful galvanometer was placed near the cabinet in full view of the observers and a small current was run through Cook's body by means of coins attached to her arms and connected to wires. If Cook had broken the electric circuit to come forth and dissemble Katie King, the galvanometer would have displayed strong and easily visible fluctuations. The spirit guide did appear on that occasion, and the electrical circuit remained unbroken, as the undisturbed flow of current displayed on the galvanometer testified. Crookes took a further precaution. He prepared a chemical solution that would produce a change in the flow of electric current and requested the spirit form to immerse her hands in this liquid. Katie King did as requested – and the galvanometer showed no significant fluctuation. In addition to these technical tests, Crookes testified that Cook and King had often been seen together by as many as eight observers in his laboratory.

FACES IN THE SEA: THE SS *WATERTOWN* INCIDENT

Two able-bodied sailors aboard an oil tanker were overcome by gas fumes while cleaning a cargo tank. Their mates on the SS *Watertown* carried out the traditional burial at sea on 4 December 1924. As the vessel continued its journey to the Panama Canal, a strange and unnerving series of observations were made: the faces of their two deceased comrades followed the ship. The first sightings were made the day after the burial. Day after day the faces were again sighted by various crew members, their features clearly visible at the surface of the water.

The observations were reported to the Cities Service Company, owner of the *Watertown*, and an official suggested that photographs be taken. A sealed roll of film was given to the captain and placed in a camera belonging to the first mate. The phantom heads were sighted again when the ship began its return trip. The captain took six photographs. The film was handed over to a company official who sent it to a commercial firm for developing. One, two, three, four, five photographs showed only the rolling sea. But the sixth shot confirmed what the crew members had been seeing all along -their two dead crewmates looking up at them.

Subsequently, Hereward Carrington, one of the most respected psychic researchers of his time, determined that the heads had always appeared at the same distance from the ship and were somewhat larger than life-size; furthermore, they were always arranged in the same way. Years later, Michael Mann, a newspaper reporter, was able to track down the original photograph which did indeed reveal the faces of the two dead comrades, formed on a crest of waves near the ship. A contemporary psychic researcher, D. Scott Rogo, commented that:

> There are other mysteries about the Watertown incident besides the faces. These faces were so clear that the entire crew saw them, yet when they were photographed only one out of six snapshots was successful in recording them. Apparently the faces were 'real' enough to be collectively seen, but not always clear enough to be photographed. On the other hand, whatever force created the images was not consistent enough to support the figures for more than a few moments. The fact that they were seen always at the same place rules out the highly unlikely possibility that the faces were caused by chance configurations in the water. Ultimately, the faces died away, and with it one of the most baffling and bizarre mysteries of the sea.[13]

A RELUCTANT SPIRIT PHOTOGRAPHER

Ed Wyllie, a reputable California photographer, was annoyed when some of his photographs came out disfigured by odd spots and streaks of light: not good for business! More odd yet, some of the spots turned into faces – faces of people who had not been there before. Becoming a most reluctant spirit photographer, Wyllie submitted his results and methods to qualified investigators. The Pasadena Society for Psychical Research investigated his work over an extended period and concluded that the images were genuine. Other investigators from both Great Britain and the United States devised their own tests.

Wyllie continued to produce photographic images of 'extras', or ghosts, and no evidence of fraud could be discovered. One of the most convincing experiments was devised by the Reverend Charles Cook, an expert in detecting photographic trickery. The results were published in the tough-minded *Journal of the American Association for Psychical Research* in 1916. Rogo calls particular attention to the following passage by psychic investigator James Hyslop:

> In the first two successful experiments, June 25 and 26, Mr J.H. Disler, a capable investigator and experienced photographer, assisted me. Disler and I made a most critical and thorough examination of Mr Wyllie's camera, lens, plate-holder, background and all accessories. Mr Wyllie at no time came in contact with them, but stood at one side as a spectator in the custody of special witnesses. On one plate there was the appearance of a 'bright spot' or 'spot of light' resembling a cube-shaped diamond near the elbow of my right arm, emitting rays of light in lateral directions. On the other plate there was a young girl's face somewhat blurred, but plainly visible on the upper part of my vest.

The forehead appeared to be under my collar, and just above it an object like a star. This plate was developed by Mr Disler, the photographer, in company with Dr Cook at Mumsey's Photographic Stores, Broadway, Los Angeles, immediately after exposure. The next experiment was made on June 27 1901, at 11a.m. Mr Wyllie focused the picture and capped and uncapped the lens. The plate-holder was not out of my sight a single instant. In the darkroom my observations were critical. My attention was tensely alert and nothing escaped my notice. I watched the developing process and saw coming out on the plate an object or face before the face of the sitter became visible. It became more clearly defined as the developing process was nearing completion.

Returning to the gallery, as Mr Wyllie held the negative up before the window, I saw on it a face that was very distinct, even more so than my own ... We saw that it was the same face that had appeared the day before. It covered my left shoulder, extended upon my breast, and was larger and much more distinct than the first attempt with additional accompaniments, flowing and wavy hair, encircled with a halo or luminous radiance, star-shaped flower or lily in the hair just above the forehead, and symbolic representations of a cross and heart below the face.

The face I recognized as that of the young lady or girl whom I first met in the month of September of the year 1866, as a student of Antioch College at Yellow Springs, Ohio. We were classmates at that institution, and passed two years of student life together. Her home was at Higginsport on the banks of the Ohio, twenty miles above my old home. She passed into the other life about four years after the short period of our student life together, that is, in 1873. The name is Flora Loudon.

Here we have the astonishing appearance of an image identified as Flora Loudon four years after her death in a photograph taken under tightly controlled conditions by a man who did not even know that she had ever existed. And there is more! Dr Cook was lecturing in Los Angeles one day some four years after the series of photographic experiments with Wyllie. A visitor to the city happened to see a handbill advertising the lecture and decided to attend. When Cook passed several spirit photographs around, the visitor gasped: "Flora!" The visitor was William Loudon, her uncle. This coincidence (for what else are we to call it?) provides independent confirmation that the image appearing on Wyllie's photograph was indeed that of Flora Loudon. Her uncle later swore a statement that the image was of his niece, adding that "So far as I know, there was never taken during the life of Flora Loudon a photograph of her, with such symbols as are seen in said photography, shown me by Dr Cook." By this time Flora Loudon had been dead for about 30 years; furthermore, she had lived a long way from Los Angeles.

THE SPIRITS ARE BLAMELESS

The visual appearance of ghosts, phantoms or spirits is not limited to the past. There continue to be many new sightings – too many, in fact, to investigate thoroughly. For example, the occupants of a small house in Belmez, Spain, were terrified when tiny faces, only a few inches in diameter began to form on their concrete floors. The faces would remain in place permanently if undisturbed, although the family at first destroyed them in fear. Local authorities became convinced that the faces were genuine if inexplicable phenomena. Hans Bender, one of the world's most sophisticated and respected investigators of unusual phenomena, explored the case and concluded that they were not created by ordinary means.

We have offered only a meagre sampling of photographic records that appear to capture ghost or spirit manifestations, selecting some of those that offer the best evidence. Many other photographs have appeared from many different sources – in family snapshots as well as the work of professional photographers. The 'extras' have included both people (and animals) known to the photographer and unidentifiable figures. It could be that many of these unexpected images are the genuine article. But because these photographs were not usually made under conditions of experimental control, resolute sceptics may not accept them as evidence.

Still another class of photograph must be mentioned: the bogus. Spirit photography soon attracted more than its share of frauds and pranksters. Some of the most visually delightful photographic images of spirit manifestations were concocted by photographers either seeking fortune or amusing themselves. There is no question that such frauds have been perpetrated: it is relatively easy to produce fake spirit pictures if motive and opportunity exist. And so we have once again a situation in which an entire class of phenomena has been tainted by misbehaviour. At times this has harmed innocent and naive people who were taken in by the tricks. But what has been harmed even more is the open minded pursuit of the truth wherever it leads. Spirit photography deserves renewed attention, especially now that advanced technology and scientific methodology would permit even more satisfactorily controlled testing.

If some among us play fast and loose with photographic and other evidence, the spirits themselves remain blameless!

RECORDING SPIRIT VOICES

And then there are the voices. Poltergeist and haunting episodes have sometimes included sounds without apparent source. Voices have been heard during occult experiences in many times and places, although the phenomenon is not as common as some others. In reviewing the history of spirit voices, how often one wishes that tape recorders had been available as, for instance, in the case of David Abbott, a notable debunker of fraud in the name of spiritism. Abbott was merrily exposing one cheat after another until he came the way of an elderly and crippled woman from Ohio whose sonic materializations had persuaded several previous investigators, including the (incognito) professional illusionist Henry Hardin. Challenged by the fact that a skilful magician had been unable to uncover Mrs Elizabeth Blake's undoubted trickery, Abbott decided the case was worthy of his own talents. After preliminary tests, the moment finally arrived when he and his confederate were listening to some faint and muffled sounds coming through the old woman's makeshift trumpet – sounds, yes, but nothing that would persuade two tough-minded men. Suddenly a perfectly clear sentence was heard: "I am your brother and I want to talk to mother. Tell her..." The voice then continued but became unclear. Abbott was startled. His attention was held further when a child's voice emerged, and then still another voice, saying: "I want to talk to my brother Davie – brother Davie Abbott." Abbott was shaken by this communication because he had come to Mrs Blake anonymously (a favourite device of seasoned 'spirit sleuths').

Abbott turned the trumpet over to his cousin and colleague, George Clawson, whose name was also unknown to the old woman. Clawson's daughter Georgia had died recently. Despite his great scepticism, Clawson had a bereaved parent's natural wish to contact his lost child again. A tiny voice spoke into Clawson's ear, using the words "Muz" and "Muzzie" – the pet names Georgia had used for her mother. How could a crippled old lady in Ohio have known that? Before the session was over Abbott heard other voices, some of them repeating the names of deceased people he had known. The two investigators returned later that day with Hyslop, and again heard distinct voices (while keeping their eyes on Mrs Blake, who did nothing to indicate that she might be producing the sounds herself – although how she might have accomplished such a feat was difficult to imagine). One of the new communicators heard a voice that Abbott knew instantly could only have belonged to an uncle who had died a few years previously. Still another session was held in an office in town, and still more voices were heard, quite distinctly giving the names of deceased people known personally by the investigators. Later Hyslop and others tried to produce similar voice effects by normal means but found it could not be done.

Unfortunately, audio-recording devices were not available then nor during a number of other episodes attested to by direct observers. Nowadays, however, we might well eventually produce overwhelming data in support of spirit voice communication. Voices from the unseen have been recorded since the mid-1950s, the first examples unexpectedly during normal tape recording. For example, Arne Weise, the director of Swedish State Television, confirmed the surprising discovery by one of his friends that extra voices were darting in and out of various tapes he had made (including recordings of bird song from his backyard).

Weise listened to the tape of bird song: "The voice spoke in German and was very weak. I became quite chilled and my wife was frightened. There was no explanation. The whole thing was too fantastic." Extra voices continued to intrude into Weise's friend's tapes, including those of several deceased relatives. Two independent psychic researchers subsequently worked with the tapes, and both confirmed the existence of the extra voices.

The audio-recording of spirit manifestations is neither immune from technical difficulties nor from the usual influx of unscrupulous opportunists. Some possible samples of spirit voices have proved too difficult to determine conclusively. Other samples have obviously been trumped up by charlatans, while yet others probably represent normal sounds misinterpreted by the over-imaginative. Nevertheless, there are tapes that are neither worthless nor suspicious. Controlled experimental work by Attila von Szalay and Raymond Bayless, for example, has produced clear voices (and whistles) under carefully monitored conditions. They have recorded literally hundreds of voices. At times the taped voices respond relevantly to questions; at other times what they say appears to have no connection to the situation. Rogo subsequently took part in this series of experiments and still further taped evidence was obtained, with ever-increasing attention being given to ruling out possible errors and happenstance. Interestingly, sometimes the voices were not heard during the course of the experiments – but nevertheless sounded forth when the tapes were played!

If seeing – and hearing – is believing, then spirit or ghost manifestations do exist today in the form of photographic images and tape recordings. Only our own time, energy and determination stand in the way of collecting further data, and only our own knowledge and ingenuity stand in the way of further refinements of method. The scepticism reflex has become simply a refuge for those who cannot bring themselves to face the facts.

ENCOUNTERS WITH GHOSTS: WHAT HAS BEEN LEARNED?

We have learned that visual, auditory and physical manifestations of ghosts occur spontaneously in natural settings and under controlled conditions. Many visitations have had several independent witnesses. We have also learned that 'ghost behaviour' can be either responsive to the living or strangely independent and absent-minded. Those manifestations in which the ghost appears to be reaching out for a purposeful contact usually make the strongest impression, as with Veronica's grandmother or some of the voices heard by Abbott, Clawson and Hyslop. And yet the seemingly meaningless behaviour observed in other situations deserves close attention as well.

F.W.H. Myers, the founding scholar of the Society for Psychical Research, pointed out that the very quality of 'meaningless' behaviour actually constitutes a significant piece of evidence in favour of authenticity. The particulars of many of the best-documented sightings found by the SPR were disappointing. The phantoms did not say or do remarkable things. Most often they spoke not a word, nor did they seem intent on carrying out some action. As a matter of fact, the 'research ghosts' were rather dull – not at all like their flamboyant counterparts in fiction and folklore. Myers reflected on this odd state of affairs:

> There is strong evidence for the recurrence of the same hallucinatory figures in the same localities, but weak evidence to indicate any purpose in most of these figures, or any connection with bygone individuals, or with such tragedies as are popularly supposed to start a ghost on his career ... The very fact that such bizarre problems should present themselves at every turn does in a certain sense tend to show that these apparitions are not purely subjective things – do not originate merely in the percipient's imagination. What man's mind does tend to fancy on such topics may be seen in the endless crop of fictitious ghost stories, which furnish, indeed, a curious proof of the persistence of preconceived notions. For they [the fictitious stories] go on being framed according to canons of their own, and deal with a set of imaginary phenomena quite different from those which actually occur. The actual phenomena ... could scarcely be made romantic ... And thus, absurdly enough, we sometimes hear men ridicule the phenomena which actually do happen, simply because those phenomena do not suit their preconceived notions of what ghostly phenomena ought to be – not perceiving that this very divergence, this very unexpectedness, is in itself no slight indication of an origin outside the minds which obviously were so far from anticipating anything of the kind.[12]

Myers also places encounters with ghosts within a broad and useful context, that of communication between minds. "A communication (if such a thing exists) from a departed person to a person still on earth is, at any rate, a communication from a mind in one state of existence to a mind in a very different state of existence." Since Myers' day, communication has become a major field of research in its own right. Contributions from psychology and many other disciplines make it clear that communication is always a complex process and is often fraught with problems and ambiguities. Myers was himself a pioneer in depth psychology, some of his observations anticipating as well as paralleling those of the early psychoanalysts. In some ways we know much more about communication (partly because of contributions from Myers and his contemporaries), but experts recognize more than ever that there is so much more that we do not know. Communication among the living is richer, more problematic and more complex than previously suspected. Communication between the living and the departed is a possibility difficult to dismiss as we continue to learn more about the powers and modalities of mind. It is even more difficult to dismiss, of course, in the light of abundant observations from many quarters that spirits of the deceased – 'ghosts', if you will – do indeed intersect our lives, even though we are certainly far from knowing the 'rules' that govern these occurrences.

Who can draw back from the evidence now? Only those who fear that such phenomena would shatter their outdated mechanistic view of the world. The comfort we take in predicting and controlling (or imagining that we control) the world might vanish in half a twinkling should ghosts and related phenomena force reality upon us. But, of course, humankind's world-view has been shattered a number of times already and we always seem to have survived and re-formed our minds. (Perhaps this is just what the spirits of the deceased do.)

The fear is understandable enough, especially when it is associated with a vested interest in the present and limited view of mind and the universe. Those whose careers seem to depend on a rationalist or bureaucratic universe are the first to sweat and grow uneasy when survival phenomena manifest themselves – and perhaps we should include the more blinkered guardians of the religious establishment as well. *A polite and distant belief in the afterlife may not stand up to the real thing!*

The open-minded person, though, has little to fear. With the ghost phenomena themselves well established, we can turn to a variety of promising explanations, ways of re-orientating our minds around the larger truth without collapsing into contradiction and confusion. We will have to delay our introduction to survival theory, however, because the critic is waiting his turn, and will have an entire chapter to thrash about with vigorous futility. Will he be able to undermine our case histories? He hasn't the ghost of a chance!

5

NO CHANCE OF A GHOST

The spiral stair was as black as pitch, and Smith was slowly making his way down its irregular steps, when he was suddenly conscious that something had passed him in the darkness. There was a faint sound, a whiff of air, a light brushing past his elbow, but so slight that he could scarcely be certain of it. He stopped and listened, but the wind was rustling in the ivy outside, and he could hear nothing else. It must have been a sudden gust of air, for there were crannies and cracks in the old turret. And yet he could almost have sworn that he heard a footfall by his very side...[1]

Careful, Smith, it might be a...

The first sensation of which he was conscious, after sinking into slumber, was a strange shivering that ran through him suddenly from head to foot, and a dreadful sinking pain at the heart, such as he had never felt before... In one moment he passed from a state of sleep to a state of wakefulness – his eyes wide open – his mental perceptions cleared all of a sudden as if by a miracle... the light in the little room was, for the moment, fair and full. Between the foot of his bed and the closed door, there stood a woman with a knife in her hand, looking at him...[2]

Careful, Isaac, it might be a...

And so it was. Smith had to contend with the ghost of a mummy in Arthur Conan Doyle's tale, *Lot No. 249*. Isaac was confronted with the ghost of a strange, beautiful and vengeful woman in Wilkie Collins' story, *The Dream Woman*. Scary? You bet! Ghost stories might well be rated by the strength of the shivers and the number of goose pimples aroused in the reader. Many writers who were famous for other creations could not resist the lure of the ghost story: Charles Dickens, Guy de Maupassant, Nathaniel Hawthorne, to name a few, and Sir Walter Scott and Daniel Defoe to name a few more. The same has been true with readers. Serious, no-nonsense people like you and me have from time to time set down our sober reading material in favor of a creepy ghost story.

Furthermore, there is just no contest when it comes to frightening small children around a campfire. "Listen. What is that sound? Do you hear it? Oh, it must be the wind. Just the wind. Nothing to worry about, right? But did you ever hear the wind moan like that? I don't think it's the ghost of the swamp man, do you? The swamp man only comes out when there is a full moon... Oh, my goodness, there is a full moon tonight... "

Ghost stories are entertaining, no doubt about it. What about 'real ghosts', though? As children, many of us had imaginary companions, friends who were always there to amuse and comfort us on rainy days. Most of us have long ago bequeathed our imaginary companions to the younger generation. Some of us, however, find it hard to let go. The belief in ghosts derives some of its sentimental appeal from our childish affection for the innocent imaginings of our early years, bolstered by the exciting fictions of novelists, and script-writers as well as religious teachings that were absorbed before we had possession of our critical faculties.

This chapter brings the clear light of day to the shadowy tricks and illusions of the impressionable mind. We will see that there is no chance of a ghost. And we will begin with one of humankind's most sordid and exploitative traditions – manipulating the hopes of sorrowing and vulnerable people for pleasure and profit.

A CARNIVAL OF FRAUD

There is a desperate shortage of real ghosts. These visions from beyond the fringes of our conscious mental life seem to have a difficult time in impressing a more sophisticated public in a technological age. The abundance of manufactured spirits has more than compensated, however, for the scarcity of real ghosts. The advocate has not done justice to the number, variety and ingenuity of those in the business of fabricating spirits. Our first task, then, is to draw a reasonable sample from among the many contrivances, devices, and schemes that have been misrepresented as though proper spirits. Surely such industry should be appreciated! To make sure that the main point is not lost as we summon up pseudo-ghosts, let it be stated immediately: *fraud is the rule, not the exception, in supposed encounters with spirit forms.*

BELIEVING IS SEEING

No cliché is more popular nor more mistaken than 'seeing is believing'. Our eyes fool us as readily as any of our other senses, perhaps even more so because we trust them more than we should. Experts who design visual displays for jet pilots and operators of other complex equipment have learned to take our normal perceptual habits and vulnerabilities into account. The illumination level inside the pilot's cabin, for example, influences the ability to react quickly to danger. At least one crash of a commercial jetliner was caused by momentary sun-blindness as the craft moved through a layer of clouds and immediately confronted the side of a mountain. The pilot's visual system could not adapt quickly enough to the situation. Specialists in perception have subsequently helped to prevent other accidents of that kind by providing a higher level of continuous illumination in the cabin. Furthermore, we are all vulnerable to visual illusions. The bent-stick-in-the-water illusion is a familiar and usually a harmless one. Other illusions, however, can prove dangerous, and have become important considerations to design engineers.

Often our visual tasks are complicated by factors not present in simplified laboratory situations. We have things on our mind. Our feelings may be stirred up. Many visual, auditory, and bodily signals compete for our attention. Our angles and perspective may be blocked, distorted and constantly changing. In the midst of everyday life, then, we have many opportunities to misinterpret visual stimuli, and sometimes we succumb. We may be able to overcome distorted impressions when we are in familiar surroundings, but when faced with novel, complex or threatening situations we have greater difficulty in assessing the perceptual information that comes at us.

Furthermore, our greatest asset – the human brain – is often an accomplice. Anatomically and functionally, the eye is part of the brain. A complex sequence of information processing is required before the light stimuli that reach the retina can be transformed into a recognizable visual image. The upper reaches of the brain, especially the occipital lobe of the cerebrum, are intimately involved in this process. But the information flow goes in the other direction as well. Expectations and memories, mediated by the brain, can tell the eyes what to see and report. The brain's contribution to visual perception becomes increasingly influential when the external situation is vague and ambiguous (e.g., dark, shadowy), and when we are in a state of intense emotional need (e.g., anxious, depressed).

There are definite limitations, then, to the truth value of the proposition 'seeing is believing'. In some situations, quite the opposite is true.

THE BLUSHING CAMERA

Now consider the far more challenging situation in which somebody is trying to deceive us. We are at additional peril when we are not aware that deception is involved. It is precisely because we place so much reliance on visual perception that the camera's eye could appear to offer prime evidence for the existence of ghosts. By collapsing this form of 'evidence' into the bag of tricks from which it emerged we will serve clear notice that the entire realm of 'proofs' for palpable spirit manifestations belongs not in the halls of science but in the carnival of frauds.

'Spirit photography' first became popular at the turn of the century through the shutter and lens of Baron Schrenck-Notzing. If productivity means anything, then this hyphenated nobleman and physician deserves the laurel wreath. He took hundreds of photographs that he offered as visual proof that spirits are not at all camera-shy. Amend that statement: *somebody* was not camera-shy. Many of the pictures are clear evidence not for visible spirits but for crude deceptions.

Schrenck-Notzing was probably not a knowing party to the deceptions, but rather an enthusiast easily taken in by the unscrupulous. The Baron decided to aim his camera where ghosts were most numerous, rather than waiting for them to pop up here and there. One of those obliging him was a (typically fraudulent) medium known as Eva C. (Marthe Beraud). He pointed the camera; she produced the 'ectoplasm'. This oh-so-mysterious substance was defined none too precisely by Charles Richet as "an unfamiliar form of matter" produced in the unconscious minds of certain mediums and modelled into recognizable shapes by a process he called ideoplasty. Perhaps idiotplasty would have been closer to the truth when one thinks of the unlimited credulity of seance visitors. Spirits simply could not resist Eva! Give her a darkened room and impressionable beholders and Eva could regularly summon up visible spirits.

The photographs Schrenck-Notzing and Eva produced are embarrassingly crude attempts at deception. The spirit forms look for all the world like two-dimensional paper cut-outs that have been introduced into a darkened visual field. Eva must have had great faith in the willingness of the public (including the ghost-happy Baron) to accept the most blatantly obvious falsifications. Schrenck-Notzing expressed some doubts himself on occasions, classifying some of the photographic images as unconvincing. Nevertheless, he lined up the weight of his photographic abilities, his medical prestige and his noble lineage on the side of the manufactured ghosts. Do not think that the phonybaloney of these photographs is being exaggerated. Not a bit. Some pictures show a 'spirit hand' that is all too clearly Eva's foot. We might say that this busy little ghost had a handy foot!

Physical mediums often employed one of their feet as a 'third hand.' The Baron's camera immortalized several of these manoeuvres. Once another observer, less impressed with the proceedings than Schrenck-Notzing, unexpectedly took a photograph of his own. What did this unexpected and unauthorized photograph show? There was the familiar spirit face all right – but it was being held aloft by Eva's hand. (On this occasion she had not even bothered with the foot-head trick.) Other independent observers demonstrated that the ghostly 'extras' in the photographs very closely resembled pictures that had recently appeared in newspapers and magazines. Repeated evidence of fraud, some of it through the Baron's own camera, did not dissuade him. Many others were also taken in. From the very beginning, then, the introduction of the camera, produced not firm evidence of spirit manifestations but simply more 'sham and humbug', to invoke a term that fits as well today as a century ago.

Schrenck-Notzing at least had a sincere belief, or will to believe, in his 'spirit photographs'. Soon, however, the market was crowded with photographers who deliberately manufactured ghosts for fun and profit. By the time the twentieth century was a few years old there were already enough vivid examples of fakery to require book-length treatment.[3] Smiles played on the faces of some photographers as they embellished ordinary pictures with fanciful spirits. A dreamy photo-portrait of a pretty child just seemed to be asking for a host of prancing little fairies. Nobody was more surprised than the playful photographer when people began to take the results seriously. Even fun-loving children could produce spirit photographs that fooled adults who were all too ready to be fooled. The success of 'fairy folk' introduced into a photograph for innocent merriment soon led to almost a full-scale invasion of miniature spirits as others joined in the sport.

But for every photographic humorist there were a score of serious deceivers who attempted to profit from the willingness to believe what (we think) we see. At least one perpetrator was convicted and jailed, and many others were exposed. Some legitimate photographers were outraged by this abuse of their craft. They provided many examples of techniques that could be used to produce pseudo-ghosts on film. This proved to be little challenge to a photographer skilled in the darkroom as well as behind the camera. Eva C. and her ilk were no longer needed. Any competent photographer could provide ghosts to order. And remember that this was in the pioneering days of photography. Today the production of visible ghosts is even easier, more convincing and more versatile. Those who know their way around computers can generate ghostly images that would have moved Schrenck-Notzing into transports of ecstasy.

The Crookes-Cook duo has been lauded by the advocate for providing proof of spirit survival. Actually, this absurd twosome provide further proof that in the heyday of spirit photography the surrender of critical faculties was almost irresistible. Sir William Crookes left his scientific credentials in his physics laboratory when he entered Florence's beguiling presence. In fairness, it should be recognized that he was entering a domain of subtle psychological interactions for which his training had prepared him not at all. Crookes' faith in instrumentation was not matched by the ability to monitor subtle and complex interactions among people – especially when one of these people was a professional medium. Stage 'magicians' who earned their living through illusionism and sleight of hand could and did replicate the shabby feats of spirit materialization.

One of these feats – and a particularly disgusting one – was obediently filmed by Crookes on many occasions. Ghosts, as we all know, are insubstantial, otherwise they would hardly be ghosts. Well, then, of what substance is an insubstantial being made? A strange question? Yes, but no matter, the answer was right at hand. Everybody soon knew that ghosts were formed out of that insubstantial substance we have already mentioned. Credit for inventing the name ectoplasm is usually bestowed on Richet, but probably belongs instead to a Professor Ochorowicz whose musings were picked up by Myers'[4] ever-vigilant antennae. Ectoplasm was certainly the right colour for ghosts – whitish – and had as well a nice indefinite shape and an apparent lack of full dimensionality. The notion of ectoplasm probably had its beginnings in spontaneous sightings of whatevers (e.g., by lads passing the cemetery homeward bound from the pub).

This was the alternative and very soon the most popular form of ghost-sighting. It came to replace the more usual encounter with a human form that suddenly 'vanished into thin air' (interestingly, fat air does not appear to be a spirit solvent). The ectoplasmic variant was as pale as a sickroom sheet and much given to hovering, and wavering, wafting and floating. A certain species of medium soon made ectoplasmic spirits their very own. The 'physical medium', i.e. the person who produced visions, noises or actions by occult means, was all the rage until the whole business collapsed under the weight of its unsupportable pretense.

Crookes, poor Crookes, was one of the first to capture ectoplasmic displays on film. Through the marvel of photography we were privileged to see a disgusting substance (sorry, insubstance) being extruded directly from Eva's mouth. This was one of Schrenck-Notzing's masterpieces. Given a little time and a good audience, the ectoplasm might form itself into various shapes: what kind of ghost would you like today?

Sir William photographed enough ectoplasm to furnish inhabitants for an entire community of apparitions. There was a lovely explanation to account for the fact that ectoplasm was sometimes observed to emerge directly from the medium's person. You see, there is an intimate relationship between the two. The spirit borrows psychic energies from the medium. This is one of the reasons why we should not think of disturbing the medium during an ectoplasmic display. It was often said in a grave and hushed voice that the medium could suffer the most serious harm should one touch her or turn on a light. True enough, a number of mediums did suffer harm – to their reputations – when heedless observers disobeyed the instructions.

This sad fate befell Florence Cook herself during one unfortunate sitting. Several sitters laid hands on the ectoplasmic visitor and found she felt much like a woman draped in a thin white garment, while at the same time others attended to Cook's chair and discovered that nobody was home. The fact that Florence Cook was repeatedly found guilty of deliberate trickery undercuts her apparent success in conjuring up ghosts with the lights on. Crookes continued to photograph Florence's creation, Katie King, even though others continued to report evidence of chicanery.

What good is the camera – or any other recording device – if the source itself is fudged? No gallery of photographic images will compensate for the fundamental flaw, namely, that the 'spirits' have their origin in human deception. John Mulholland warns us in the very title of his book: *Beware Familiar Spirits*.[5] He was able to get his hands on some real, genuine, authentic ectoplasm. One sample proved to be very much like gauze. Another sample had a striking resemblance to tangled string.

Harry Price went a step further by demonstrating that one could produce ectoplasm on demand by swallowing and regurgitating "various textile products". Other determined observers discovered goat-bladders on the person of physical mediums shortly before they were to fill the air with ectoplasm. Next time you see a ghost forming itself ectoplasmically, do notice the incidental resemblance to a balloon (or goat-bladder) being puffed up. The point is that there were many ways to achieve an ectoplasmic display, and a photographic record of them does not really demonstrate survival of death.

The occasional snapshot of ghost-like figures taken outside the medium's turf holds more interest. Yes, it is curious that what could be interpreted as two faces can be seen in a photograph said to have been taken from the *SS Watertown* (although it is far from being a clear and precise image). And, yes, it is worth noticing that every now and again an image will show up on film that the photographer did not notice when the camera blinked. One of the most intriguing is a picture in which a young child is holding a perfectly normal-looking kitten. The photo itself is something we might find in an ordinary family album and not think twice about. Supposedly, however, the kitten had died a week previously and the child's hand had been empty when the picture was taken.

Hmmm!

It is in the nature of these spontaneous images that one cannot form a definite opinion. Often the 'extras' were not expected, nor did either the photographs themselves or the conditions under which they were taken allow for a clear determination. Prank, self-deception and fraud cannot be ruled out, but there remains the tantalizing possibility that something both unusual and 'real' has been recorded on film. The bulk of 'spirit photography' comes to us from people who are quite capable of concocting the results or entrapping trusting photographers into unwitting partnership. But let us keep alive the possibility that photography might reveal the presence of spirits, assuming that spirits are photogenic in their nature and assuming also that in this ideal case all likelihood of accident and fraud can be ruled out. I am still waiting for the first definitive example.

Let us suppose, however, that a 'valid' photographic image has finally been obtained. There it is! Look at it. Examine it. Here at last (hypothetically) is a documentary photograph that could be interpreted as a visible spirit manifestation. Would we now have evidence for survival of death? No, not in the slightest! Why not? We will return to this question after some additional phenomena have been examined so it can be answered within an even richer context. Before we do move on, however, let us drape and conceal the camera in its moment of embarrassment – the pursuit of spirit images has given it much to blush about.

POLTERGEISTS AND OTHER NUISANCES: THE MORNING STAR OF SPIRITUALISM

What about those 'noisy ghosts' who, too shy to let themselves be seen, nevertheless make a nuisance of themselves through their mis-behaviour? If the camera's eye has failed to document alleged ghosts with a talent for visibility, then we must subdue our expectations here as well. Fraud, that all too familiar word, must be invoked again and again when considering many of the phenomena. But another explanation must be added as well: *psychopathology*. Poltergeist phenomena often occur, as we shall see, around people of disturbed mind and seething emotions. Let us begin with fraud, however, and follow with madness.

THE LITTLE FOXES DISCOVER MR SPLITFOOT

The spiritualism that infected vulnerable minds throughout Europe and the United States in the nineteenth century was touched off by a pair of young sisters dwelling with their parents in Hydesville, a quiet rural village in upstate New York. The Christmas season of 1847 apparently did not bring enough excitement for sweet little Margaret and innocent little Cathie Fox. Fortunately, Mr Splitfoot did. The two girls started to receive messages from an invisible party to whom they gave that name. Mr Splitfoot communicated by causing rapping sounds to be heard – usually on the walls, but he was versatile enough to make them appear in other places as well. Their mother later recounted a typical manifestation of the Hydesville poltergeist:

> I had just lain down. It commenced as usual. I knew it from all other noises I had ever heard before. The children, who slept in the other bed in the room, heard the rapping, and tried to make similar sounds by

clapping their fingers. My youngest child, Cathie, said: 'Mr Splitfoot, do as I do,' clapping her hands. The sound instantly followed her with the same number of raps. When she stopped, the sound ceased for a short time. Then Margaret said, in sport, 'Now, do just as I do. Count one, two, three, four,' striking one hand against the other at the same time; and the raps came as before. She was afraid to repeat them. Then Cathie said in her childish simplicity, "Oh, mother, I know what it is. Tomorrow is April-fool day, and it's somebody trying to fool us.'[6]

April Fools' Day lasted much longer than 24 hours! The incredible, astonishing, mysterious rappings soon had all Hydesville excited (except for the usual few sullen sceptics who could easily be ignored). Rappings from Mr Splitfoot and other denizens of the Great Beyond continued to follow the Fox sisters wherever they went – including theatres and ballrooms where they gave poltergeistic performances for a fee. A decade after the first ghostly rappings were heard on the walls of the simple little farmhouse, the phenomenon had spread to other walls, both humble and elegant, throughout Europe as well as the United States. Exchanging knocks with Mr Splitfoot and his host of ghosts became the source both of spiritual experiences and cheap entertainment (this was all well before the motion picture, radio and television, of course).

Famous and sophisticated Europeans gave themselves to this mystery as well as the rural folk of upper New York State. Victor Hugo, for example, was much enamoured of dining-room tables that would rap out the answers to his questions about the fate of lives after death. Indeed, tables around the world seem to have rebelled against their customary muteness and joined in the family chatter.

It was all nonsense, of course. Fraud and nonsense. The baffling and inexplicable raps had been produced all along by little Margaret and Cathie. As ridiculous as it may seem, spiritualism started with the pranks of two sisters looking for a way to entertain themselves. At first they did not believe that grown-ups would take this diversion seriously. But when their parents and later much of the world fell for their pranks, the sisters decided to make a career out of it, with tutoring from their older sister, Leah, who quickly became part of the plot.

There are at least three important lessons to be learnt from the sisters Fox. These characteristics showed up in this first outbreak of spiritualism and can be found again and again in the dreary and simple-minded 'manifestations' that continued to astound the naive: the other-worldly phenomena are produced with great ease by this-worldly folk.

- Exposures and confessions do not necessarily terminate belief.
- There is very little that is 'spiritual' about spiritualism.

Manufacturing the phenomena. Margaret and Cathie created the mysterious poltergeist knockings and rappings by a variety of means.

When conditions were favourable, they would simply tie a string to an apple and let it bump on the floor while pretending to be asleep. A crafty manoeuvre: no wonder that adults had such difficulty in determining the cause! Under more challenging conditions, the sisters Fox turned to another sophisticated technique: flexing their knee-joints! A little practice (and perhaps a special talent in that direction) enabled them to produce satisfyingly alarming raps from the Great Beyond. Later they perfected still another method. One hesitates to reveal it: should some mysteries not remain forever behind a discreet veil? In respect for this further incredible and innovative method, we will not say a word about it (however, we will let one of the sisters Fox speak for herself in a moment). Subsequent practitioners usually took their cue from these girls and had a variety of methods at their disposal, most of them rather simple: why get fancy when people are fooled well enough by childishly obvious devices?

The good folk of Hydesville made their investigations, to be sure. On at least one occasion a committee of respectable ladies stripped and searched the sisters, but of course could not find any poltergeist machinery labelled as such. The first point to remember, then, is that what all the shouting is about – the basic phenomena of poltergeists and spiritualism – can be produced by almost anybody with the interest to do so. Try it yourself – or send a bucket of money to me and receive your official Mr Splitfoot apple and string.

The stubborn persistence of belief. The sisters Fox were exposed as fraudulent – repeatedly. The earliest exposure occurred about three years after the first contact from Mr Splitfoot. A faculty committee from the University of Buffalo observed closely while the girls carried out their customary rap session with the spirit world. Their report clearly established that the sounds had been produced by flexing of the kneejoints. Caught!

When a newspaper account of this investigation was published, independent confirmation was provided by a woman who had married into the Fox family. The *New York Herald* published Mrs Norman Culver's statement that the sisters had admitted to her that they had produced the baffling rappings in precisely the manner detected by the professors. These double exposures did not even slow down the spread of spiritualism nor shake the belief of many who had accepted the rappings as authentic. Well aware that they still commanded the attention and belief of many people, the sisters Fox embarked on their career as professional dabblers with the Great Beyond. And the exposures continued as well – with as little effect as before on the true believers. P.T. Barnum, the famed promoter, quite naturally contracted the sisters and brought them to New York for public shows as well as elite private performances. Yes, this is the same Barnum who expressed his philosophy in the memorable phrase: 'There's a sucker born every minute.'

A climactic occasion occurred on the night of 21 October 1888. How we would have enjoyed being there! *The New York World* had on that very day published an exposé of spiritualism based largely on testimony from Margaret Fox Kane herself. That evening she appeared before a sold-out house at the Academy of Music. The audience was divided between sceptics and ardent spiritualists (a riot was feared, as you can well imagine). The moderator, Charles Richmond, listened to the boos and hisses of the spiritualists, then said: "I am not attacking the theory of spiritualism, which is a very pretty one indeed, as anyone who ever read Swedenborg knows, but the thing I attack is the fraud, the humbug, that is called Spiritualism."

While that whole evening deserves to be recalled, we will limit ourselves to Margaret's contribution. Joseph Rinn,[7] one of those present, describes the scene:

> *The doctors then left the stage, and Mrs Kane came forward in her stocking feet and stood on a pine table only a few inches high. 'Silence, please,' called Richmond. It was a memorable moment, full of suspense. The vast audience held their breath as they watched.*
>
> *All knew that they were looking at the woman mainly responsible for Spiritualism, that the demonstrator was its high priestess – its founder.*
>
> *As Mrs Kane stood motionless for a few moments, one could indeed almost have heard a pin drop. Then all heard loud, distinct rappings that seemed to be now in the aisles, now behind the scenes. The audience listened in suspense, for they realized that history was being made, that those rappings which had brought spiritualism into life were most likely rapping it out of existence with the same toes.*
>
> *It was a weird and ludicrous sight, this black-robed, sharp-faced woman working her big toe.*
>
> *Mrs Kane became excited and danced about the stage, clapping her hands while she cried: 'It's a fraud! Spiritualism is a fraud from beginning to end! It's a trick. There's no truth in it!'*
>
> *It was a remarkable, a dramatic spectacle; and when she stopped, a whirlwind of applause drowned out the hisses of the spiritualists.*
>
> *Mrs Kane, stepping down from the stage, then gave demonstrations as she went among those in the audience. She stopped when she reached where Newton and I were sitting, and she placed her foot on Newton's and made several raps with her big toe, which all of us who were near could hear and see done. She continued her demonstrations as she went down the aisle of the orchestra, and convinced everybody that the raps came from her big toe when she pressed against some solid object.*

Who could ask for a more direct and potent exposé? This particular evening did not do much to advance the cause of spiritualism, but belief in such phenomena remains endemic to this day, fuelling itself now from this, now from that shoddy source. On question remains, though:

why do you suppose the advocate neglected to tell us about those wonderful sisters whose dealing with Mr Splitfoot initiated the international spiritualist movement?

The lack of spirituality in spiritualism. What do you understand by the word spiritual? To me, it signifies something rather extraordinary, transcending the petty thoughts and motives of everyday life. I think of religious devotion at its most heartfelt, and of the most sublime experiences and states to which a person might aspire. This meaning deserves respect because it conveys that occasional impulse within the human race to be somehow better, nobler, more profound than we are amid our daily concerns and occupations. And this meaning is entirely debased by spiritualism. The stringed apple knocks... the knee-joints flex... the big toe presses. This is not spirituality, but its parody and degradation. The nature of the supposed communications themselves has nothing of grandeur or insight about them. In the case of the sisters Fox as well as their many imitators, the spiritualistic messages are as petty and self-concerned as the minds of those who perpetrated the hoax.

The sisters Fox, the morning stars of spiritualism, stand then revealed as simple tricksters, taking advantage of an astounding will to believe in the ridiculous despite ample evidence to the contrary, and, perhaps most appalling of all, as shameless exploiters of the genuine impulse towards spirituality.

THE FONDNESS OF POLTERGEISTS FOR UNBALANCED MINDS

Taken episode by episode, poltergeist fraud is often entertaining. Examined as a pattern, however, it becomes rather depressing: so much crude, dreary, manipulative behaviour on the one side, so much willingness to be deceived on the other.

The other major factor associated with poltergeist phenomena is perhaps more interesting, certainly more deserving of sympathy and of further inquiry. Many poltergeist episodes have been shown to centre on a particular individual. In the words of R.G. Roll,[8] one of the leading investigators associated with the late J.B. Rhine's Psychical Research Foundation at Durham, North Carolina, poltergeists tend to be 'person-oriented'. The disturbances (usually odd noises and displacement of objects) occur when one particular individual is present and seldom if ever in that person's absence. This partiality does not in itself explain anything; rather, it is just one more fact that requires explanation.

What advocates of spiritualism prefer not to face, however, is that a disturbed emotional state frequently exists in the person whose presence seems to cue off the phenomena. Somebody is disturbed, in other words – but not necessarily the poltergeist!

Roll's examination of the mental and physical health of people closely associated with the poltergeist phenomena is worth careful attention. He examined the best available reports from four historical periods between 1612 and well into the twentieth century. This survey, then, includes observations made long before the rise of spiritualism, as well as those from our own time. He uses the phrase *recurrent spontaneous psychokinesis (RSPK)* to denote poltergeist-type phenomena.

Of the 92 RSPK agents, 49 appeared to have more or less severe medical or psychological problems. In the accounts, 22 agents were described as having seizures or dissociative states, or as being prone to such states. Sixteen of the 22 were observed one or more times as having muscular contractions, comas, convulsions, fainting fits, trances, seizures, or other dissociative episodes. Of these, three were treated for the disease at the time of the RSPK outbreak and one had previously shown epileptic spikes in their EEG (electroencephalogram) patterns. A fifth, whose EEG was taken some months after the incidents, produced a short burst of such spikes. This RSPK agent and one other were prone to dissociative episodes according to their psychological tests.

Would we find so much disturbance in a random sample of 92 people? Very unlikely! Furthermore, not only was there an exceptional amount of disturbance among the RSPK agents, but the high incidence of dissociative phenomena was also significant. Some of the most dramatic and extreme psychiatric cases ever recorded involve people with strong dissociative tendencies.

It is within this set of people, for example, that cases of multiple personality appear. It is also curious that the heyday of multiple personality cases was during the years when spiritualism flourished most grandly. The syndrome that has come to be known as multiple personality is marked by a severe splitting-off between one organization of the self and another. Robert Louis Stevenson's famous story, *Dr Jekyll and Mr Hyde*, described a split between the respectable gentleman and the violent fiend who led an uneasy existence within the same body. Although a fictional character, Jekyll behaves much like a person who has repressed half his nature in order to function in the world of polite society, while Hyde bursts out periodically as representative of all the primitive impulses that have not been allowed expression.

This analogy (ours, not Roll's) illustrates something rather Freudian in poltergeist phenomena. The bursts of unruly noises and the dropping or hurling of objects are behaviours characteristic enough of an angry, frustrated person who is 'breaking loose'. Many reported poltergeist manifestations have the pattern of a dissociative episode. Both the nefarious Mr Hyde and the misbehaving poltergeist represent what happens when a person suddenly releases 'forbidden' impulses in a violent burst instead of integrating this side of his nature into his total personality and behaviour.

NO CHANCE OF A GHOST

Back to Roll. The number of RSPK agents with dissociative characteristics was actually greater than Roll's tally. Somnambulism (sleep-walking) and hysteria were noted in some of the people whose presence sparked the appearance of poltergeist phenomena – and both these conditions can be considered dissociative as well. Furthermore, the agents also included people afflicted with schizophrenia and alcoholism, as well as sufferers from nightmares or a general state of 'nervous collapse'. Furthermore, Roll himself comments that the number of RSPK agents with clearly described and dissociative characteristics would probably have been larger in the earlier historical periods if improved methods of investigation (e.g. use of the EEG test) had been available.

What has been learned, then, about RSPK agents – those lightning rods for poltergeist phenomena – who have been studied using modern techniques? Roll reports that 13 such individuals had been assessed in professional psychological or psychiatric examinations. They were all found to have "repressed aggression or low tolerance of frustration". In other words, they harboured an intense and unstable complex of angry impulses that, on the right occasion, would be likely to flame forth in some form of disruptive behaviour. Roll notes that "repressed aggression was probably also part of the problem for many of the RSPK agents in the previous periods". He suggests that some of the dissociative episodes and hysterical outbreaks may have been the result of "the psychological stress associated with the RSPK disturbances".

While this possibility cannot be ruled out, Roll (a philosopher and researcher but not a clinician) does not take sufficiently into account what psychiatrists and psychologists have learned over the years in their work with dissociative personalities. Yes, the episodes might be triggered by certain problems, vexations and temptations. However, there are pre-existing types of personality organization that respond to problems through dissociation. The report of strange goings-on, then, may be attributable more to the individual's well entrenched personality characteristics than to anything in the environment. Furthermore, the very fact that a particular individual has this kind of personality structure itself predisposes it to certain stresses and frustrations. The breaking point will often come sooner, and it will take that form known as dissociative.

The classic literature on multiple personality also reveals that sexual repression permeates the lives of such people. Prim and nearly asexual when functioning as their usual, everyday selves, they become creatures of open and exaggerated sexuality in their dissociative episodes. The power of repressed sexuality as well as general rage at life is thus available to people who match the profile of the RSPK agent.

Further information can be gleaned from Roll's useful work on this topic. Many of the RSPK agents seemed "to have been subjected to more psychological stress during childhood than others at their age". In some instances it was possible to identify a precipitating event in the life of the RSPK agent before the first poltergeist manifestation. Roll found that significant changes or problems in the family had occurred in 41 per cent of the poltergeist cases he examined. This figure, if anything, is likely to be an underestimate. Every case in which a significant life change preceded the poltergeistery had to be based on a documented event (e.g. a death in the family) – but it is entirely possible that undocumented life changes also occurred. Common to all these life changes was the need for the individual to adapt, to cope somehow with an altered reality. The frequency of such life changes and disequilibria prior to poltergeist manifestations should pass unnoticed.

Based on his own research and that of other investigators, Roll concludes that "the RSPK agent at the time of the incidents is often in a poor state of health, either mentally or physically. The existence of precipitating factors reinforces the impression of pathological conditions which are triggered into overt expression when the situation becomes overly stressful."

What are we to make, then, of poltergeist phenomena that are not blatantly fraudulent? It is clear that a large proportion of such reports center on people who are emotionally unstable, under high stress and predisposed toward dissociative reactions. Such people are entirely capable of perpetrating the phenomena themselves while in an alternative and altered state of mind. They themselves are the 'noisy spirits'. Unlike the fraudulent, they do not do this with conscious deliberation, nor do they necessarily seek to deceive others or gain a profit. One split-off mind knows not what the other has done.

This dissociative split preserves the 'normal' self in a state of sincere innocence that is likely to convince others that the RSPK agent could have had no direct role in creating the phenomena. The power of 'dissociative poltergeisting' can be amplified easily enough when others who witness or hear of the events also have dissociative tendencies. The same holds true when there is a circle of ready believers conditioned by certain philosophical or religious orientations and requiring little evidence to confirm their cherished preconceptions.

We are not quite through with poltergeistery. There are other phenomena to consider, as well as some additional explanations. For the moment, however, we have reviewed sufficient evidence to indicate that fraud and unbalanced minds compete for dominance in this realm.

WISHING MAKES IT SO

"The heart has reasons that reason knows not," said the philosopher Blaise Pascal. Psychological studies over the past century require an addition to this statement: when the heart's closest desires are at stake, reason exits the scene. We were regaled with some choice anecdotes in the previous chapter: most (although not all) fit the pattern of wish-fulfilment. This is characteristic as well of the entire range of spirit-contact anecdotes from which the advocate made his rather cautious selection. The wish-fulfilment explanation has already been presented in another context. It applies here as well and can do with some further explication.

We have already seen that an entire sect established itself around the spurious rappings of the sisters Fox and their imitators. No doubt many of the people who willingly abdicated their critical judgment at the first movement of Margaret's big toe did exercise greater care in everyday matters. Not all of them purchased the London or the Brooklyn Bridge from a fast-talking stranger. Nevertheless, the same person who shrewdly evaluates a politician's promises or a salesman's spiel will then turn around and greet fraud, pathology, hearsay or coincidence as evidence of spirit survival.

This disparity requires an explanation, and the explanation is wish-fufilment. Belief in a spirit basis for the phenomena brings such comfort and allays such anxieties that one willingly suspends critical judgment.

Numerous psychological studies have demonstrated that even lesser needs and anxieties often influence our interpretations of events. This is especially true when the events themselves are fleeting or ambiguous or occur under less than ideal conditions of observation. The concept of *need-determined perception* became well established in psychology after a variety of experiments which showed, for example, that people tend to 'see' what they expect or want to see depending on their dominant need-state of the moment. These tendencies express themselves under virtually any condition that makes it a little difficult to perceive the stimulus. Flash a word quickly using the laboratory instrument known as a tachistocope, for example, and the slightly hungry person will report having seen 'dinner' while the slightly anxious person sees 'danger', and the respondent with money on the mind replies 'dollar'. Present ambiguous face-like stimuli that actually represent nobody in particular and people will give identifications consistent with their own experiences, needs and expectations.

Add a stronger emotional component to the situation and people will make systematic errors in perception even when the stimuli are perfectly clear. This has been repeatedly demonstrated in studies of rumour and prejudice. One respondent may be given a picture to view, for example, the interior of a bus with many passengers. The respondent is allowed to hold the picture himself and examine it for a reasonable period of time. His task is then simply to describe what he saw to another participant in the study who has not seen the picture. This second participant in turn describes the picture to another participant and so on. By the time this description has made the rounds, the received version of the picture usually differs appreciably from what was actually viewed by the first respondent.

In the particular example I have in mind, it was routine for respondents to tell each other about the 'knife' in the hands of a black man. This weapon is not to be found in the picture: he is holding a comb. The systematic misperception was in this case fostered by the heritage of racism that on occasion trips up people who sincerely believe that they are free from this prejudice, as well as by indications of tension and anger among passengers on the bus. It does not take long for such distortions to show up – often enough the misperception is made by the person who actually saw the picture. If not, it is soon enough created by minds that have been conditioned by racial fears.

We bring unrecognized assumptions and expectations with us wherever we go. These expectations can suddenly rise to dominate our perceptions and interpretations of new situations, especially when a strong emotional component is present, and even more so when the conditions of observation are imperfect. This statement can stand as summary both for laboratory studies of need-determined perception and for very many of the ghost and poltergeist anecdotes. The controlled psychological experiments have been inspired in part by the heightened awareness of unconscious processes.

The clinical work of Freud and other leading psychoanalysts, provides abundant examples of wish-fulfiling mechanisms in everyday life outside the laboratory. We find, for example, that troubled people may employ the psychological defence known as projection. This mechanism, touched on earlier, involves treating some aspects of our own thoughts and feelings as though part of the external world. Banquo's ghost in Shakespeare's *Macbeth* has no reality to the innocent people around the banqueting table, but seems all too palpable to Macbeth: his own guilt takes the form of an external representation.

Psychologists and psychiatrists today are well aware of the mechanism of projection. Their awareness of our tendency to project our own thoughts and feelings into external reality is an important tool in psychological assessment and treatment. It is just as important when we hear reports of ghosts and poltergeists. One must always ask: what psychological function might these phantoms serve for those who report them?

Wish-fulfilment, projection and other psychological mechanisms are well documented and understood. Ghosts and poltergeists are not. It is always useful to examine the likelihood that 'spirit manifestations' are in reality need-driven perceptions.

Example: there is no objective evidence for the persistence of Veronica's grandmother's post-mortem existence. What we do know is that Veronica and her late grandmother had cared a great deal for each other, and that bereaved people often do feel a sense of presence for some time immediately after the death. From a psychodynamic standpoint, it is probable that Veronica had internalized the personality of the old woman who had been such an important part of her life, in effect keeping Grandmother alive in her heart. This internal representation – and not the projected-out spirit – gave the warning. One part of Veronica, in other words, informed the other.

From the standpoint of probability, the book falling off the shelf could well have been an accident or coincidence that Veronica would not even have noticed were she not 'primed' by her grief for her lost grandmother and her unconscious perception that all was not right with her body. And if we cared to pick up on the dissociative possibilities here, Veronica herself might have produced the falling book incident in a transient split-off episode which her everyday self would not have acknowledged. Every event and manoeuvre described above has been observed repeatedly in the realm of psychiatry and the social/behavioural sciences. Deceased grandmothers lingering in the vicinity and moving objects around have not.

Example: the mother of that cigar-smoking English businessman died happy in her belief she would rejoin her favourite daughter in a better world. And who would have wanted to deprive her of that comforting belief? And yet the intense wish-fulfilment function served by this belief is impossible to ignore. Her unconscious collaboration in creating and validating this ghost story served the double function of relieving her guilt about having marred the face of her dead daughter and assuring herself that there was a 'better world' after death.

Example: Mr D., that irascible old New Englander, demonstrated a commendably strong grip on reality. He could not ignore the repeated perceptions of his deceased wife because these had become part of his reality. On the other hand, he admitted, "I don't know what to make of it." This apparently simple way of managing such an unusual experience reveals strength of mind and character. Other people with similar experiences would have forced a resolution: either the experience was not real, or it proves survival of death. It is much more comfortable to force discordant experiences into some kind of resolution rather than to live with uncertainty. Mr D. was able to accept the lack of resolution rather than to leap to a conclusion: "I can't explain it, but I can't let go of it either." It can be done, as Mr D. exemplifies: one can have unusual experiences and even derive some comfort from them without surrendering the good judgment and respect for evidence that one has arduously developed and practised throughout life. We all have our temptations, but we are not obliged to become the slaves of wish-fulfilment.

PERSONAL INVOLVEMENT MAKES A DIFFERENCE – BUT SHOULD IT?

Some of the examples given by the advocate were part of my experience as well. Veronica was a student and friend, Mr D. a patient, and Ms Y. a business associate. It must be admitted that this personal involvement does have its effect on the critic as well as the advocate. Recognizing this sense of connection to the reported phenomena, I also recognize how difficult it must be for people to dismiss their first-hand experiences of possible spirit contact. Personal involvement does make a difference in how we evaluate apparent encounters with deceased people. I am like most people in this respect. The same type of paranormal report that I would criticize and reject when coming from others would be more insistent in its claims on my belief if it was my own experience.

This common tendency divides us up between people who have had personal experiences of spirit contact or other paranormal phenomena and those who have not. The haves and have-nots might be expected to persist in their convictions indefinitely with neither being able to persuade the other because they are using different methods and criteria for establishing the truth. Traditional logic and science would insist that we should disregard the experiential differences and attend only and with greatest rigor to the objective evidence. This approach will almost always lead to rejection of the claims – but will seldom persuade those who have a personal involvement with the paranormal experience.

It would serve my role as critic to endorse this traditional view and let it go at that. However, there are significant issues at stake here regarding the whole enterprise of knowing ourselves and the world. For this reason I am not rushing to the conclusion that all experiential reports necessarily involve naiveté, misrepresentation, or distortion. Let us be strong enough to leave this critical question unresolved for the moment, but to keep it in mind as we complete our analysis.

WHAT IF THERE REALLY IS SOMETHING OUT THERE?

Suppose – just suppose that amid fraud, pathology, error and wish-fulfilment there actually are some ghost/poltergeist phenomena that must be considered 'real'. We mean, of course, not simply 'real' in the sense that some people believe in them, but that they have an objective status in the universe. If purely mental, ghosts possess a subjective form of reality akin to dreams and hallucinations. This is not enough 'realness' to satisfy most apologists for spirit phenomena. Let us take a step beyond where the sober and cautious mind would ordinarily tread. But let us also be sure to bring our common sense with us! Let us, in other words, suppose for a moment that there is some truth in some of the reports. *If something or someone is there – what?*

"A MANIFESTATION OF PERSISTENT PERSONAL ENERGY"

F.W.H. Myers, early leader of the Society for Psychical Research, wanted desperately to believe in survival, but was not about to swallow the available evidence hook, line and sinker. He began with the same approach we are applying here. Assume that there is or might be 'something out there'. What would be the most sensible, least fantastical explanation consistent with what has been observed?

Myers rejected the vague though popular notion of 'ghost' and in its place substituted the idea of "a manifestation of persistent personal energy" after death. This is more than a substitution of words. The concept has changed as well. Myers makes it clear that "this force or influence, which after a man's death creates a phantasmal impression of him, may indicate no continuing action on his part, but may be some residue of the force or energy which he generated while alive."[4] Something is there all right, something that can be perceived by the living under certain conditions that we do not well understand. But this 'something' is not the ghost or survivor of the deceased. It is instead – well, what is it?

Agreeing with his colleague Edmund Gurney, Myers characterized this 'something' as an afterimage. It is an impression created on the observer by residual energies or forces. To emphasize the point, Myers and Gurney actually used the term *veridical afterimage,* meaning that the perception has its basis in reality, not hallucination or some other subjective condition affecting the observer. It "communicates information... as to a former habitant of the haunted locality", as Myers puts it. This phenomenon, then, brings to mind the afterimages we sometimes experience when we close our eyes after seeing a bright light or certain other types of visual stimuli. The two types of afterimage probably represent very different psychophysiological processes, but both involve the perceiver's reaction to a stimulus generated by something that has already disappeared or changed.

There is another and even more common experience to which the afterimage phenomenon could be likened. Our naked eyes as well as the sophisticated instruments of modern astronomers both register light waves propagated millions of years ago by distant celestial bodies. 'Star light, star bright' is objectively real as stimulus for our perception, but the astral bodies themselves have changed, and have sometimes 'died' since they beamed the light we perceive tonight. Again, we are not speculating about the specific process that might be involved in the afterimage phenomenon, but simply pointing out that it is possible to receive stimuli from a source that has altered its position or condition by the time we have completed our perception.

The advocate quoted earlier Myers' rather clever argument that some of the apparition sightings must be genuine because people would not have bothered to invent reports of such "fragmentary and apparently meaningless" hauntings. This argument, however, is more persuasive regarding the possibility of a genuine afterimage rather than full-fledged ghosting. The afterimage theory would account for the reports just as well and would place less strain on our credulity.

The incoherent and boring behaviour reported in the files of the

Society for Psychical Research makes no case for visitations by spirits of the dead. These same reports, though, do make a slightly more credible case for some type of *residual* phenomenon. We can expect less from the afterimage of a once-living person than from a spirit with its whole bag of supernatural tricks. The advocate would like to have it both ways: to argue for spirit survival on the basis of the fragmentary, incoherent type of phantom-sighting, and then turn round and slip old-fashioned ghost stories in when he thinks we're not looking. Myers' argument applies only to the first type, and this type of sighting is better explained as an afterimage or residual.

It should be emphasized again that most apparitions or phantom-sightings have been of the limited-action type. As Hornell Hart summarizes it: "The fact that most apparitions have been largely or wholly tongue-tied, and that their behaviour is usually confined to a single idea or purpose seems inconsistent with the hypothesis that apparitions are vehicles for the fully surviving consciousness of the deceased."[9] Hart also reports the independent conclusion of Raynor C. Johnson, Master of Queens College at the University of Melbourne:

The apparitional behaviour is usually confined to a semi-automatic type. Anything beyond this is generally of a single idea or purpose – e.g., to stroke hair, to wave the hand, to exhibit a wound, to frequent a neighbourhood, or to demonstrate continued existence; having done which the sustaining persistent thought (or object) has expended the impulse which gave it birth, and it fades away. Such mono-idealism is far removed from the wealth and complexity of mental structure of the normal living person.

What Hart describes as 'tongue-tied' and Johnson as 'semi-automatic' does not require the concept of an actual surviving spirit entity. The observations would fit in well enough with the more conservative concept of an afterimage or residual. And it is a cardinal rule of science – and of good sense in general – to give priority to the explanation that requires the fewest assumptions while still encompassing the facts. The afterimage hypothesis is thus the clear winner over the spirit-survival hypothesis.

There have been variations on Myers' concept. Some characterize the apparitions as similar to marionettes, others liken them to a motion picture or some other form of projected representation. The modern holograph would be another, more sophisticated, candidate along the same lines. The common thread running through these variations is that *one has not perceived an actual spirit in action, but rather some type of representation,* such as a residual energy-field or whatever else one cares to guess at.

We must keep this fact in mind, namely, that the phenomena, if 'real' in a certain sense, do not justify acceptance as independent, surviving spirits. We will encounter precisely the same situation later, should the advocate decide to impose 'evidence' from so-called 'mediums' upon us.

OUR OWN MINDS ARE THE REALITY

Fraud, pathology, error, coincidence, and wish-fulfilment – let us put all these explanations aside for the moment, knowing that in doing so we are also putting aside much of the 'evidence' for spirit survival. This leaves us mostly with perceptual phenomena that can be encompassed by the afterimage hypothesis or a variant thereof. But some of the phenomena lend themselves better to an alternative hypothesis. The afterimage hypothesis is well suited to the 'tongue-tied' and 'semi-automatic' type of phenomena. The second hypothesis comes into play when we consider the 'cream of the crop', the most interesting, complex and detailed ghostly sightings.

Many classic examples of what might be called 'intelligent' phantoms appear in the publications and records of the Society for Psychical Research. Illustrative cases were cited by the advocate in Chapter 4. Neither these nor the other examples are beyond criticism. But here we are being charitable to the point of imbecility, so we will continue to assume that there might actually be something in some of the cases. First, let us review the criteria that the best or most nearly evidential cases must meet (based upon the standards devised by Gurney and others). As Alan Gauld says:

> Such apparitions (of deceased persons) may be classified as 'veridical' if either (a) the percipient did not know and had no reason to suspect that the person in question had died, (b) the apparition was of some deceased person not known to the percipient but subsequently recognized by him from a photograph or detailed description, or better still picked out by him from a series of photographs or descriptions, or (c) the apparition conveyed some information once known to the deceased person concerned, but previously unknown to the percipient. Of especial interest here is information the conveying of which seems calculated to fulfil some desire characteristic of the deceased.[10]

Perhaps most important is the requirement that the apparition "convey some information once known to the deceased person ... but previously unknown to the percipient." Gauld chooses an example from the SPR collection. A Miss Lucy Dodson was wide awake one evening when she heard her name called. She thought it was her uncle and invited him in. The voice repeated her name and she her reply. Once again the voice called her name and now she recognized it as not Uncle George at all, but rather her mother, dead for about 16 years. Miss Lucy cried out, "Mamma!" A moment later the apparition of her mother came from behind a screen near her bedside. There were two children in her arms. She gave the children to her daughter and asked her to take care of them "for their mother is just dead." Miss Lucy promised to do so. She implored her mother to stay and speak with her, "I am so wretched." "Not yet, my child," said her mother, who then rounded the screen again and vanished from view. Miss Lucy felt that the children were still in her own arms and eventually fell asleep. When she awoke the next morning neither her mother nor the children were there.

What gives this anecdote its distinction was the following event. Two days after the apparition appeared to Miss Lucy, she learned that her sister-in-law had died. "She had given birth to a child three weeks before, which I did not know till after her death."

So here we have what passes for a high-quality episode of ghost-sighting. The apparition spoke and behaved in a purposeful manner (it even brought along two more apparitions!). Furthermore, the phantom conveyed information previously unknown to the percipient and, in this case, information of a personal and significant matter.

The Lucy Dodson case obviously goes beyond the mute and fragmentary sightings that are more easily explained by the afterimage hypothesis. Could this apparition then be explained as a valid example of spirit survival? Yes, it could. But, again, this would be giving preference to the most exotic and extreme hypothesis when there is a more plausible explanation available. The alternative explanation is itself far-reaching enough and would require substantial revision of the current scientific view of reality. It does not, however, go nearly as far nor introduce nearly so many assumptions as does the survival hypothesis.

We are speaking, of course, about ESP (extrasensory perception). Many researchers are unhappy about this term. ESP suggests that the phenomena occur without the participation of our ordinary sensory modalities. We don't know how we came to know the information. There must be some weird and wonderful modalities of communication available to us that are not as obvious as our eyes, ears, and other familiar modes of perception. Just what are these weird and wonderful modalities? Your guess is as good as anybody's.

It is obvious, however, that our ordinary senses do sometimes play a role in unusual communications, and nobody has yet been able to demonstrate the existence of other modalities. Some investigators, then, prefer to leave their options open and not have to defend the proposition that an unknown, purely hypothetical extrasensory process is involved.

Furthermore, the realm of paranormal events includes more than the purely sensory. A more accurate classification system would include at least telepathy, precognition and psychokinesis (PK). Telepathy refers to communication from one mind to another independent of normal means, e.g. gesturing, speaking, writing. Precognition (also known as clairvoyance) describes paranormal knowledge of an event before it actually occurs. PK refers to the effect of the mind on external objects or processes without the use of known physical energies or forces. In addition to these standard concepts, some investigators also include *autoscopy*, the phenomenon of seeing one's own body as though from the outside. As noted in the NDE chapter, autoscopy is known more popularly as the out-of-the-body experience (OBE). All these phenomena are objects of study in the field of research that has come to be known as *parapsychology*. The term *psi* is sometimes employed to encompass all types of paranormal event. It is a useful term because of its neutrality – it does not imply a particular explanation for the phenomena. No doubt, though, people will continue to speak loosely of ESP, even if it makes the researchers cringe.

Let us now make our own analysis of the case described above. The Lucy Dodson episode displays possible characteristics of one and perhaps two forms of psi. The more obvious phenomenon is precognition. Miss Lucy seems to have received a hint through paranormal means both of her sister-in-law's delivery of a child and of her subsequent death. On the surface of things, it appears that a deceased person provided this knowledge. This type of event, however, has often been reported in the psi literature without calling upon the services of an apparition.

The law of parsimony holds that a complex explanation should not be accepted when a simpler one will do. And it is simpler to interpret this episode as having two components: (a) an authentic precognition that was (b) presented through the form of an hallucination. In other words, Miss Lucy needed a way to move the precognitive information from an obscure corner of her mind into conscious awareness. This transfer of information was accomplished through the vision. G.N.M. Tyrrell,[11] offers a number of examples consistent with this explanation.

You will have noticed, however, that there is something a little odd about this particular display of precognition. The actual events themselves – birth of the child and death of the sister-in-law – had occurred before the hallucinatory episode. This meant, of course, that a number of people – ordinary living people – had known of these events for some time. *Telepathy?* A very good possibility! Any of the people who knew the two key events through normal means might have conveyed the information telepathically to Miss Lucy. In fact, the telepathic communication could have developed through the combined psi of several people.

And how about the sister-in-law herself? Facing the prospect of her imminent death, she might have wanted to assure love and nurture for her children. This need could have intensified her crisis and given a powerful impetus to her psi abilities. The fact that Miss Lucy experienced the communication on a conscious level several days after the death does not require the assumption that a surviving spirit of the sister-in-law made the contact. Again, a more parsimonious explanation is available: the paranormal message, being of such an emotional and extraordinary nature, required time to be processed through Lucy Dodson's thoughts and feelings. We have no basis to expect that psi communications should be instantaneous in objective time. Indeed, many examples in the research literature involve delayed comprehension and articulation of the message.

Every case of apparent spirit-conveyed knowledge can be analysed in a similar manner. At times we may find it credible to accept the possibility that knowledge has been conveyed through paranormal means. But this is not at all the same thing as accepting the phenomena as proof of survival! One must always look for the possibility that one or more living people possessed the knowledge that came to the percipient as though from beyond.

Make no mistake: it is much more in keeping with the observed facts to interpret such phenomena as demonstrations of psi rather than of survival. This may seem odd at first. Psi phenomena themselves remain surrounded by controversy. The scientific community in general has not accepted these phenomena as valid. Nevertheless, this interpretation remains clearly superior for the following reasons:

- Psi research has applied sophisticated methods under controlled conditions, while the investigation of ghosts and poltergeists has usually been limited to second-hand anecdotal reports, many of them distant to us in time and place. While not all psi research has passed muster, one can find well-crafted studies.
- The spirit hypothesis is riddled with inconsistencies. As we have already seen, for example, Chinese ghosts are a good deal more menacing and dangerous than the Euro–American variety, and the Navajo's *skinwalker* is really not the ideal person we would like to meet while wandering through the desert. Such differences would not make much sense if spirit survival were universal. It makes very good sense, though, to anthropologists who rightly view the reports as creations of their respective cultures instead of glimpses of the beyond.
- Belief in spirit survival requires a whole set of problematic assumptions about life and the universe, including the independence of mind from matter. We are asked not only to accept dubious philosophical positions, but also to deny our practical experience with the world. All the king's horses and all the king's men could never put Humpty Dumpty together again. Few children would allow themselves to be persuaded that a broken egg can be made whole, yet adults are expected to believe in much more than the reconstitution of the egg from the omelette. They are expected to endorse nothing less than the continuation of personality after death. Psi phenomena do require some rethinking of our relationship with the world. They certainly require an open mind. Belief in survival, however, requires much of the world to be misinterpreted, and requires a mind capable of believing in almost anything.
- The psi alternative consistently provides a simpler explanation for the same phenomena. To cite one more type of example: many apparitions of deceased people have the same characteristics as

autoscopic experiences, or as perceptions of people who are still alive although not on the scene. The close parallel between apparitions of the living and of the dead has been affirmed again by Stevenson,[11] even though he acknowledges a sympathy for the survival hypothesis. And so again we must ask ourselves: why accept the most extreme and fantastical explanation when other interpretations are just as satisfactory?

POLTERGEISTS AT PLAY?
NO – PSYCHOKINESIS AT WORK!

The psi interpretation takes good care of those noisy and sometimes ill-tempered poltergeists as well. Some laboratory experiments (notably those of the late J.B. Rhine and his colleagues) have produced evidence suggesting psychokinesis. Individuals with exceptional PK talents seem to have influenced the way that dice fall, producing results well beyond those to be expected by chance. PK effects have also been demonstrated in several other types of experiment in which the individual has had no obvious opportunity to influence the outcome by normal means. These findings obtained under laboratory conditions suggest that such phenomena might also occur spontaneously in the midst of 'real life'. Knocks? Rappings? Well within the range of PK! (We are excluding, of course, playful little girls flexing their knee-joints or bouncing apples on a string.)

Even more dramatic spontaneous PK phenomena have been observed. A clue to their origin is provided by two items in the glossary of the *Handbook of Parapsychology*.[13] In defining poltergeist phenomena, it is noted that the "unexplained movement or breakage of objects ... often seem to center around the presence of an adolescent." Again, the term poltergeist medium is defined as "a person, often a teenager, who appears to be the focal point of a poltergeist outbreak; the poltergeist 'agent'."

Why should the *Handbook* single out adolescents in this context? For very good reason. The aggressive and sexual energies of the teenager seem to fuel rampant PK phenomena, including the sort frequently misattributed to poltergeists. Consider this example. I once asked Robert Brier, the noted psi researcher, if he had ever personally witnessed phenomena that were immediately convincing to him – in other words, something that did not demand painstaking research and statistical analysis, but which instead revealed itself persuasively in the moment. Brier told of his experience with an adolescent whose reputed PK powers had been creating nothing but trouble for him. The youth, Julio Vasquez, had emigrated to the United States under difficult circumstances, leaving behind his family, friends, and home in South America. He found employment in a gift shop in Miami, Florida. Unfortunately, PK seemed to follow him as he went about his duties.

The souvenirs on the shelves would explode spontaneously, or fall to the floor and shatter. These mishaps occurred so frequently (in other words, an RSPK pattern) that his employers became upset, although nobody accused Vasquez of breaking the items with his own hands or of doing the damage deliberately. It had become clear to his co-workers, however, that these inexplicable destructive events occurred regularly in his presence.

After police and a professional magician confirmed that the breakages had not occurred by normal means, Brier and R.G. Roll entered the picture. They conducted an investigation on the premises during one of the sustained outbreaks of PK, including as much control and documentation as could be arranged in a field situation. They discovered that the PK force had a form and trajectory distinct from the linear action of electromagnetism. Objects affected by Vasquez's PK were not suddenly knocked over. They were carried along as though by a wave of energy until they lost their stability and toppled. The phenomenon resembled radioactive decay in its pattern of activity and fading. Brier and Roll came up with numerous specific findings and themselves observed the phenomena occurring on several occasions. Significantly, Vasquez admitted that he felt better, as though some of his tension had been relieved, after these incidents occurred.

Eventually, Vasquez was accepted as an experimental subject by the Psychical Research Foundation with some reluctance as they did not want to be drawn into a case that might be picked up by the media and sensationalized. He first participated in some of their standard tests of psi ability. The tense and unhappy young man did not show any unusual abilities for a while. But now we come to the sequence of events that made a vivid impression on Brier as one of the direct witnesses. Vasquez was asked to 'make' the dice come up 'boxcars' (two sixes) by willpower. The dice-throwing machine broke – yet, even so, it did come up with the target dice-sides. This was a highly unusual event at the PRF. Vasquez was then escorted into another testing room where there was another dice-throwing machine. Yes – that machine broke as well! Brier could not recall seeing either machine ever become dysfunctional; now both had gone down in rapid succession.

The finale was even more spectacular. Somewhat shaken by the double breakdown, Brier and his colleagues suggested that Vasquez come with them to their main office. Walking down the hallway together, they passed a table on which a valuable vase rested. Nobody touched the vase or the table. You know the outcome, of course: the vase simply shattered as the young man walked by. Needless to say, Brier was impressed.

There are enough other examples – from our own time – to demonstrate a special affinity between tense adolescents and PK/poltergeist-type happenings. This explanation itself requires an explanation. How does PK operate? Why does PK occur when it does and not at other times? Psi research continues to pursue key questions of this kind. The definitive answer is not yet at hand. It is frustrating not to have a more complete understanding of PK and related phenomena. Nevertheless, enough is already known to demonstrate that poltergeist-type events closely resemble, and are probably identical with, PK.

Let us take one more example that reveals something additional about PK and alleged spirit survival. There is science and there is experimental science. We can observe situations, events and processes in a scientific manner (e.g. when Roll charted the time-space distribution of Vasquez's PK destruction of souvenirs). It is even more desirable, however, to introduce experimental variations, to make things happen under adequate observational conditions (and Roll even did a little of that in his field research on Vasquez). However, best of all is actually to create the phenomena! This, for example, is what a number of scientists around the world are currently doing with the question, 'What is life?' Their theories earn a lot of extra credibility when supported by an actual synthesis of living matter.

LET'S MAKE A GHOST...

Does this mean we should go out and create a ghost of our own? We would not be the first to do so. A group of psi researchers in Toronto claim that they created a poltergeist by the name of Philip.[14] The group met regularly at the home of one of its members and, resolved to create a ghost or poltergeist by their combined psi powers. This took much time and concentration with, at first, little to show for the effort. Eventually, however, 'Philip' made his presence known. While Philip never made a visual appearance, he did answer questions intelligently through a rapping code. His personality, formed as a composite from the individual personalities of the group, developed its own distinct characteristics, such as an aversion to anybody smoking cigarettes at the table.

Philip's behaviour tended to represent the mood of the group on any particular occasion. He could be teasing and playful or sullen and distant. In a co-operative mood, Philip could levitate the table off the floor, or move it around the room. When in a particularly devilish mood, he would even chase someone around the room with a table or chair. Although Philip had a particular table at his service for the regular sessions, he was also able to raise and move other tables and other items, in various locations (including a television studio). It was claimed that an acoustical analysis found that the nature of the sound waves produced by Philip's rappings was not the same as those produced by an ordinary person knocking on the table.

Philip's behaviour was frequent and persistent enough to qualify both as RSPK and poltergeistery. In fact, his manifestations were so similar to what has been reported in many hauntings that they would not have been mentioned here except for the singular fact that Philip was deliberately created by group effort. In so doing, the Toronto group added some interesting additional evidence for the existence of PK, and strengthened this explanation for so-called poltergeist phenomena. Indeed, they demonstrated that it is no longer sufficient to look for one particular 'poltergeist medium' when there are hauntings to investigate. Osis and McCormick[15] conducted a reasonable investigation of the phenomena reported at that old gift-shop house, and did not find that the phenomena depended entirely on the presence of any one person. This finding, however, does not necessarily eliminate PK as the answer. Individual psi powers seem capable of being multiplied in certain group situations, and it has also been frequently observed in the psi literature that association with lively phenomena tends to endow others with a temporary boost to their own powers.

To Philip (and his creators) must go the honor of being the first officially manufactured poltergeist. It is more than likely, however, that many poltergeists of the past are intimate relations of Philip: not manifestations of the surviving spirit of the deceased, but the product of psi energies produced by the living. Unfortunately, the taint of misrepresentation and exaggerated claims also detracts from the Philip experiment as it does from so many other claims of ghost encounters. Philip's 'people' promised to supply me with evidence to support their claims in reasonable detail. They never came through, nor replied to my subsequent correspondence. The segment from a television studio shows only a clumsy, noisy, indecisive episode with one table and many hands. Alas, poor Philip: I did not know ye well!

O GOOD AND INNOCENT DEAD

The advocate opened his plea with a prayer from the Mende of Sierra Leone and an excerpt from the *Tibetan Book of the Great Liberation*. These texts served well his intention to soften us up by reminding us that many people in the humanity's past have believed that they were still in the company of ancestral spirits. As he put it:

> ... *they lived within a sacred and coherent world. Bodies changed and eventually perished... but spirit moved on to its next phase of existence. The living and the spirits of the deceased had their own agendas and concerns, but still cared about each other.*

He followed with some high-toned sociological blather. The cosy arrangement between living and dead was disrupted by the rise of industrialization and technology, "the roar of the locomotive, the heat of the blast furnace, the numbing monotony of the assembly-line, and the impersonal face of corporate and governmental bureaucracy..." People became alienated from the land, from the past, from each other. Give the advocate a little credit here: he just might be on to something!

NO CHANCE OF A GHOST

The world is in many respects a different place than it was for our ancestors in the long ago. I can work up a sense of nostalgia for those wonderful old days when we walked together with the spirit – and I wasn't even around then! It is possible that, as a race, we humans still feel a sense of loss and a craving to compensate for that loss. I want my ghosts! I need my ghosts!

Suppose that we become uncontrollably sentimental at this point and make a huge – though only temporary – concession to the advocate. In ancient times people felt, believed, assumed that spirits of the dead continued to go on about their business and could interact with the living? All right: so be it. During those millennia in which this belief system prevailed without question, it can be said that ancestral spirits also prevailed. It would not be irrational or false to assume living – dead interaction. From this thesis it is but a very small step to conclude that we are subject to interaction with the dead and that our own spirit will survive death. A very small step – but a slippery one!

There are two reasons to hesitate before taking that tempting little step. The first reason has already been furnished by the advocate: things have changed, things have changed a lot. Perhaps there were indeed spirit entities or ghosts way back when. Perhaps our distant ancestors lived in a kind of intimate communion with the natural (non-human) world that we can scarcely imagine today. Perhaps a strong primitive sense of identification with the forces of the universe contributed to a consciousness within which spirit entities were as real as anything else, if real in a somewhat different aspect. A small band of humans under the vast canopy of the evening sky might have had powerful and exquisitely sensitive experiences. Indeed, the human mind in concert with nature might have generated astounding phenomena. The world might – just might – have been a place in which both psi and spirit communication was possible.

But – this does not mean that such phenomena are possible today. The human mind has changed in many (although not all) respects, and so have the socio-physical and symbolic characteristics of our existence. Mostly we do not live in the midst of undisturbed nature under the vast canopy of the evening sky: mostly we live in the midst of each other, and do a great deal to disturb each other at that. Mostly we scheme at ways of gaining more and more control over the world. Mostly we live within belief systems and mass media messages that have little to do with the original or 'pure' state of the human/world relationship. Ghosts, if ghosts there were, have had a progressively more difficult time in sustaining themselves. Social history reveals that ghosts have become increasingly marginalized and deprived of status and useful employment over the past several centuries.[16] It is likely that the decline and virtual disappearance of ghosts started even earlier as the human mind turned to exploring its many potentials that had been limited by the primitive union with nature. We created new worlds of thought and achievement but, in the process, we lost our ghosts and we still miss them from time to time. The possibility that there might have been something resembling authentic spirit entities in the remote past of humankind does not prove that this phenomena is still with us today.

The other reason is a little more subtle. It has to do with the nature of the mind that conceives of ghosts. When we ask if there is sufficient evidence to accept the proposition of survival, we are asking a kind of question that would not have made sense in the dawn of the human mind. The concepts of evidence, truth, and rationality had not yet been articulated. Survival belief was neither irrational nor false, then, because these categories of thought themselves had not been firmly established. Furthermore, people seemed at ease in holding a variety of beliefs at the same time that would strike us as incompatible or contradictory. It would be a long time before the demand arose for systematic and logically consistent thought, and even longer before the demand for credible evidence.

When people started questioning their gods and each other and exercising their higher cognitive powers, the ghosts shrugged, sighed, and faded away.

The "good and innocent dead" to whom the Mende of Sierra Leone address their prayer are useful projections of their own reflective higher nature. The Buddhist's conception of the One Mind and its All-Deliverance does not certify vagrant spirits, but enshrines the insight that

Nothing save mind is conceivable.
Mind, when uninhibited, conceives all that comes into
existence.

It is in the conceiving mind that ghosts are most at home. They are welcome, for the most part, but we would be naive to assert that our inspirited thoughts have any other form of existence.

6

HOW SPIRITS HAVE THEIR SAY –
FROM MEDIUMS TO CHANNELERS

Those with the most steadfast belief in survival do not require evidence. Faith is sufficient. Nevertheless, even these people, completely secure in their beliefs, might find it a stirring and affirming experience to encounter palpable signs of a life after death. Events suggestive of survival would be even more welcome to those who very much want to believe, but who could not suppress questions and doubts. And the person who hardly knows what to believe, who perhaps has given up the hope of ever knowing the answer this side of the grave – think how significant an experience it would be to observe a credible proof of survival.

What kind of sign, proof, evidence, or event might impress the firm believer, the shaky believer, and the chronically agnostic? We have already considered several possibilities. In this chapter we explore the type of experience that has perhaps been the most persuasive to the largest number of people over the past century.

We refer to hearing from departed spirits through the mediation of a person who appears to have a special talent or calling. Throughout the nineteenth and much of the present century such people were known as *mediums*. In recent years, this term has been almost completely replaced by *channelers*. Whether or not these terms denote identical, similar, or markedly different processes is one of the questions we will take up later in the chapter.

We begin as usual by inviting the advocate to make his case. And, as usual, it doesn't take much inviting to get him started.

THE ADVOCATE'S CASE

Doubt, even skepticism, is swept away when one personally has access to spirit communications. In this section we first will draw upon some of the classic examples of mediated communication. These are by no means the only examples, nor is mediated communication of historical interest only. These phenomena continue to occur throughout the world day after day. Later we will sample the new wave of mediated communication through people who are known as channelers.

ON BEING A MEDIUM

A medium is, by definition, a person with the ability to serve as a go-between with spirits of the deceased. It may be that all of us have some ability of this type, but the medium is an individual with exceptional powers of receptivity. The relationship between mediumship and psi has not been fully determined. Sometimes the same event can be interpreted either as psi or mediumship. Suppose, for example, that we are meeting for the first time and know little or nothing about each other. After a few minutes you start to give me 'messages' from my long-deceased Uncle Waldo. These messages include information and characteristics that are very much like Uncle Waldo – and yet you had no obvious way of knowing that I had such a relative, much less the specific details conveyed by the communication.

Does this prove that you are a medium, one who serves as a vehicle for communications from beyond the grave? Or does it suggest instead that you are a first-class telepathist, drawing your information from various levels within my own mind? This question arises all the time. Sometimes the weight of evidence favours one interpretation, sometimes it favours the other.

It may be that what has been learned about conditions that favour psi performance applies to mediumship as well, taking into account the fact that the same person sometimes shows both types of ability. The most productive mediums seem to have functioned at their best when they could be spontaneous, make use of their favourite methods of responding, and be in the presence of friendly and encouraging people. The same is true of the most productive 'sensitives' in psi research!

These are important points. Skeptics are fond of snarling that mediums sometimes falter when asked to perform under highly restrictive and controlled conditions. Well, who wouldn't! Few of us do our best even at ordinary tasks when subjected to great pressure. The phenomenon of 'test anxiety' is well recognized in many types of situation. Competent students may draw a blank or become confused in a high-pressure testing situation even though they knew all the answers upon entering the room and will shortly recall them after leaving. How much more difficult it must be to achieve a relaxed and receptive state for spirit communication while a grim and suspicious crew stares at one's every move! It is hardly surprising that mediumship, a chancy state at its best, is subject to failure under the uncomfortable conditions of super-scrutiny. What is really surprising is the opposite finding – that sometimes spirit communication does take place, despite all the tension and restriction.

Other findings on psi functioning are also instructive here. Mediums may lose their abilities after a while, either temporarily or permanently. This, in fact, seems to be rather the rule than the exception. The uncivil skeptic likes to imply that if it comes to an end the ability never existed in the first place. The same critic would not dare offer such a preposterous claim in other realms of human functioning. Athletes at an advanced age can no longer run as fast or leap as high – does this erase the feats they accomplished earlier? Did the composer not write several masterpieces simply because his well of creativity has now run dry? As you can see, a host of unfair and rather illogical objections are raised both to mediumship and to psi phenomena. We are identifying some of them at this early juncture so that we shall not have to fret about them later.

Studies have shown that psi performance is not improved when participants are offered financial rewards. The same may well be true of authentic mediumships. Setting aside the usual collection of unscrupulous opportunists who have masqueraded as mediums, the genuine article has often shown little or no interest in payment for services. Furthermore, the more impressive mediums have often been solid, well-adjusted people, by no means mentally deranged. We would have to take mediumship seriously even if the best practitioners were in fact mentally disturbed. There would be additional problems to disentangle were it true that only psychotic individuals could receive messages from beyond. Nevertheless we would still have the fact of authentic communication before us. In actuality, however, mediumship in general cannot be dismissed as a form or correlate of pathology. Yes, it is common enough for people to hear hallucinatory voices while in a psychotic condition, but the mediumships that compel our attention have nothing in common with such aberrations. In short, the best mediumships deserve to be taken seriously, and have indeed been taken seriously by many distinguished investigators. Sceptic – stand back! We are about to consider some formidable evidence in favour of the survival hypothesis!

EVIDENCE THROUGH MEDIUMSHIPS: MRS PIPER OF BOSTON

She was a quiet, refined person. The phrase, 'a proper Bostonian', comes readily to mind when we think of this rather private and well-to-do lady. She lived on Beacon Hill, the refuge of cultured Bostonians at the turn of the century. Her life was passed in a comfortable and unremarkable manner – except for the fact that Mrs Piper was also one of the most remarkable mediums of modern times. She will receive particular consideration here not only for the nature of her spirit work *per se*, but also because she allowed herself to function under the scrutiny of some of the most critical investigators who have ever entered this field of study.

HOW SPIRITS HAVE THEIR SAY: FROM MEDIUMS TO CHANNELERS

Leonora Piper made her reluctant debut as a medium at the encouragement of the great philosopher and psychologist William James. A Harvard professor, James struck the difficult balance between critical thinking and an open-minded attitude toward the mysteries of the universe. Many of his articles and books are classics and continue to be consulted today. Mrs Piper had not been aware that she harboured any special abilities, least of all in this realm. (A number of other mediums have also not recognized their abilities until well into their adult lives.)

Her first clue was an experience she found rather disturbing, a sudden trance state that left her confused and alarmed. Both at the very beginning of her mediumship and many times thereafter, Mrs Piper expressed her preference to close and lock the door on this undesired secret chamber. She was as far removed as possible from the opportunist who seeks fame, fortune or power from special abilities. It required the encouragement of James and others, including a respected Massachusetts judge, for Mrs Piper to do anything but turn and run from her new-found abilities.

Let us first sketch the overall character of Mrs Piper's achievements during the early phase. She would hold sittings only with family members and close friends. She refused to be a sensationalistic attraction for the public. James did manage to arrange a series of visits for himself and his wife. Sceptical at first, James was soon impressed by the richness of accurate information Mrs Piper provided both about the details of their present lives and the status of deceased friends and relatives. Mrs Piper would not only convey information highly specific to a particular deceased friend, but would do so with gestures and nuances that could be immediately recognized as their little personal quirks.

James next arranged sittings for many of his friends and colleagues unknown to Mrs Piper. He made these sittings more difficult for her by giving them pseudonyms. Despite the fact that James' friends came to her under false names, Mrs Piper continued to reveal startlingly accurate information about their lives and to convey what appeared to be authentic information about – or from – their deceased friends and relatives. Person after person entered her presence sceptically, only to come away astounded. In modern terms, Mrs Piper seemed to be possessed both of exceptional psi abilities and of an even more exceptional ability to pick up messages from spirits of the deceased. It would not have been easy to determine where one ability left off and the other began, but the frequency and specificity of communications in the name of deceased people strongly suggested that more than telepathy with the living had to be involved.

Professor James had too many other commitments to continue working with Mrs Piper. However, he succeeded in gaining the interest of other qualified investigators, and for many years thereafter her activities were closely monitored by a variety of individuals whose integrity and scientific approach were never in doubt. Several investigators started out convinced that it must all be trickery, imagination or misperception. It was just too much to believe that this sedate little woman was actually a medium for spirits of the deceased! Yet one after another, the investigators became convinced that this was precisely the case.

What happened during a typical sitting? Sooner or later Mrs Piper would behave as though she had come into contact with what some people called a 'spirit guide'. Through this guide she would establish contact with the spirits of deceased people who were known to those present. Mrs Piper had several spirit guides, or at least used various names to describe her primary contact. Her readings would range back and forth over both living and dead friends and relatives of those attending the sitting. Sometimes she would venture very specific information; other times she felt less sure and was more hesitant or general in her observations. It was not unusual for her to say things that were not understood by the sitters and to be mistaken now and then on some details. Nevertheless, it was also not unusual for her to come up with information that absolutely amazed the sitters and which could be confirmed.

Frank Podmore,[1] one of the investigators who began as a sceptic and ended as a believer, reported some typical sittings. In one, a stranger, Harlow Gale, was brought to the sitting. Neither his name nor any other information was provided to Mrs Piper. The visitor was given highly specific information about his living father, brother and sister (e.g. "What is the thing your father wears over his shoulders? He looks quite important in it. He wears it because of his throat. He is in a different place from here.") Later Gale disclosed that the most conspicuous aspect of his father's appearance was a white silk handkerchief which he wore because of "a sensitiveness of his throat". Gale's father also lived in another state, and his other attributes were as the medium stated. After describing Gale's living relatives, she then told him that

> there is a minister in your family, an uncle, in the spirit. Tall, fine physique; wears spectacles, with a high forehead; something like you. He is your father's brother. He died some little time ago – away from you across the water. He died suddenly. He used to wear a cape – a long coat thing. He was not Episcopal, but like a Methodist – that sort of doctrine.

All these statements were right on the mark, except that the deceased uncle was not a particularly tall man.

Sometimes Mrs Piper would only be able to describe the deceased person. At other times she would convey messages. On still other occasions she would apologize if a particular spirit did not want to make itself available. "Your mother is nervous. I can't get her to come near,"

145

she told another visitor who was a stranger to her. However, she was able to make contact with his deceased father who "has a solemn, graceful manner, as he had on earth. He had trouble with his throat – irritation [points to bronchial tubes]. The boys used to call him Tim at college." These were correct statements about the life and personality of the visitor's deceased father.

Let's take another example in more detail. The following observation comes from quite a distinguished source, Sir Oliver Lodge, an eminent scholar who also investigated Mrs Piper's mediumship. Here is an excerpt from one of his official reports published in the *Proceedings* of the Society for Psychical Research:

> It happens that an uncle of mine in London, now quite an old man, and one of a surviving three out of a very large family, had a twin brother who died some twenty or more years ago. I ... wrote to ask if he would lend me some relic of his brother ... I received a curious old gold watch, which this brother had worn and been fond of; and that same morning, no one in the house having seen it or known anything about it, I handed it to Mrs Piper when (she was) in a state of trance.
>
> I was told almost immediately that it had belonged to one of my uncles – one that had been mentioned before as having died from the effects of a fall – one that had been very fond of Uncle Robert, the name of the survivor – that the watch was now in possession of this same Uncle Robert, with whom he was anxious to communicate.
>
> After some difficulty and many wrong attempts Dr Phinuit (Mrs Piper's name for her favourite spirit guide) caught the name, Jerry, short for Jeremiah, and said emphatically, as if a third person was speaking, 'This is my watch.' All this at the first sitting on the very morning the watch had arrived by post, no one but myself and a shorthand clerk who happened to have been introduced for the first time at this sitting by me, and whose antecedents are well known to me, being present.

Sir Oliver did not rest content with these communications, but instead pressed for additional and more detailed information.

> I pointed out that to make Uncle Robert aware of his presence it would be well to recall trivial details of their boyhood, all of which I would faithfully report.
>
> He quite caught the idea, and proceeded during several successive sittings ostensibly to instruct Dr Phinuit to mention a number of little things such as would enable his brother to recognise him.
>
> References to his blindness, illness and main facts of his life were comparatively useless from my point of view, but these details of boyhood, two-thirds of a century ago, were utterly and entirely out of my ken. My father was one of the younger members of the family, and only knew these brothers as men.

> *'Uncle Jerry' recalled episodes such as swimming the creek when they were boys together, and running some risk of getting drowned; killing a cat in Smith's field; the possession of a small rifle, and of a long peculiar skin, like a snake-skin, which he thought was now in the possession of Uncle Robert.*
>
> *All these facts have been more or less completely verified. But the interesting thing is that his twin brother, from whom I got the watch, and with whom I was thus in a sort of communication, could not remember them all. He recollected something about swimming the creek, though he himself had merely looked on. He had a distinct recollection of having had the snakeskin, and of the box in which it was kept, though he does not know where it is now. But he altogether denied killing the cat, and could not recall Smith's field.*
>
> *His memory, however, is decidedly failing him, and he was good enough to write to another brother, Frank living in Cornwall, an old sea captain, and ask if he had any better remembrance of certain facts – of course not giving any explicable reasons for asking. The result of this inquiry was triumphantly to vindicate the existence of Smith's field as a place near their home, where they used to play, in Barking, Essex; and the killing of a cat by another brother was also recollected; while of the swimming of the creek, near a mill-race, full details were given, Frank and Jerry being the heroes of that foolhardy episode.*

Some of the details provided by Mrs Piper could not be verified. This was also true in many other sittings. Other details Lodge could check out directly. 'Phinuit' (in Mrs Piper's voice) asked Lodge to take the watch out of its case and examine it in a good light at a later time. He was told he would see some nicks near the handle which (the deceased) Jerry said he had cut into it with his knife. Oliver did as instructed.

> *Some faint nicks are there. I had never had the watch out of its case before; being, indeed, careful neither to finger it myself nor to let anyone else finger it.*
>
> *I never let Mrs Piper in her waking state see the watch till quite towards the end of the time, when I purposely left it lying on my desk while she came out of the trance. Before long she noticed it, with evident curiosity, evidently becoming conscious of its existence then for the first time.*[2]

An occasional flash of inexplicable knowledge might perhaps be overlooked. One could always try to explain such events as a 'coincidence', but such an explanation quickly became overstrained as Mrs Piper continued to produce evidence suggesting contact with deceased spirits. As in the examples described here, she would occasionally falter and had to work hard to receive the message, and it was not unusual that some of the details were incapable of definitive verification. Nevertheless, she provided an amazing flow of accurate information about deceased people that she could have had no opportunity to obtain through ordinary channels, even if she had invested all her energies in trying to do so.

Through all the excitement that followed, Mrs Piper remained her quiet, genteel self. She was not one to seize the centre stage, nor did she show much curiosity either about her powers or about the substance of what was conveyed through them. In fact, her powers became an increasing burden to her as one investigator after another tried to verify her feats and discover how she achieved them. Verification was not difficult. For many years Mrs Piper continued to produce information about both the living and the dead that she could not have obtained through ordinary means. Discovering her supposed secret bag of tricks proved impossible. There were no tricks to discover. Indeed, even the most sceptical investigators were hard-pressed to imagine any motive she might have for trickery. She was not interested in earning money from her powers nor, as has already been said, did she even show much curiosity about the phenomenon. What was astounding to everybody else was more or less routine for Mrs Piper.

Consider with what energy and determination Richard Hodgson tried to catch her out. This young psychic investigator had already made his mark. Among his other achievements, he had conclusively exposed Madame Blavatsky, a fraudulent medium who had attracted a large cult following. Hodgson knew his way around and in accepting Professor James' invitation to pick up the investigation of Mrs Piper he was confident that he would soon have another skin to nail to the wall. Of course, nothing of the kind happened! During their first meeting, Mrs Piper calmly presented fact after detailed fact about Hodgson's family at home in Australia. Hodgson sent his own series of anonymous sitters who in turn heard Mrs Piper give names, facts and events from their private lives as well as descriptions of deceased friends and relations. Not ready to admit defeat, Hodgson hired private detectives to follow the medium and determine if she had been obtaining her information by conventional means. The detectives collected their fees from Hodgson but had nothing to report that might support his hopeful suspicions.

Hodgson eventually had to bow to the accumulating weight of evidence from Mrs Piper and the complete absence of any suspicious behaviour on her part. This did not end his investigation by any means; there were many other questions to pursue. Hodgson's work with Mrs Piper took a strange but very instructive turn when a new spirit control appeared one day – a man who called himself George Pellew. He and Hodgson had known each other, before Pellew, a writer, died in an accident at the age of 32. At least three highly significant aspects of the Piper/Pellew connection deserve the most serious consideration.

Firstly, Pellew, communicating through Mrs Piper, revealed an extraordinary amount of specific and accurate information about his previous life and about Hodgson as well. This was an excellent opportunity to test medium communications against objective reality, and Piper/Pellew passed the test with high grades.

Secondly, information given in the name of Pellew continued for about seven years. It was a far from transient phenomenon. All scientists look for consistency and duration in their subject-matter. Hodgson found much of his through the medium communications of his deceased acquaintance whom, odd to say, he came to know more intimately after death.

Thirdly, Pellew passed another post-mortem test: he correctly identified about 30 people that Hodgson had known during his life. When such a person entered the Piper/Pellew presence, he would speak to him or her on a familiar basis, mentioning the names of friends and relatives and discussing specific topics important to them. Apparently he never missed a 'positive'. Perhaps just as important, Pellew did not recognize or address in familiar terms more than 100 other people introduced to him (negatives) whom he had not known during his life. Let us not forget that this astonishing sequence of mediumistic proof of survival occurred in the presence of a notoriously tough-minded investigator who had persistently sought other explanations for the phenomena until gradually overwhelmed by the substance and nature of the data.

Hodgson was joined by another investigator who was at first just as sceptical. James Hyslop, a Columbia University professor of philosophy, did his best to lead Mrs Piper astray and keep all personal information from her. He, too, became convinced of her powers, particularly after she provided much detailed information about Hyslop's deceased father. Hyslop proposed alternative interpretations of these phenomena, but finally concluded that the most efficient, least strained explanation was that he actually had been conversing with deceased relatives through Mrs Piper.

Hyslop inherited the investigation when Hodgson died suddenly in 1905. And this led to still another surprising development. Not long after Hodgson's death, a new spirit control appeared in his name. This 'post-Hodgson' did not come in clearly at first. Eventually he provided Hyslop with so much detailed information that he had to reject the alternative hypothesis that this material was somehow coming from Mrs Piper's mind. This evidence was shared with William James, who also raised the possibility that the Hodgson communications arose from Mrs Piper's telepathic powers. The scientist and critical thinker in James would have preferred that interpretation, but, like Hyslop, he believed it did not accord with the facts of the case. James seemed to stop just short of accepting these communications as definitive proof of survival and remained in his characteristic position of honest doubt. Many other vigorous and critical thinkers were persuaded by the massive evidence, filling many pages of observation and of documents produced through automatic writing (a modality that Mrs Piper employed later in her career to receive spirit communications).

Well-documented ... subjected to searching investigation by a variety of researchers in both the United States and Great Britain ... incorrect or unverifiable at times, but never guilty of fraud or deception ... and, through it all, as normal a person as one can be when possessed of exceptional powers that defy ordinary explanation ... These are some of the main facts about Mrs Leonora Piper, medium.

Evidence for survival of death? Most certainly! We will return later in this chapter to this remarkable source-person for another set of perhaps even more startling data.

EILEEN GARRETT: THE SKEPTICAL MEDIUM

The case for survival based on the evidence of mediumship does not rest entirely on Mrs Piper, imposing as her achievements were. We will sample more briefly a few other individuals who have demonstrated the clear ability to attract communications from deceased spirits.

Eileen Garrett was an author, an executive and much else in addition to being a remarkable medium. A woman of our own times, she is remembered today with great affection and respect by many who knew her well. She employed her astounding psi powers in the interest of human values and scientific research. It was Garrett herself, for example, who insisted that investigations into psi and survival phenomena must be conducted under the most rigorous scientific conditions possible. Not only did she serve as a key participant in a number of controlled studies, she herself also funded, and helped to raise additional money for, high-quality research. Remember also that, unlike almost all other mediums, this healthy, vibrant Irish-American did not have a firm belief in survival. Despite the testimony of her own powers and of much other material, she believed the evidence had to be evaluated with great care. With Eileen Garrett we are in an entirely different world from the money-grubbing pretenders who have recoiled from the searching light of inquiry. The Parapsychology Foundation (New York), one of the most distinguished centres for research in this challenging area, owes its existence to her, and she served a term as president.

Since survival is our main interest here, we will not dwell on Garrett's psi achievements, which have been described in the research literature[3] and also in two of her own books.[4, 5] Instead we will focus our attention on a single specific incident that demonstrated the powers of her mediumship in a most striking manner.

An investigator by the name of Harry Price had arranged for Eileen Garrett to attempt communication with the recently deceased Sir Arthur Conan Doyle – the creator of Sherlock Holmes and himself active in the spiritualist movement. Price's secretary and a journalist were also present.

This type of session was not unusual at a time (1930) before researchers turned to elaborately controlled laboratory studies that, for all their technical improvements, tended to move away from the most dramatic and fascinating phenomena. As Garrett settled herself into a receptive state, the others adjusted themselves to what would probably be a long wait until contact could be established with Conan Doyle – if, indeed, it was to be achieved at all.

But something else happened instead...
Garrett quickly entered her familiar state of trance.

The first voice that came from her lips was that of an Arabian soldier of the fourteenth century who was one of Garrett's primary spirit controls (although she did not give much credence to this term herself). Uvani first brought greetings from the late Dr Albert von Schrenck-Notzing, the psychic researcher best remembered for his spirit photographs. He then brought greetings to Ian Coster, the journalist, from an old woman who Coster took to be his grandmother.

Suddenly, the voice shared by Uvani and Garrett became fraught with agitation. Another voice had broken in, and it was not that of Sir Arthur Conan Doyle. A man was speaking in great distress. He gave his name: "Flight Lieutenant H. Carmichael Irwin." The sitters, waiting expectantly for Conan Doyle, were at first annoyed at this intrusion. But as the voice, shaken with anxiety, continued, they tingled with the realization that an even more extraordinary – and tragic – phenomenon had pierced the barriers between life and death.

> I must do something about it... The whole bulk of the dirigible was entirely and absolutely too much for her engine's capacity. Engines too heavy. Engines too heavy. It was this that made me on five occasions have to scuttle to safety. Useful lift too small. Useful lift too small... Gross lift computed badly – inform control panel. And this idea of new elevators totally mad. Oil pipe plugged... Flying too low altitude and never could rise. Disposable lift could not be utilized. Load too great for long flight... Load too great for long flight.

None of those listening to this strangest of broadcasts knew much about lighter-than-air flight. But, of course, they listened most intensely to the next few words which then broke off inconclusively into unending silence:

> Cruising speed bad and ship badly swinging. Severe tension on the fabric which is chafing... Engines wrong – too heavy – cannot rise. Never reached cruising altitude. Same in trials. Too short trials. No one knew the ship properly. Weather bad for long flight. Fabric all water-logged and ship's nose is down. Impossible to rise. Cannot trim. Almost scraped the roofs of Archy. Kept to railway.

HOW SPIRITS HAVE THEIR SAY: FROM MEDIUMS TO CHANNELERS

The very last words proved to be exceptionally important:

> *At enquiry to be held later it will be found that the superstructure of the envelope held no resilience and had far too much weight in envelope. The added middle section was entirely wrong... too heavy, too much overweighted for the capacity of the engines.*

And then – silence.

Let us now put this extraordinary episode into its historical context. Commercial air travel was in an early phase, and many people believed that the future belonged to lighter-than-air vehicles, usually known as dirigibles. A passenger service had been inaugurated in Great Britain and hailed as a triumph of modern technology. As we know today, this did not prove to be the case. Several disasters took a high toll of human life and led most people to abandon this form of air travel. One such disaster occurred just two days before the session we have described. The R101, pride of the British sky fleet, crashed into a hillside in France. Most of the passengers (48 out of 54) died in the crash or were burnt by the flames that rapidly consumed the airship. It was the commanding officer of this ill-fated dirigible who spoke during Garrett's trance – after his death.

The R101 catastrophe was alarming. It proved to be one of the failures that destroyed much of the confidence in such airships. Naturally, an official inquiry was launched. *The facts established after six months of expert investigation confirmed – in detail – the information given by Commander Irwin two days after the accident.*

The details conveyed through Garrett were too numerous and specific to have been a matter of guesswork and coincidence. For example Archy

> is a tiny railway stop that does not appear on most maps, including the authoritative **Michelin Guide to France**. In 1930 it did not appear either in the equally reputable Baedeker's **Northern France** (5th edition), or in a variety of other detailed commercial maps Price and others consulted all over London.
>
> They found it finally on a large railway map used only by professional railway and some military people. It was such a map that Irwin must have had to identify the small village between Amiens and Beauvais.[3] (p. 34)

This episode arouses a powerful, mixed reaction even today. People bold enough to trust themselves to a new means of transportation died suddenly in a terrible accident that, in reality, was not entirely accidental. It was instead a natural consequence of design errors, insufficient testing procedures and other human failings. Out of this unnecessary catastrophe, however, emerged a striking body of evidence for survival of death. The information provided through Garrett in the name and voice of Irwin was at that moment unknown to anybody (except Irwin). And yet his observations were amply confirmed by a team of experts. Evidence, and evidence enough!

But even more evidence for survival came from this same episode. Major Oliver Villiers of the British Ministry of Civil Aviation asked Garrett to attempt further communication with those aboard the doomed airship. She agreed, and the Major became not only a witness but an active participant. Villiers heard testimony from several other (deceased) people who had been aboard R101. Here is an excerpt from his conversation with a crew member by the name of Scott:

Villiers: *What was the trouble? Irwin mentioned the nose.*

Scott: *Yes. Girder trouble and engine.*

Villiers: *I must get this right. Can you describe exactly where? We have the long struts numbered from A to G.*

Scott: *The top one is 0, and then A, B, C and so on downward. Look at your drawing. It was the starboard of 5C. On our second flight after we had finished we found the girder had been strained, not cracked, and this caused trouble to the cover… it split the outer cover… The bad rent in the cover on the starboard side of 5C brought about an unnatural pressure, forced us into our first dive. The second was even worse. The pressure on the gas bags was terrific; and the gusts of wind were tremendous. This external pressure, coupled with the fact that the valve was weak, blew the valve right off, and at the same time the released gas was ignited by a backfire from the engine.*[6]

These and other statements taken by Villiers through Garrett's trance communications were verified by the subsequent official investigation of the R101 disaster. An officer of the Royal Airship Works where the airship had been built asked for a copy of the seance transcript, as did an airship pilot who had been a friend of Irwin. These two experts discovered forty detailed technical references in the transcript that would not have been known by or comprehensible to anybody other than an air ship specialist acquainted with the project. Furthermore, the pilot who had been Irwin's friend was impressed by the peculiar manner of speech that came through Irwin/Garrett. In life, Irwin had a quick and jerky speech pattern (Garrett did not).

The evidence developed from Garrett's R101 communications has the characteristic which researchers sometimes describe as 'sturdy'. Despite the astonishing nature of the data (communications with deceased people previously unknown to those present), the information came forth both spontaneously (the first session) and upon demand (the second session), involved more than one deceased person, consisted of a series of highly detailed observations that were well verified later by independent investigation, and even permitted two-way communication involving a non-medium (Major Villiers).

THE REMARKABLE GLADYS OSBORNE LEONARD

Mrs Gladys Osborne Leonard was another medium whose trance communications were closely observed over an extensive period. In fact, her biographer reports that "this quiet woman of common sense and integrity" was "the most carefully researched and documented medium in history"[7] (pp. 11-12). Born in 1882 at Lytham on the Lancashire coast, she was a happy child in a happy family who sometimes saw things that others did not. She assumed for some time that everybody else also saw those beautiful scenes that she called 'Happy Valley'. When she learned that this was not the case, young Gladys did her best to suppress these visions. The effort of denying part of her unique reality was laborious and unpleasant. Some years later a medium told her that she had been selected for important spiritual work. Gladys still intended to go about having a normal, ordinary life if possible. One night, however, when Gladys was staying with friends in a neighboring town, she awoke suddenly at 2 a.m. with the feeling that something alarming was taking place. She saw a large, circular patch of light above and in front of her.

> *In this light I saw my mother distinctly... A pink flush of health was on her cheeks, her eyes were clear and shining, and a smile of utter happiness was on her lips. She gazed down on me for a moment, seeming to convey an intense feeling of relief and a sense of safety and well-being. Then the vision faded. I was wide awake all the time, quite conscious of my surroundings. (p. 19)*

She learned the next morning that her mother had died at 2 a.m. Her mother had not been well, but she did not seem to have been seriously ill and in imminent danger of death.

It was a while before Mrs Leonard was ready to accept the fact of her mediumship. She considered it repugnant and improper to lose one's identity during a trance state. Nevertheless, one day she took a little nap and later learned that she had been in a trance state and conveyed a voice by the name of Feda. Mrs Leonard eventually did accept the reality of her powers and the inconveniences associated with them. Over the years she earned the respect and affection of many people whose own integrity were never in question. During her most active years as a medium, (about 1915 to 1930) she was observed, investigated and tested relentlessly. Her work survived the unprecedented length, scope, and variety of examination.

After a brief period of offering public sittings, Mrs Leonard restricted her trance activities to private sittings, mostly with people of education, achievement, and distinction. The communications conveyed by Mrs. Leonard were recorded in detail. For example, Rev. Charles Drayon Thomas attended her private sittings for many years and, himself a psychic researcher, made his detailed records available to the Society for Psychical Research. One after another, the leading investigators of survival phenomena sought out Mrs Leonard and made their own independent observations and determinations. Some even imposed experimental procedures on her. One of the most persistent and ingenious of these investigators was W. Whately Carrington. He was a mathematician and philosopher as well as a first-rank psychic researcher, and had earned the respect of distinguished people in other fields, such as the famous American psychologist, Gardner Murphy.

This hard-nosed investigator pursued a question that continues to be raised today, especially by the skeptic who will once again be trying to distort and confuse the facts a little later in this chapter. Carrington wondered if the voices that seemed to speak through Mrs Leonard were real and independent individuals or only alternative forms of the medium's own personality. It is important to appreciate just how Carrington came to this question: he had been so impressed by the accumulation of evidence from Mrs Leonard's trance states that he had to find a sound explanation. He could no longer doubt that she was providing accurate information that she could not have obtained through normal or known modalities of communication. Even so, he was not ready to concede that she was really in contact with spirit entities: perhaps these communications were produced through what we now call psi abilities.

Carrington applied a variety of experimental tasks in the effort to distinguish between spirit and psi explanations. He was particularly persistent and resourceful in using the *word association* technique that had been introduced recently by the renowned Swiss psychiatrist, C.G. Jung for the study of mental processes. As you probably know, the basic task here is to come up with the first word that pops into one's mind after seeing or hearing a stimulus word. The respondent is given a series of stimulus words and his/her response times as well as the replies are recorded. As another example of Carrington's familiarity with then-current research methodology, he also made psychogalavanic measurements, i.e., changes in electrical conductivity of the skin during the word association task. Psychogalvanic measurements are still in use today as a component of so-called lie detector tests.

In none of his experiments did Carrington find any indication that Mrs Leonard was engaging in behavior intended to mislead or defraud. Regarding his central question, Carrington concluded that two of the regular trance-voices ('John' and 'Etta') showed response patterns that were definitely independent of Mrs. Leonard's personality. This finding was consistent with the conclusion that Mrs Leonard was indeed communicating with spirit entities. The very cautious Carrington, however, would not go quite that far. He realized, quite properly, that proof for survival of death 'arrived at for the first time in history by the use of exact quantitative methods, would open up prospects beside which the achievements of the relativity theory would be of no more than parochial interest. I prefer to make precaution doubly cautious... (p.181)

Even the doubly cautious Carrington might have found it impossible to cling to his last thread of science-spun doubt had his own life been as intensely involved in the proceedings as say, that of Sir Oliver Lodge. Raymond, Sir Oliver's son, was killed in action during the First World War. Communicating through Mrs Leonard, Raymond provided highly detailed information that only he could have known. The trance-communication information was verified repeatedly, e.g., through a photograph taken shortly before his death that he described in great detail. This photograph had not been seen by his father and was not known to exist. A determined investigation located it, and it turned out to be precisely as described. There is a wealth of detail in the Raymond episode that cannot be adequately summarized here. Among other sources, Lodge's book, *Raymond*[8] is especially worth consulting for its first-hand account.

The people who found Mrs Leonard to be an authentic medium were not gullibles who were ready to believe anything. In fact, some of them devised new methods to test her powers. Some of the efforts of the professional investigator Carrington have already been noted. Consider what a person without scientific credentials contributed: Nea Walker, secretary to Sir Oliver Lodge, was one of those who wondered whether the medium was acquiring her information from deceased spirits or, by telepathy, from living minds. She came up with the technique known as the *proxy sitting*. In this procedure, the person who desires information from a deceased loved one does not actually visit the medium. Instead, a representative is sent. The medium cannot successfully 'pick the brain' of the proxy because that person simply does not have a store of intimate, particular information available about the real (absent) sitter. This is obviously a superior procedure for those in doubt about spirit survival. Mrs Leonard had a number of impressive successes with proxy sitters.

Like the other notable mediums whose work has been sketched in this chapter, Mrs Leonard left us a rich heritage of evidence for survival. Few outstanding mediums have been carefully studied over a long period of time: it is an arduous process. The results of the available investigations, however, are decidedly favourable to the survival hypothesis.

There might have been more cases of thoroughly investigated and verified mediumship if the fashion in research methodology had not changed drastically over the past 40 years or so. The early psychic investigators most often studied the phenomena whenever and wherever they occurred. Later generations have been more inclined to study whatever aspects of their subject-matter can be made to fit within the tight and narrow confines of laboratory research. There is a gain: more complete control over the proceedings. But there is also a loss: less opportunity to study some of the most important phenomena because these cannot easily be turned on and off in the laboratory setting. At present, however, there seems to be a more adventurous spirit among investigators of psi and related phenomena. It is entirely possible that we may yet see a new generation of mediumship research in which the essential phenomena will be studied using the most modern techniques of scientific inquiry.

THE ALMOST PERFECT EVIDENCE: CROSS-CORRESPONDENCES

We have explored many types of evidence in support of the survival hypothesis, both in this chapter and throughout the book. Those capable of fair-minded judgment (and for whom the prospect of an afterlife holds no terrors) will already have been well satisfied on this score. And yet we have not opened the files on still another type of evidence that might well surpass all the others in its sophistication – and, for that matter, in its methodological ingenuity. We have arrived, then, at the phenomenon of cross-correspondences, evidence as nearly perfect as our minds can comprehend on this side of the grave.

A NATURAL EXPERIMENT OF A SUPERNATURAL SORT

Some scientific research requires the construction of elaborate equipment and the establishment of highly particular experimental conditions. At other times it is possible to achieve a similar degree of rigour and value by making clever use of situations that already exist. If two groups of scientists hold differing theories about celestial events, they cannot very easily settle their differences by inducing a planet to deviate from its orbit to such-and-such a degree and then observe the results. However, astral physicists and a variety of other scientists are able to take advantage of exceptional circumstances that arise on their own (e.g. a solar eclipse or the approach of a seldom encountered comet). The natural experiment has an accepted place in science and has contributed much to our knowledge.

Cross-correspondences can be regarded as a kind of natural experiment as well, although the substance is of the sort that some would be inclined to call 'supernatural' (a mischievous and unnecessary term best left to sensationalistic thrill novels and movies). Let us begin this time not with the historical sequence of events but with a brief reflection on what would constitute superior evidence for survival. Let us further restrict this matter to evidence obtained through mediumship. Carefully studied examples of 'ordinary' mediumship have provided strong evidence for survival, but some people have felt the need for even more. We are not concerning ourselves here with those who are dedicated to spurning all evidence no matter what – the sort of person who would continue to sulk and complain even when he passes through death and finds himself still surviving. (Imagine the scene: "So, here I am, dead but still living. Humph! It will take more than that to convince me!") No, we are thinking instead of people blessed with first-rate minds who feel they must withhold their definite acceptance of survival until they encounter evidence even more precise and overwhelming than what has already been reviewed. William James was such a person, Eileen Garrett another. But it is of F.W.H. Myers that we must first speak when we turn directly to the evidence from cross-correspondences.

Our question is: how might evidence from mediumship take an even more convincing form? Would it be sufficient simply to identify more mediums and study them even more extensively? Probably not. This would be interesting, of course, but would essentially just add more data of the same type already available. What then?

Suppose then that we dispatched a seasoned investigator into *terra incognita*. We ask this person to pass from earthly life into the beyond. ("It's for science, you know – be a sport!") Instead of limiting himself to efforts at piercing the curtain from this side of death, our 'advance man' would be in a position to observe the core phenomena directly. Our plan would have to be more elaborate, however. Once 'on the other side', how would our investigator communicate his findings? 'Through a medium' would be the most obvious reply. If we limited ourselves to this procedure, however, we would not really have advanced a great deal. We need, then, a research strategy whose yield of evidence could dispel any lingering doubts about survival.

There is a way to do this. It is, in fact, rather simple in principle although not so simple in practice. The investigator must be instructed to fragment and distribute his messages so that the meaning cannot be ascertained until all the pieces have been assembled. The total message must be a puzzle to be solved through detecting and interrelating all the pieces. This can best be done by communicating each piece of the total message to a different medium or sensitive. If the experiment succeeds, several people in different places will independently receive fragments of message that make no sense until they have been put together. The odds against such a process taking place 'by chance' or by any explanation other than survival would be overwhelming. We would, of course, make sure that the message itself is not commonplace. The assembled message could not simply say, "Having wonderful time. Wish you were here." It would have to be unusual, specific and somehow characteristic of the sender.

We might call this novel procedure an experiment in *cross-correspondences* to distinguish it from direct communication of a message through one medium. The message here takes shape only when several different people have independently received its fragments.

Perfect? Almost. It is possible, however, to strengthen this rigorous experimental design even further, in two ways. First, distinguish between the function of the medium and of the 'code-breaker'. In other words, create the message and select the mediums in such a way that the person who receives a particular fragment has no data base for making sense of it. Other people – not those who receive the message-fragments – will have to perform additional work in order to reconstruct the original message. Second, do not even let anybody know that the experiment is being done! This will completely by-pass expectations, psi, whatever.

Here, then, is an extremely tough experiment in which inordinately high odds are stacked against success. Notice, for example, that even if our 'advance man' survives and flourishes in the afterlife, the experiment with cross-correspondences could fail because of insurmountable difficulties at any of the points involved. We could very well have a 'false negative', that is, an experiment whose results should have been positive but do not register as such. A 'false positive', however, would be out of the question. An accurate message could make it through cross-correspondences only if there is survival of death and some living people are sensitive enough to receive the fragmentary and coded messages.

Share this research design with your favourite scientist. He will think it rigorous and ingenious, but then give you a funny little smile and say, "But, of course, it just can't be done." And, of course, he would be mistaken, for this is precisely what was accomplished (and repeated over and again) by the remarkable F.W.H. Myers and an international network of sensitives. We will now describe – all too briefly, considering the richness of the material – some of this superb evidence for survival.

THE DEATH OF MYERS

The scholarly and much-respected president of the Society for Psychical Research had just completed his research for what would be acclaimed as a monumental contribution to our understanding of extraordinary phenomena, *Human Personality and Its Survival of Bodily Death*.[9] He was in Rome for what should have been a long-overdue vacation. But Myers had been taken grievously ill and the massive two-volume set would later be prepared for publication by Richard Hodgson and Alice Johnson. As Myers struggled for breath in his last hours, an intense little scene occurred that has escaped general notice. Here it is in the words of an eye-witness, the Swedish physician and psychiatrist Axel Munthe,[10] who had just been called in as a consultant by the attending physician:

Judge of my surprise when I recognized in his patient a man I had loved and admired for years as did everybody who had ever met him…

159

His breathing was superficial and very difficult, his face was cyanotic and worn, only his wonderful eyes were the same. He gave me his hand and said he was glad I had come at last, he had been longing for my return. He reminded me of our last meeting in London, where I dined with him at the Society for Psychical Research, how we had been sitting up the whole night talking about death and thereafter... There was nothing else for us [the physicians] to do but help him not to suffer too much.

As we were speaking, Professor William James, the famous philosopher, one of his nearest friends, entered the room... [and] told me of the solemn pact between him and his friend that whichever of them was to die first should send a message to the other as he passed over into the unknown, as they both believed in the possibility of such communication. He was so overcome with grief that he could not enter the room, and sank down on a chair by the open door, his notebook on his knees, pen in hand, ready to take down the message with his usual methodological exactitude. In the afternoon set in the Cheyne-Stokes respiration, that heart-rending sign of approaching death. The dying man asked to speak to me. His eyes were calm and serene.

'I know I am going to die,' he said, 'I know you are going to help me. Is it today, or is it tomorrow?'

'Today.'

'I am glad, I am ready. I have no fear. I am going to know at last. Tell William James, tell him...'

His heaving chest stood still in a terrible minute of suspense of life.

'Do you hear me?' I asked, bending over the dying man, 'do you suffer?'

'No,' he murmured, 'I am very tired and happy.'

These were his last words.

When I went away William James was still sitting, leaning back in his chair, his hands over his face, his open note-book still on his knees. The page was blank.

Both Myers and James were the sort of people who placed exceptional barriers in the way of their own belief in survival. While often brought to the very threshold of belief by much good evidence, they would hesitate, seeking some further and even more definitive proof. Myers expressed this difficult attitude of suspended belief in what was almost his last breath: "I am going to know at last." He died not only with the intense motivation to discover the reality for himself but also to pass it on to William James and other seekers of truth. And, soon enough, he found the way. The evidence that started to appear not long after his death made it clear that Myers, ever resourceful, had invented the method of cross-correspondences after he left this life.

MYERS' MOST ASTOUNDING EXPERIMENT

We have already described – in the abstract – the conditions that would be required to prove the survival hypothesis by communicating through cross-correspondences. These conditions have, in fact, been fulfilled, and amply so. The only discrepancy between the abstract requirements and what actually happened was itself simply a matter of experimental conditions: while the first cross-correspondences came as a surprise to the mediums and interpreters, naturally the subsequent communications were not so unexpected.

It is not possible to delve into the cross-correspondences in adequate detail in less than a book – and it would have to be a massive book at that. Transcripts derived from communications received by a single medium are very difficult to summarize; this problem, which originates in the extreme richness of the material is multiplied in cases involving cross-correspondences. Those willing to invest the time and energy in exploring this literature in detail are best advised to consult the accumulated *Proceedings of the SPR* from Volume XX onward. Unfortunately, still other material continues to be withheld from publication because of the personal details given. Here we can present only a brief sample of the kinds of data obtained.

Much of the cross-correspondence material came by way of automatic writing. The person gifted with this ability often (but not always) enters a state of consciousness somewhat akin to a trance, giving over the writing hand to whatever influences might be able to employ it. The script written out by the dissociated hand is often quite different from the individual's customary style of writing, while, in evidential cases, the substance of the material is also foreign to the scribe's own experience and personality. The frequent use of automatic writing in cross-correspondences has thus given us permanent access to the source materials or 'raw data'. It should also be made clear that most of the key cross-correspondence (C-C) evidence for survival comes from the work of 'automatists' who were not professional mediums but individuals who attempted to keep their private lives private and sometimes covered their actual identities with pseudonyms. Neither fame nor fortune were motives for their cross-correspondence activity, but simply the willingness to serve as a medium for these precious messages.

(We will italicize the name Myers, and those of several other communicators, when referring to their spirit or after-life status in order to keep matters clear.)

Let us first establish the intensity of *Myers'* desire to communicate across the barrier, to share his discovery with those he left behind. In one of his simple (non C-C) messages, the following words appeared in the hand of a woman who preferred to be known as Mrs Holland: "If it were possible for the soul to die back into earth life again I should die

161

from sheer yearning to reach you to tell you that all we imagined is not half wonderful enough for the truth." On another occasion he also wrote through her that "I am feeble with eagerness – how can I best be identified?" In a communication through Mrs Piper he reiterated this theme: "I am trying with all the forces...together to prove that I am *Myers*." While messages of this sort were conveyed at various times through more than one medium, they are not to be confused with well-developed C-Cs.

Here is an example of a relatively simple form of C-C, (for this and several other examples presented here we are indebted to the patient labours of H.F. Saltmarsh,[11] who examined and evaluated the voluminous primary material with rare persistence).

The Selwyn Gardens sequence:

- *Myers* signs himself through Mrs Holland's automatic writing in a scrawl characteristic of his actual style.

- Mrs Holland replies through her automatic writing, indicating that her hand feels shaky and wondering if she should continue.

- *Myers:* "Yes let it go on quite freely just exactly as it likes." He continues with an extensive message which includes an accurate description of a Dr Verrall and gives his address. The message concludes: "Send this to Mrs Verrall, 5, Selwyn Gardens, Cambridge."

- Mrs Holland had come across Mrs Verrall's name in Myers' book, but did not know her personally, nor had she ever been to Cambridge or heard of Selwyn Gardens.

- The address turned out to be correct, and the two women made their acquaintance for the first time through the mediation of *Myers*. Presumably, *Myers* could have contacted his old friends, the Verralls, directly. Instead he mediated the contact through a person who had not known him during his life. Here we have a real if very simple form of C-C, involving only two people but including the transmission of accurate information (the address) not previously known to the first person.

A great many subsequent C-Cs followed between Mrs Holland and Mrs Verrall (as well as between other people in years to come). Some of these simple communications demonstrated unusual knowledge on *Myers'* part of little events taking place in the lives of these women (e.g. "a new dress, not a black one this time."). Bit by bit, evidence was sifting through that *Myers* could not only communicate but could also somehow observe and report phenomena that were occurring among the living. In fact, *Myers* seemed to tap into telepathic as well as ordinary events, as suggested by the following sequence.

The Rhododendron sequence:

- Mrs Forbes, a friend of Mrs Verrall's, had been attempting – without success – to communicate telepathically "the idea of lilies". Mrs Verrall did not know that her friend was attempting this experiment.

- One day, Mrs Verrall's automatic writing contained this message from *Myers:* "If you had seen her picking lilies you would have understood... The house is large and there is a belt of rhododendrons. In the north you have seen it. Not you, I mean, but Mrs Forbes."

- This message did not make sense to Mrs Verrall. She inquired of Mrs Forbes who replied: "I looked at the lilies and cut some, and mentally asked if it would be possible to tell our friends at Cambridge [the Verralls] about them. We have been planting a belt of rhododendrons to the north of the garden." Neither of the Verralls had previously known of the rhododendrons planting.

Sequences of this type suggested that *Myers* (and, quite possibly, other deceased people) can function as amplifiers or clarifiers within the telepathic network of the living. The implications of this possibility have not yet been pursued systematically.

We are ready now for a more complex C-C sequence, one that closely approximates the ideal conditions described earlier, although with an interesting variation. An SPR investigator by the name of J.G. Piddington had reviewed some of the available C-C evidence, and decided to make a specific request for new material. This is the sequence, reduced to its essentials.

The Hope-Star-Browning sequence:

- Piddington asked *Myers* – in Latin and through Mrs Piper – to communicate between two mediums, who did not know each other, and then involve a third medium with a further message that would serve to 'cap' the previous communications. He volunteered the specific suggestion to *Myers* that he might try some kind of drawing exercise, such as placing a triangle within a circle.

- Piddington did not have long to wait. About a month later, *Myers* replied through Mrs Verrall (not Piper) "an anagram would be better. Tell him that rats, star, tars and so on... or again, tears, stare."

- In a further contact through Mrs Verrall, *Myers* did communicate two drawings (an inverted triangle within a half-circle resting on a straight line and another inverted triangle along with a much smaller triangle within a larger, rather ovalish circle). The drawings were accompanied by a wildly poetic written passage:

Aster. Teras. The world's wonder. And all a wonder and a wild desire. The very wings of her. AWINGED DESIRE. **Upopteros eros.** *Then there is Blake. And mocked my loss of liberty. But it is all the same thing – the winged desire.* **Eros potheinos.** *The hope that leaves the earth for the sky –* **Abt Vogler** *for earth too hard that found itself or lost itself – in the sky. That is what I want. On earth the broken sounds – threads – in the sky, the perfect arc. The C major of this life. But your recollection is at fault.*

Surely, whatever else might be said about this passage, it is far from commonplace, displays great erudition, and is characteristic of *Myers'* more imaginative flights of thought while he was still Myers.

● As this series of C-Cs between Mrs Verrall and Mrs Piper continued, *Myers* specifically mentioned the name of Robert Browning (a caustic critic of spiritualism), one of whose poems was called *Evelyn Hope*. He also corrected one of his own errors in transmitting a piece of the message. Careful analysis of the accumulated C-Cs disclosed many internal matchings between bits communicated to one medium or the other (e.g. another Browning poem, *Abt Vogler*, and more communications through drawings). Furthermore, the additional demand set by Piddington was fulfilled: Mrs Verrall's mother suddenly joined the C-C circle with messages from *Myers* that added new dimensions to the previous communications. The words 'hope', 'star' and 'Browning' found their way into the automatic writings of all three women.

The Hope-Star-Browning sequence was a good deal more complex than can be summarized here – and it was exceeded in complexity and richness of material by a number of other sequences. One in particular, too complex to describe without writing another book involved no fewer than seven people in the same C-Cs. The material communicated by *Myers* often reflected his enormous fund of knowledge, especially in obscure corners of world literature that were unknown to most people. And the mediums often could make no sense of the information as it came to, or through, them. In some instances it required years of patient investigation on the part of others, involving literary detective work, before the connections emerged. When the various links were put together, however, the results sometimes were beautifully precise (not all communications worked perfectly, of course). *Myers* had not only convinced himself but had devised a most effective means of convincing others as well.

Nor did this experiment end with Myers/*Myers* and the circle of people around him in the early years of this century. Cross-correspondences continued to flourish for many years. As several other pioneers of the SPR died, they also succeeded in communicating through a variety of automatists. And, yes, the transition from critical investigator to spirit communicator was made by Richard Hodgson as well. The sceptical young man who once was certain he would detect Mrs Piper's trickery eventually became an important 'control' or 'guide' himself and as *Hodgson* provided further detailed evidence for survival.

One person who joined the Myers C-C network after it had been functioning for a while lived a quiet and private life for many more years. But Mrs Coombe-Tennant (using the pseudonym of 'Mrs Willett') continued to receive automatic writing communications from Myers and others. And when Mrs Coombe-Tennant died in 1956 (in her 83rd year), she in turn communicated with a member of a younger generation of automatists, Geraldine Cummins. Myers' experiment is, in a sense, 'alive and well', and there may be many more chapters to write. Incidentally, C.D. Broad, the eminent British philosopher, independently examined the Coombe-Tennant/Cummins material and its historical context – and then agreed to write the preface to *Swan on a Black Sea*, [12] the combined work of older and younger automatists.

Next to all this extraordinary evidence I would like to place a few humble items of my own. I once taught a course in parapsychology at the University of Massachusetts-Boston simply because I felt like doing so, welcoming the opportunity to improve my knowledge in this field. (My usual courses were concerned with the psychology of adult development and ageing, and the psychology of dying and death.) There was no shortage of students interested in exploring this topic with me. I thought a lot about Myers and his work, puzzling it over and over in my mind, accepting certain conclusions on Monday and rejecting them on Tuesday, etc. For a period of several weeks F.W.H. Myers was almost a tenant in the portion of my brain that I did not need for everyday activities. And during this same period of time, *Myers* seemed to pay some rather playful visits as though to demonstrate that he was still available when the circumstances were ripe.

On one occasion I was driving home from the University and thinking about the examination I would need to construct for students in the parapsychology class. "Seven!" said a voice in my head. *"Myers!"*, I smiled to myself, but did nothing. A moment later, the voice made itself more obvious: "Seven! Radio!" I turned on the car radio and heard a Beethoven symphony in progress: Beethoven's *Seventh*. I felt somehow that *Myers* was pleased, and I felt happy for him. *Myers* had not finished for the day, however. With what I hoped was his permission, I turned the radio off before the symphony was over so that I could be alone with my (or our) thoughts. *Myers* spoke again: "Swansy." At least, that's what I thought he said. I was a little irritated at him because I didn't care for the sound of the word. What a stupid word, "Swansy!"

Immediately I felt that *Myers* was brooding because I didn't care for his new message. After a moment or two, another word formed in my head – I didn't 'hear' it this time, but visualized it spelled out: Swansea.

In this form, the word sounded vaguely British to me and marginally less irritating. In a burst of unfounded confidence and good feeling, I said (perhaps aloud, I don't remember for sure) "Radio!" I turned the radio on again, and this time I was not even surprised to hear the suite from Tchaikovsky's *Swan Lake* – although I was surprised to discover later that Mrs Coombe-Tennant, the automatist of *Swan on a Black Sea*, had lived in Derwin Farr – close to Swansea! (This piece of information is given by Broad in his introduction, which I had not previously read.)

Myers has not made himself known to me for a while now. But why don't you turn on your radio?

THE CHANNELS ARE STILL OPEN

Piper, Garrett, Leonard, and Myers are among the great figures in spirit communication who now are themselves on the other side. Furthermore, the term 'medium' is seldom heard these days. Not to worry! Mediated communication between the living and the dead continues to occur and may well be as frequent and widespread as in the halcyon days of nineteenth century spiritism. The desire of human spirits to embrace each other across the subtle boundary of death has not been destroyed by the massive technological and socio-cultural changes that have occurred in the past few decades.

We begin with studies by reputable investigators that retain the traditional term, 'medium', and then sample the burgeoning area of communication through channelers.

FROM ITALY TO ICELAND: MEDIUMSHIP SURVIVES

The research enterprise is subject to changing fashions and trends. A hot issue that engages the attention of many scientists for several years may be set aside when another issue emerges – or when there is a shift in the sources of potential funding. The earlier issues have not vanished, however, and they are likely to reappear as the wheel of socio-scientific interest turns and as new phenomena or methods are identified. For example, in my own experience I saw the problem of suicide and its prevention become a priority concern for the U.S. Institutes of Health, thereby encouraging many new investigators to work in this area. Within a few years, though, sickle cell anemia (a condition with a strong genetic component) became the 'disease of the day' and the suicide prevention effort was essentially abandoned. Just a few years later, the strengthened cadre of sickle cell anemia researchers witnessed the sharp reduction of their support as other conditions seized the imagination, anxiety, and resources of the establishment (e.g. Alzheimer's disease... AIDS...). Meanwhile, neither suicide nor sickle cell anemia had disappeared. The problems remained and the promising research and prevention efforts had to struggle on at a much reduced level of support.

So it is with the study of mediums. Once many of the best investigative minds devoted their attention to the survival question in general and to mediums in particular. Today there are still honest and effective mediums at work, and it is still possible to confirm and extend our knowledge of their spirit communication process. Relatively few qualified researchers are available, however, to pursue these studies. I am emphasizing this point to make it clear that the reduced output of scientific reports is almost a function of the state of affairs in the sciences rather than the disappearance of the phenomena.

Here are a pair of examples to remind us that mediumistic communication continues to provide evidence for survival.

Luigi Pisano (born in 1913 and, at last report, still among the living) was a trance medium who has also been associated with a number of psychokinetic effects (in which mental activity has an effect on physical matter). His activities as a medium occurred during the years 1937-1952. He had several controls through whom it appeared that he communicated with about a hundred spirits. Something out of the ordinary – even for a medium! – occurred during one of his seances in 1948, given in a village in the vicinity of Florence. One of the ten sitters present made close to verbatim notes of the proceedings. During this seance an unfamiliar and unexpected voice was heard. His story included the following statements:

> I cannot see you, but I feel that you exist just as I once existed. I was a priest. I am happy. I am glad that you finally know the truth. I was killed with a revolver. I bear no grudge. I was a priest in Canton, Ohio. Giuseppe Riccardi. I do not know who you are; I only know that we are brothers...
>
> A woman shot me after I had celebrated mass...When shot, I felt very warm. I raised myself to ask this woman why she had shot me with a pistol. She was in a sort of hysterical state, and she paid no attention to me. She did not seem aware that I had asked her to lift me up. But that does not matter, any more.[13] (p. 259)

Nobody in the seance room knew anything about a priest named Giuseppe Riccardi of Canton, Ohio. His voice was heard again with brief statements similar to the above at two subsequent seances, and then, silence. The seance had been held at the home of a psychic investigator, Silvio Ravaldini. He was interested in attempting to verify the information conveyed by this 'drop-in' communicator (a voice unexpected by the medium), but could see no way of doing so (e.g., the priest had not given the date of his death, and Ravaldini had no contacts in Ohio). Ravaldini tried repeatedly to have American investigators look into this matter, but they were already fully occupied with their own studies.

Almost four decades after this series of seances, Susan Adams, a research assistant to Ian Stevenson, contacted the Youngstown, Ohio diocese office and learned that a "Father Giuseppe Riccardi of St Anthony Parish, Canton, had died on 10 March, 1929." That was the only information provided by the diocese office. From this point, however, it became possible to learn a little more about Riccardi's life, mostly through newspaper accounts of his murder in 1929. The additional facts confirmed and supplemented the information conveyed by the drop-in communicator. Father Riccardi had been shot as he prepared to baptize a baby. His killer was a woman who had objected to the relocation of the church, a move that had been supported by the priest. She had also accused Father Riccardi of molesting her five-year-old daughter, a charge that the priest denied and a medical investigator determined to be false. The newspaper accounts described the women as "apparently suffering from mental illness".

A Father Riccardi had existed, then, in an Ohio city whose very existence was not known either to the medium or the sitters (they associated Canton with China). He had met a violent death in 1929, and somehow managed to communicate with people he felt comfortable with two decades later – and, after another four decades, what he said was verified and the possibility of fraud carefully ruled out.

Other investigated reports have come to us from Iceland. Why Iceland? Probably because one of the leading investigators of paranormal phenomena is a citizen of this nation and therefore available to notice and study significant cases. Erlendur Haraldsson with the assistance of Ian Stevenson has reported two cases that are also of the drop-in type. The example we will share here is of Hafsteinn Bjornsson, a trance medium.[14] Bjornsson's sittings have been observed extensively and been the subject of many publications in Iceland. Some of his communications are consistent with the most common pattern observed with other mediums (and channelers): receiving information from 'controls' while in a trance state. There are two other characteristics of his activities, however, that are more unusual: firstly,in a waking, non-trance state he experiences impressions of deceased persons who he sees or visualizes around the sitter; and secondly, some of his communicators are from two generations prior to the sitter; e.g., he may talk in detail about grandparents whom the sitting relatives barely recall.

A visit by Bjornsson to the U.S. in 1972 provided the opportunity for a controlled experiment at the Chester F. Carlson Research Laboratory of the American Society for Psychic Research (New York City). The ten sitters recruited for this study were given headphones to wear during the proceedings and listened to Mozart's clarinet concerto played at a rather loud volume so they could not receive auditory clues from the medium. Bjornsson did the readings into a tape recorder without going into a trance state and without the sitters being able to hear him. Furthermore, the medium and the sitter could not see each other either; they were separated by a heavy opaque curtain.

Later the sitters were called in one at a time and asked to read the transcripts of all ten sessions. Each sitter was asked to determine which report was most applicable to himself and to substantiate his choice with detailed information. Here is an excerpt from one of his readings:

> *There comes a man around fifty... A quiet man, but a determined and resolute man. He says his name is Thordur Thorsteinsson. He has lived up in the country in Iceland, close to, very close to a village or town.*
>
> *There comes with him an old woman, a very old woman by the name of Gudbjorg. They have known one another and have known this person [the sitter] when he was a boy... But another man is also there... who has known him. He went [died] suddenly, very suddenly.*
>
> *A man of average height, rather slim, both around his body and in his face, with long-drawn facial features who says his name is Gunnlaugur Jonsson... He went very suddenly. I have a feeling of choking and suffocation. Somehow something happened to his breathing organs and he died as a result... Along with him very close to Reykjavik. (pp. 198-199)*

Thordur Thorsteinsson's name and fate was immediately recognized by the father and other family members of the sitter. Further inquiry revealed that Gunnlaugur had choked to death when a piece of food got stuck in his throat. The main facts and most of the details of this communication from Bjornsson were found to be accurate. There was an error, however, in speaking of the sitter as having been a boy: the sitter was a woman. Bjornsson did not claim to knowing the gender of his invisible sitters.

The results varied from sitter to sitter, especially with respect to the amount of verifiable detail. For example, sometimes Bjornsson provided only a first name and the sitter could not identify that person. Interestingly, there was a high proportion of violent deaths among the spirits who appeared to have been communicating through the medium. Perhaps there is something to the nearly ancient and nearly universal belief that people who die a violent death are more likely to seek the opportunity to communicate. Another characteristic of his readings was the grouping of communicators; the spirits seldom came alone. In fact, Bjornsson occasionally complained about the 'crowding' of spirit communicators when he was trying to pay attention to just one.

The investigators were impressed by the *combinations* of verifiable facts that Bjornsson was able to provide for several of the sitters. They judged it extremely unlikely that these combinations could have occurred by chance. These positive results could be attributed either to authentic spirit communication or to a high level of telepathic information exchange. The spirit/survival interpretation is fully consistent with the results, but those who favor the psi hypothesis are free to conduct follow-up studies based on experimental approach taken here.

CHANNELING THE SPIRITS

Young people today and those who have just recently become interested in spirit communication are more likely to have heard about channeling and channelers than about mediums. Nevertheless, the medium and the channeler have much in common. There may be some individual variations, but in general:

- Both receive communications from the spirits of deceased people.
- Both have one or more spirit guides who mediate their communication with particular spirits. There is usually a primary spirit guide that makes itself available to the channeler/medium over an extended period of time.
- Both are likely to close their eyes, alter their breathing patterns and enter a trance-state.
- Both provide the channel for voice communication from the spirits.
- The communicating voice may be of the same or opposite sex of the channeler/medium, and may be similar or vastly different in personality, race, and ethnicity.
- There may or may not be the opportunity for sitters to interact with the spirit communicators; this seems to depend entirely on the way a particular channeler/medium operates.

Along with these significant commonalities, there is another characteristic that most channelers share with some of the most respected mediums. I refer to the absence of the darkened room and physical phenomena. There was a time when people purporting to have exceptional psychic powers would insist on plunging the room into darkness, forbidding the sitters to speak or move around, and otherwise exercise considerable control over the setting. Furthermore, they would often astound their sitters with such physical phenomena as table rappings and tippings, contact by phantom hands, or even full body levitation. The Fox Sisters, previously mentioned, were early practitioners of this kind. Others famous as both mental and physical mediums included Eusapia Palladino, D.D. Home, and, of course, the ineffable Madame Blavatsky (all of them spectacular cheats, at least some of the time). There is reason to believe that some mediums of the dark-room, physical-manifestations type did have 'the real stuff' even though they could not perform at peak efficiency in every sitting. It must be admitted, however, that this kind of set-up invited suspicion, criticism, and parody.

The typical channeler today does not insist that the room be plunged into darkness or that the sitters hold their breath in worshipful tension all evening. The channeler may be comfortable in sitting in your own living room, chatting congenially with everybody present and then, when the time seems ripe, slipping easily into a receptive state. As we have seen, credible mediums such as Bjornsson often do not require special arrangements or make unusual demands on their sitters. The quality channeler and the quality medium therefore have a lot in common.

The similarities between medium and channeler are sufficiently impressive to raise the question: has only the name changed? I would say that channeling represents a variation on mediumship, a variation that deserves its own designation. Only a person ignorant of the history of spiritism could assert that channeling is completely different in its *modus operandi* and results – yet there are distinctive features of the contemporary channeling approach, as we will see.

EDGAR CAYCE: SAGE OF CHANNELING

Channeling owes much to Edgar Cayce, who is considered by some to have been "America's greatest psychic".[15] Cayce (born in Kentucky in 1877) would have been recognized as a notable person even if he had not given us the fundamentals of the new channeling approach to spirit communication. He was an excellent interpersonal communicator, the sort of individual that others intuitively seek out for advice, counseling, and support. By many accounts, he was, indeed, invested with a high level of psi powers. Possessing significant psi ability does not necessarily translate into using this power in a positive and effective manner. Some people feel very uncomfortable with this ability, and others never learn how to use it for human benefit. Cayce was a shining example of a wise and good person who also happened to have exceptional psi abilities.

It was Cayce's concern for his fellow humans and his ability to think things through in a fresh and reflective manner that distinguished his approach and helped to form the character of the channeling movement. We can appreciate this better when we compare Cayce's ideas with those of the most influential mediums. Piper and Leonard were highly effective and solidly authenticated practitioners of mediumship. Neither, however, had much of an idea about either the how or the why. They seemed to have conventional Christian beliefs, and did not trouble themselves any further about it. They had no theory to explain, let alone to sell. Garrett was an exceptionally bright person with an inquiring and critical mind. She had the intellectual qualifications to propose a conceptual framework for spirit communication. Instead, she took the admirable pathway of demanding and supporting quality research to test the existence of psi and spiritual processes. The neighborhood medium was usually content with some vague theory learned at second or third hand that could not be taken seriously by educated people. Basically, mediums were engrossed in being mediums and touched on metaphysical issues only to the extent that their clients seemed to expect some philosophical chit-chat from them.

Not so with Cayce. Over the years he developed ideas about the human mind and spirit and its place in the universe. In a word, he had a philosophy. Channeling therefore became more than a technique; it became one facet of a comprehensive world view. We must therefore understand something of Cayce's world view in order to appreciate the nature and significance of channeling. This is not the place to present his views in their entirety, but it will be useful to identify some of his propositions that are most relevant to the survival question.

- Mind is not exclusively the personal property of any one individual. Although we all have our unique experiences and sequences of thoughts about daily life, on the deeper level, all of us share in a universal mental activity. Essentially, our minds are *transpersonal*.

- This deeper and universal reservoir of mind remembers everything that the human race has experienced. This enduring and ever-accumulating archive of the human experience is known as the *Akashic Record*.

- There is another level of mind that exists between the conscious, personalized stratum and the deep vein that is shared by all humanity. This *subconscious* mind is free of the restrictions and boundaries that characterize our usual everyday thought processes. The everyday conscious mind is functional and analytic, helping us to cope with information presented to our senses by the external world. It is at the subconscious level that all minds are in contact with each other – including the minds of the 'living' and the 'dead'.

- Each level of mind is a distinctive information channel:

Conscious   Sensory information from external world

Subconscious   Telepathic information from subconscious minds of others

Transpersonal Universal information from the oneness of all life

- *Intuition* is an ability that makes use of all the other mind channels. It can be described as a super-channel.

  We find intuition at work when a person has prophetic visions, takes just the right action because it 'feels' right, or expresses a truth in symbolic language.

To these elements of Cayce's world view we must add his conception of the *higher self*. This is the person we are, in a sense, just waiting to become, although in another sense this person already exists as an ideal and guide. Intuition and the higher self are closely related. The person who is in harmony with both the natural world and his/her own self is able to experience intuition to its fullest extent. The alienated, isolated, withdrawn, conflicted, or angry person has much less ability to integrate information from the three mind channels through the super channel of intuition.

We see at once that Cayce's approach does not require 'supernatural' elements, nor does it assume that completely different forces come into operation when living and dead communicate. Throughout our lives we are potentially open to communication with both the living and the dead. We vary among ourselves in our ability to receive, acknowledge, and interpret these communications. I may be a poor communicator who has failed to make effective contact with my inner self and therefore cannot make the most of contacts with others. You may be well in touch both with your higher self and with the natural world, and, therefore, more awake to communicational transactions with other minds, living and dead. *We do not start channeling when we first attempt to communicate with a deceased person. We have been channeling all our lives, in many ways, and with greater or lesser success. Channeling is part of life.*

There is a strong moral and self-development component in channeling. Those who follow the lead of Cayce (and many do) are not focused exclusively on the mere fact of communication with the deceased. They are more concerned with discovering the truths that are within themselves and within all of nature. They attempt to be increasingly open to experience from all sources, and to recognize 'the voice of intuition'[15] whether it comes from themselves, another living person, or the subconscious of a person no longer alive. Dreams are given serious attention as a source of insight and a way of becoming better acquainted with one's higher self. As compared with the general run of mediumship over the years, channeling has more of a self-improvement motivation and morally informed perspective.

Cayce's thoughts about survival differ appreciably from the assumptions that have accompanied much of the mediumistic activity. Reed has summarized Cayce's position as follows:

> *When a person dies the personal conscious mind dies with the body, but the subconscious mind remains unaffected... our dream images, or subconscious desires and fears, continue their existence after the death of the body. Cayce makes an important distinction about this continued life. There are the continued effects, which arise from the permanent records of all thoughts and experiences... and those thoughts live on in eternity. There is also the continued activity, which is the soul's spirit journey in other dimensions of being. Much of what passes for contact with the activity of the spirit, however, is actually contact with the effects of the records of the entity's experience patterns in the subconscious regions.*[15] *(pp. 178-179)*

There is survival of the spirit, which continues its journey beyond this life. However, sometimes what we contact are traces of a deceased person's thought patterns. Our access to these traces and our ability to interpret them depends much on our personal affinity with the personality and needs of the deceased. But we may also be able to contact the active spirits of the deceased, again depending in part on the 'fit' between their desires and intentions and our own.

Channeling has taken a firm hold today in our critical – make that a skeptical, a cynical – world. Intelligent and responsible people have been persuaded, one by one, that our minds have potentials that are too seldom actualized. Contacts are made with both the residual thought patterns and the active spirits of the dead for the serious purpose of continued self-development and world harmony, not for the simple thrill or reassurance of exchanging greetings with a deceased companion. Perhaps the finest accomplishment of the medium has been to prepare the way for the enlightened channeler.

THE CRITIC'S RESPONSE

On and on the advocate labours! We note with approval that he has improved his skill at steering clear of out-and-out fraud and also has seen fit to admit that the scientific method does have its points. Yet his latest collection of picturesque stories is still a long way from demonstrating survival of death. Fortunately, we will be able to present the actual state of affairs in but a fraction of the verbiage required by the advocate for spinning his few promising threads into an entertaining if insubstantial fabric. Here are some of the principal objections I must raise to mediumship evidence even of the 'higher' (not clearly fraudulent) type.

The analogy with psi abilites is not convincing. It is true that the abilities of humans vary considerably, speaking now of those abilities whose existence is beyond doubt (e.g. athletic prowess, mathematical facility, etc.). Nevertheless, the existence of psi abilities is problematical, to say the least. The doubt remains despite years of psychic research that has become increasingly sophisticated. The supposed phenomena cannot be produced and documented reliably under specified conditions. It is not very helpful, then, to support survival claims by drawing comparisons with psi research. Psi research has enough troubles of its own.

Much less scientific evidence can be seriously put forward for the survival hypothesis, and the meagre evidence there is also of poor quality. And so we are being lured into accepting the range of possible psi abilities as a model or proof for the existence of a similar range of abilities in mediumship. The unlikely is asked to guarantee the incredible! I am willing to grant the possibility of authentic psi phenomena because in this realm there are some observations that are worth taking seriously although not fully validated. This does not mean, however, that we can allow claims for communication with the dead to slip by on the coat-tails of psi. Yes, it is plausible enough that there are individual differences in the ability to communicate with the dead, but only if this ability has itself been established as authentic. The sly argument by analogy with psi abilities begs rather than answers the question.

HOW SPIRITS HAVE THEIR SAY: FROM MEDIUMS TO CHANNELERS

Mediumship failures, errors and deceptions are tolerated and excused by their advocates. This is painfully obvious in the larger domain of so-called mediumships from which the advocate has made a few very careful selections. It is not only commonplace for mediums to be exposed in the midst of their deceptions, but almost as commonplace for many people to continue to believe in their powers. We discovered this phenomenon in the very first appearance of spiritism, the Fox sisters, and it has come up again and again. Phony mediums have been defended in spite of repeatedly being caught in the act of deception. Eusapia Palladino, for example, amazed a number of well-educated people with her feats. A versatile performer, she could make chairs, even sofas move about at her command, as well as summon up miscellaneous spirits from the great beyond. On several occasions she was discovered in the act of producing her phenomena through simple trickery. And yet the same witnesses were inclined to shrug their shoulders and apologize that Eusapia was just having a bad day, and had stooped to cheating because her powers had not quite been up to the mark. This same kind of slippery logic is implicit in the advocate's comparison of psi abilities with mediumship. The medium is given a whole set of ready-made excuses, e.g. somebody in the group had a suspicious attitude, so how could she work her wonders? Has science ever had to make excuses for authentic phenomena? "Gravity is a little tired today and doesn't feel up to pulling things down… "

People who should know better have continued to believe in mediums despite evidence of fakery. Let's take an example that was studiously avoided by the advocate. 'Margery' was one of the dominant mediums in the years following World War I. The wife of a prominent Boston physician, Mina Stinson Crandon was the very model of a model medium. Such a respectable person. Such a charming woman. So open. So cooperative. So little interested in financial rewards for her astounding psychic performances. After one spoke reverently of Piper and Leonard one would add the name of Margery as an honest soul and gifted medium. Those with the good fortune to know Margery could not for a moment imagine that she was anything less than a person of complete integrity.

She was, nevertheless, a cheat. It was a while before investigators caught on to her methods, and a longer while before, quite grudgingly, there was general agreement that her mediumship had been shot through with fraud. She might have escaped history's verdict even so, had not investigators come up with very damaging physical evidence. Her primary spirit control was her deceased brother, Walter. He was an entertaining fellow as well as a first-rate solicitor of spirits. Walter, like Margery, was usually quite willing to meet the needs of sitters and investigators. The more pushy investigators sometimes asked for physical manifestations of spirit presence. Walter obliged by leaving his fingerprints on blank wax tablets that were placed in the seance room.

The prints made by Walter would be compared with the prints of everybody else present. No match. The mysterious fingerprint had been made by some other agency – in all likelihood, the ever-resourceful and cooperative Walter. Alas, poor Walter, and, also, alas poor Margery! A resourceful bit of detective work disclosed that Walter's fingerprints were actually those of a Dr Caldwell, Margery's very own dentist. Confronted with this evidence, Caldwell phoned Margery in a panic, and this act provided further evidence of collaborative fraud, if further evidence was needed.[16]

The reputation of Gladys Leonard has fared much better as far as fraud is concerned. Inexplicably, though, the advocate neglected to inform you of her most outstanding skill outside of trafficking with the spirits: she had been a professional actress. It is not just that the skills of a trained actress might come in handy when performing seance-room feats. It is also that the ability to construct or call upon a variety of performing personalities would be invaluable in assembling a repertoire company of spirit communicators. Sitters and even investigators are likely to be impressed by the appearance of spirit personalities who are markedly different from the medium. This, in fact, was one of the main points in Carrington's word association experiment that the advocate so kindly summarized for us. Actually, the results of this study were rather a mess, as Carrington himself soon recognized. In retrospect we can see that although Carrington was a mathematician, he did not have available at that time the kind of sophisticated, computer-based statistics that might have yielded clearer findings. The one clear finding that did emerge would be more interesting to a psychoanalyst than to a person looking for survival evidence: 'Feda', her control, showed a personality pattern that was the mirror image of Mrs Leonard's. This finding strongly suggests that so-called spirit controls are actually alternative or split-off selves of the medium. A person who is somewhat more disassociated than others or who for any reason has developed a larger stock of partial selves could have a decided advantage when it comes to playing medium. By the way, despite several determined efforts by investigators, no actual person matching up with 'Feda' was ever discovered. They were looking in the wrong place, as we can see now.

There's more, too. Gladys Leonard made her reputation by having persuaded Sir Oliver Lodge that she could communicate with his beloved son, a war casualty. The pain of emotional loss and the intense desire for a sense of reunion made Sir Oliver vulnerable to skilfully performed acts purporting to be mediumship. Gladys became 'certified' in the public's mind and highly sought after once Sir Oliver accepted her offerings as authentic. Many other English families were grieving the death of family members in the War that unfortunately did not end all wars. Similar phenomena would occur in the other nations who suffered casualties in that grinding and brutal war. All too predictably, war brings violent death, pestilence, social disorganization, widowhood, orphanhood – and mediums.

Perhaps Gladys Leonard really believed that she could communicate with deceased spirits. Perhaps she really wasn't sure but kept doing whatever it was that she was doing because so many people desired that of her. It would not be fair to accuse her of intentional deception on the basis of the available evidence, but neither does the available evidence support the extravagant claims for spirit survival on the basis of her mediumship. It is not just that she identified some spirit communicators as deceased spirits while the actual people were still hale and hearty. It is that we have a welter of reports but no clear evidence that she was ever actually dealing with deceased spirits.

In retrospect, such claims will also have to overcome the barrier first recognized by Myers and later reformulated by Cayce (whose thoughts, though enticing, were hardly original). Myers suggested and Cayce asserted that when people die they are survived by a trace pattern of thoughts and memories. This is not the kind of survival most people have in mind, but it is very interesting on its own terms. The gaps, errors, and inconsistencies in the communications offered by the most illustrious mediums, such as Gladys Leonard, could derive from the difficulty in making sense of these floating clouds of residual thought.

Leonora Piper has also been treated kindly by history, and perhaps will continue to enjoy a high reputation in the absence of verified misdoings. Nevertheless, questions can be asked of her mediumship as well. Consider, for example, her faithful 'Phinuit'. This celebrated spirit guide claimed to have been a French physician. One investigator finally got around to asking Phinuit to converse with him in French. *Sauve qui peut!* He could not. Phinuit was then asked to discuss medical subjects. Ah … um … sorry, time to go. Given this response, it is difficult to understand why investigators did not press further into Phinuit's alleged spiritual identity as well as undertake more critical analyses of Leonora's communications, which vagueness (see below) was not uncommon.

Eileen Garrett's approach to psychic phenomena was unique among those with strong reputations. As already noted, she created an outstanding career for herself in publishing, and neither needed nor sought financial compensation for use of the powers that were attributed to her. She even supplied her own money to support improved research on the survival question and other psychic phenomena. At this point, Garrett would be the person whose psi powers I would be most willing to consider as possibly authentic. The R101 episode still haunts me. It is one of the best (most evidential and documented) cases of possible spirit communication to have come our way. One could design a more perfect situation for evaluating the possibility of communication between the living and the dead, but one could not reasonably expect that reality would spontaneously give us so challenging an episode.

HOW SPIRITS HAVE THEIR SAY: FROM MEDIUMS TO CHANNELERS

It would be convenient to my position if I could say that deception and fraud has been exposed in the R101 case, but no such evidence has surfaced over the years. (I am patient, though, I will wait … has anybody cross-checked on those who cross-checked on the seance transcript?) I might say that Garrett obtained the mass of technical information by telepathy rather than spirit contact. I would hate to concede even that much! Recall that the R101 crashed two days prior to the seance. Now add a fact that somehow the advocate again neglected to share with us. Garrett had previously experienced a vision of a dirigible that seemed so real to her that she could not believe that everybody else had not seen it as well. The lighter-than-air craft was sailing along beautifully, high above, when suddenly it started to discharge smoke and fall from the sky. It was difficult for Garrett to come to terms with the fact that this incident had taken place only in her – Her what? Her imagination? her psychic-scope? She remained anxious about the dirigible from that point on, not being able to erase the memory of her vision. This sequence suggests that Garrett already had a special sensitivity towards the possibility of a dirigible catastrophe. She was on the wave-length. This special sensitivity could well have made her receptive to telepathic communication from the R101 pilot when the catastrophe actually occurred. Additionally, she might have absorbed information about the crash without conscious awareness prior to the seance, although this would not account for the wealth of detail that she produced. The communication, then, could be interpreted as a slightly delayed telepathic report, rather than ongoing contact with deceased spirits. The trance situation might have been needed to bring this information to the surface. I am aware that this interpretation itself has some problems, however, and I must be content for now with placing the R101 episode in the elite category of experiences that should not be too hastily dismissed.

The basic point here is this: all the little nuggets of apparently positive evidence for mediumship have been extracted from a much larger mass of failure, error and deception. The 'yield' in favour of the survival hypothesis is thus presented in an unrealistic light because a great many negative and suspicious cases have been quietly set aside as unimportant. Wouldn't you like the licence to discard all your errors and mistakes without taking responsibility for them? Perhaps you would have too much moral fibre to take advantage of this opportunity. The mediums, however, have thrived on it.

Many of the 'spirit communications' have been vague to the point of being useless. The answers given by deceased parties to specific questions were often empty and imprecise, and the personality of one 'control' often blended into that of another.[17] No one has examined so much of the detail of mediumship 'evidence' as thoroughly as Mrs Henry Sidgwick,[18,19] one of the original group of SPR investigators. She discovered many examples of vagueness and banality in the alleged communications – in fact, triviality was more the rule than the exception. Furthermore, alleged communications from historical figures such as Julius Caesar came across in a singularly unconvincing (although unintentionally comical) way. (In fairness it should be stated that the mediumship of 'Mrs Willett', or Coombe-Tennant, may be exempted from these problems.)

All this suggests that what we now know as the *halo effect* exercised its influence on those who frequented mediums and even those who believed they studied them. In social psychology, the halo effect refers to an overgeneralization of favourable expectations – a new witticism, for example, is quickly attributed to a person who already has a reputation as a humorist, a gifted athlete or actor is deemed to be a political expert when he steps up on the platform, etc. Occasional 'revelations' or interesting bits from a medium induce people to credit him with additional successes when, in fact, the material is vague, imprecise and far from illuminating. And how are these few successes themselves obtained? Unusual knowledge is most likely to be obtained either through telepathy or through the powers of the mind to retain information obtained through ordinary means on an unconscious level (i.e. what we once heard 'out of the corner of our ears' but paid little conscious attention to at the time). Success through memory upshoots or telepathy can easily lead, through the halo effect, to someone being attributed with powers of communicating with the dead – which is quite another matter entirely.

Telepathy remains a more reasonable explanation than survival. In the previous chapter we pointed out that psi, usually of the telepathic type, is a superior alternative explanation for much of the so-called survival evidence. This holds true even when a person sees a medium anonymously or with a pseudonym. If the 'medium' is actually a psi sensitive, he or she might have little difficulty in getting through to the personal information encoded in the visitor's mind, and lack of the correct name should not be a major barrier. In fact, the sitter's preoccupation with suppression of his/her real name might make this very easy indeed.

It is probable that in many cases the medium was able to work not only with his psi abilities but also with the many verbal and non-verbal cues offered by the sitters. Did this man enter the room heavy-footed, his head drooping, his eyes sunken in grief? Is that woman trying hard to keep her nervousness under control as some people do when they have a guilty secret? In everyday life we provide each other with many clues about our state of mind. A psychologist or clever salesperson will pick up many of these – a sensitive or medium may be even more adept. When a combination of telepathy and subtle behavioural clues can account for mediumship survival phenomena this more parsimonious interpretation should be preferred.

And this alternative interpretation is appropriate in a great many of the situations that have been offered as proof of survival. Accepting this approach will place us alongside the estimable Mrs Sidgwick and all others who are not keen on playing the fool. To believe in the psi hypothesis requires more than enough risk-taking. Why commit unnecessary intellectual folly by swallowing the survival hypothesis as well?

The 'cross-correspondences' do not provide clear evidence for survival. It is appealing to think that Myers became *Myers* and then hit upon this rather clever technique. We do not know for a fact, however, that either Myers or *Myers* had anything to do with these products of psychological dissociation (automatic writing). What we do know is that the idea of C-Cs occurred to some living people (who were already tuned into exotic phenomena) after Myers' death. Just because some people decided to put a variety of phenomena together and describe them as 'cross-correspondences' does not prove much of anything. Gurney, Johnson and others may simply have credited their late mentor with their own bright idea, the notion of a puzzle-solving exercise across the life-death barrier.

Automatic writing is itself a dubious proposition. Supposedly, the writer is not aware of what he or she is writing. At times, it is claimed that the writer did not even know that he or she was writing. The writing is usually done at a rapid pace and in what is assumed to be an altered state of consciousness. The examples of automatic writing that played a role in the cross-correspondences and other psychic transactions are usually thought to have involved the intercession of a visiting personality – some agency other than the person whose hand is at work. Ian Stevenson, one of today's leading investigators, points out that automatic writing is subject to the operation of the individual's secondary personalities, just as is the case with the so-called spirit controls of mediums.[20] It is likely that what really happens during automatic writing is the emergence of hidden memories, memories whose very existence had been forgotten. The information then strikes readers as coming from some source other than the writer. In a sense, this is true: it comes from behind previously locked doors in the writer's memory vault. It does not come from discarnate spirits.

Stevenson concludes that:

> *Some uncritical enthusiasts of automatic writings know that other persons have doubts about the source of their productions. They know that para-psychologists, and many skeptical laymen also, question the claims of most trance personalities to be discarnate persons. Yet they want to believe, and want others to believe that their communicators are different. (p. 325)*

In addition to the alternative psi explanation, the evidence favouring survival through C-Cs is excessively complex. With so much material to rummage through it is not surprising that one can occasionally come up with apparent correspondences and confirmations. Social scientists have learned that even in the most straightforward and non-exotic studies there may be 'false positive' findings. Make enough observations and something is likely to show a relationship to something else. This is why mathematical models of chance and probability are applied to research findings and why investigators are careful to report statistical levels of significance. It is not enough simply to discover a relationship. There must be appropriate and rigorous statistical tests to permit an estimate of probability: how likely is it that this particular correlation or correspondence could have arisen by chance?

This is the accepted approach in a wide variety of research, notably in the social and behavioural sciences. Nothing of the kind has been applied to the C-Cs – and it would, in fact, be extremely difficult to abstract and prepare the C-C material for meaningful statistical analysis. We would probably not get beyond the early steps of identifying and coding each item of information. Some degree of correspondence in the automatic writings would be expected by chance, and a further degree would have been expected both from psi and from the fact that many of the automatists knew each other and had common interests. In principle, the C-C method might be applied to the scientific evaluation of possible survival communications. The existing material, however, interesting though it may be, has not been evaluated in this manner nor does it lend itself to such evaluation. Lacking a critical test of the 'data', then, we have no reason to accept that most extreme of explanations, the survival hypothesis.

We can gain further insight into the chance and probability explanation by conducting simple little experiments of our own (no spirits need apply). Saltmarsh suggested several experiments, the simplest being:

> *Choose a book by an author with whose works you are well acquainted, and from it pick a passage by chance. You could open it at random and, with the eyes shut, put your finger on the page, then take the passage indicated. Do the same thing with another such book and then try to work out a cross correspondence between the two passages. This experiment will give an indication of how far pure chance is likely to have been responsible for the concordance found between the scripts of the automatists.*[11]

Many people have attempted such experiments (including some more complex than the example above), with results sometimes approximating the famous C-Cs, while at other times yielding little or nothing. In other words: just about what we might expect by chance. In this post-Freudian world, we should add another consideration. Take the simple experiment proposed by Saltmarsh for illustration. Why did you choose the first book? What led you to purchase this book in the first place and now 'just happen' to pick it up for the experiment? And why did you choose the second book? The pointed, sometimes rather uncomfortable, observations made by Freud and other psychoanalysts make it clear that much of our apparently random or chance behaviour is intimately connected with our motives and personality. Psi, chance and unconscious motivation! Taken together, these factors offer a much more soundly based approach to the better C-C phenomena than does the increasingly tattered survival hypothesis.

Channeling is mediumship rigged out in new clothing. The advocate has already noted some major commonalities between the medium and the challenger. He might have mentioned still another: mediumship did not prove survival of death, and neither does channeling. Good old-fashioned seances with all their hocus-pocus have lost much of their appeal as the 20th century staggers to its close. The need to believe is still with us, however, as well as the need for a sense of contact with those who have passed on. Mediumship required a new cover story that would not sound too much like the old discredited stories. Furthermore, it had to deal with our anxieties about our lives here today as well as our questions about the afterlife. The shelves of book stores and libraries are groaning with how-to-live-better treatises. Judging from the plethora of such books, few of us are satisfied with ourselves as we are. (Perhaps the satisfied ones don't read books and, therefore, don't realize that they should not be satisfied.) Some of this dissatisfaction arises from a sense of stress, conflict, and alienation within our society. Neighborhoods are not as friendly, streets are not as safe, authorities are not as trustworthy, youths are not as respectful, and so on. Competition's nasty edge, merchandising's unrelenting assaults on consumers, and mass media's replacement of traditional values with sensationalism, violence, and trivialities gives many of us the uncomfortable feeling that we are not so much living our own lives as we are enacting roles in somebody else's script. People who are attracted to channeling often are those who have become disaffected with brash, materialistic, and impersonal mainstream society. The other primary attraction to channeling begins with the personal side. Somewhere along life's journey we might come to feel unsure about our identity and destination. We may have been accomplishing what we set out to accomplish in life, but now we wonder if we might not be missing something important.

Channeling may be seen as an opportunity to explore our own needs and potentials. This approach has been described variously as getting in touch with 'the inner child', 'the universal self', or 'the higher self'. Channeling offers legitimation, encouragement, and companionship to adults who are motivated to learn more about themselves.

This inclination to turn inward and explore the recesses of our own minds and feelings is a natural response to the present condition of society. It is also an adventure that is worth undertaking by any thoughtful man or woman who is willing to accept the risks that go along with self-exploration. I have no problem with the idea of getting better in touch with our inner selves which, after all, is just what the Delphic oracle told Socrates: "Know thyself."

None of this, however, provides acceptable evidence for survival of death. Cayce's main ideas can be found in the writings of other speculative thinkers, especially Carl Gustav Jung.[21] First a disciple then a rival of Freud, Jung was a brilliant, idiosyncratic, and mystically-orientated psychiatrist. Cayce's speculations about the mind will offer little that is new to those who are familiar with Jung's. This similarity is important because Jung's ideas have been around for some time now. His assertions that bear most closely on the nature of mind and the possibility of survival have been known to mental health specialists, scholars, and researchers for about seven decades. Many people still find these ideas interesting, myself included. Nevertheless, his theories remain theories. Evidence that would be acceptable to the scientific community at large has not been forthcoming. For example, Jung's *collective unconscious* is a universal mental stratum that is the common property of all humans. He has some provocative things to say about the contents and function of this deep level of mental life.

Some people accept and some reject this theory. Nobody has proven it. Cayce's assertions about the structure of our mental life owe a great deal to Jung, but neither the original nor the popularized version has been subjected to appropriate and systematic test. And if proof remains lacking for the Jung/Cayce version of mind, then the survival assertions that depend on this theory are left without secure foundation.

Furthermore, if we do accept Jung's conception of the collective unconscious despite the lack of firm verification, then we also will have trouble persuading ourselves that the channelers find anything other than alternative selves and *archetypes*:

> *Archetypes are typical modes of apprehension, and wherever we meet with uniform and regularly occurring modes of apprehension we are dealing with an archetype, no matter whether its mytho-logical character is recognized or not.* The collective unconscious consists of the sum of the instincts and their correlates, the archetypes. Just as everybody possesses instincts, so he also possesses a stock of archetypal images.[21] (p. 57)

Channelers encounter their own archetypal images, then, not discarnate spirits of the deceased. This would be the most direct and parsimonious interpretation to make of claimed spirit communication by channelers, along with encountering alternative versions of one's everyday conscious self. The Jung/Cayce theory may or may not be verifiable in principle. This is a debatable proposition. It has not been verified in practice, however. Furthermore, as we have just seen, if the theory is correct in its fundamental assumptions, then it presents us with a complex inner world of symbolic-mythical images, not with active spirit communications.

Now we must face up to a side of the channeling phenomenon that is not quite as admirable as the pursuit of self-knowledge. Channeling is a positive and serious endeavor for some people and seems, indeed, to contribute to their peace of mind and continued self-development. Whatever really happens during the 'channeling' process, it can be a valuable experience for some people. However, channeling has also become a lucrative industry, a mindless entertainment, and a refuge for the mentally ill and the sociopathic. Although many turned to channeling as an alternative to materialism, others have exploited it as a cash cow. The suspension of critical thinking and loosening of logical demands has made channeling a haven for those who are unable or unwilling to come to terms with reality. Almost anything goes. Saying something is as good as proving it. An adult's re-invention of Never-Never Land, now retitled, Ever-Ever Land. Those who are unfortunate enough to be afflicted with a serious mental illness may find themselves more attuned to the free-floating phantasia of the channeling experience than to the harsh demands and risks of everyday life. To put this another way: channeling has attracted much the same crowd that formerly paid for the medium's groceries: a mixture of the curious, the questing, the manipulative, and the unbalanced.

When the advocate (remember him?) dealt with mediums he perhaps conveyed the impression that there was invariably a team of highly trained and objective investigators on the job at every seance. Actually, by far the greater number of seances included nobody who was equipped to examine the proceedings from a critical perspective. The same may be said of channeling. By and large, people do not go to a channeler to test their claims for spirit communication, but to derive comfort and enjoyment, if not also to soothe some deeper needs. The channeler is more likely to launch into a vague and vapid discourse regarding cosmic principles and the nature of the human spirit than to provide credible information from departed souls. Say the same things without claiming to be an entranced channeler, and the audience would quickly zone out. The claim that it is 'channeling' that is going on serves as a cover story for a lot of boring claptrap. The last bit of channeling rap that I heard reminded me much of a particularly uninspired sermon that would have emptied the pews had the listeners not already fallen into slumber.

Have we run completely out of spirits through this dispiriting examination of pro-survival claims? Not to worry. Turn the page and marvel at the wonders of reincarnation.

7

FROM LIFE TO LIFE: REINCARNATION

Our birth is but a sleep and a forgetting:
The soul that rises with us, our life's star,
Hath had elsewhere its setting
And cometh from afar.
Not in entire forgetfulness
And not in utter nakedness
But trailing clouds of glory do we come...[1]

I have just rediscovered the key of the lost staircase... The staircase in the wall, spiral like the coils of a serpent, winds from the subterranean depths of the Ego to the high terraces crowned by the stars. But nothing that I saw there was unknown country. I had seen it all before and I knew it well – but I did not know where I had seen it before. More than once I had recited from memory, though imperfectly, the lesson of thought learned at some former time (but from whom? One of my very ancient selves...).[2]

During regression therapy, Betty began choking and gasping for air. She related to me that she was being burned at the stake, sometime in the later Middle Ages. The smoke was overpowering; her lungs were being seared...[3]

It would be tempting to say that reincarnation has itself been reincarnated in recent years. This belief has been openly avowed by an increasing number of people, and the topic given renewed currency through the media. It is more accurate, however, to say that reincarnation never was very far from our minds. Although usually associated with Asian and African religious belief systems, reincarnation seems always to have fascinated some Euro-Americans as well. Furthermore, the idea of previous as well as continuing existence often occurs to children in an apparently spontaneous manner. Whether or not we believe in reincarnation as reality, we are likely to have had some affinity to reincarnation as both a natural and a provocative thought.

We will soon be opening the cages to give advocate and critic their opportunities to contest the question of survival through reincarnation. To the advocate will also fall the primary task of providing basic information on reincarnation doctrine from the past to the present. It might be useful, though, to set the stage a little before the adversaries have a go at each other.

Poets, their antennae ever alert, have often picked up on the reincarnation wavelength. This has been true even of poets whom one would regard as the upholders of traditions in which reincarnation had barely a foothold. Wordsworth, for example, the very model of a model major poet in British Christendom, seemed an unlikely partisan of reincarnation. Yet he believed in the pre-existence of the soul before birth and eventually confirmed his belief in repeated births. With each new birth the reincarnated soul is thought to come forth "not in entire forgetfulness", but "trailing clouds of glory". Sadly, we lose this child's touch of heaven and joy in our adult years as the vision fades "into the light of common day". Tennyson, his younger contemporary and eventual successor as establishment poet, also felt that we had been through all of this before, some of us knowing each other well in previous existences.

A couple of generations later Romain Rolland, as French as Wordsworth and Tennyson were English, became convinced that his "very ancient selves" were still sleeping within the subterranean depths of his mind, every now and then allowing an astonishing memory to emerge into consciousness.

It says something for the appeal and tenaciousness of the reincarnation idea that it has never quite released its hold on the imagination despite centuries of disapproval by the major religious establishments of the Western world. Moreover, reincarnation has endured beneath the surface and around the fringes despite the dominance of a world-view fabricated by society's industrial-technological preoccupations. Meanwhile, people by the hundreds of millions in the Asian-African sphere have never doubted that they were on a journey from body to body, from life to life.

Does the resurgence of interest in reincarnation represent the irresistible break-through of a truth that Euro-American techno-society had been afraid to hear? Or does it instead represent a desperate escapism from the grind, alienation, and info-babble of postmodern society? Experiences that have taken place during past life regression therapy ("Betty began choking and gasping for air ... She was being burned at the stake") could be interpreted either as a new source of evidence for reincarnation or as fantasy excursions away from the crush of everyday reality. As usual, advocate and critic have all the answers – but which, if either, has the right answers?

THE ADVOCATE'S CASE

We would all accept the truth of reincarnation if social pressures did not interfere. The idea forms itself naturally in our minds as children and accords just as naturally with our subsequent experiences – until anxious authority demands that our thoughts travel in the dull, worn grooves where adult minds trudge their weary way. Let us begin by recovering and celebrating our heritage. Reincarnation has been the ultimate traveller's guide long before the first map attempted to enclose space and the first calendar dared to mark time. As we shall see, this tradition belongs to the West as well as the East, although more steadfastly maintained by the latter.

THE BASIC CONCEPT

There is a soul that survives death. This belief is not specific to reincarnation. It is shared by orthodox Christianity and Islam and by those who subscribe to the Messianic tradition in Judaism. Reincarnation parts company with the other views, however, when it comes to the origin and destination of the soul. In Western religions the prevailing idea is that each infant leaps into the world with a fresh soul of its very own. This belief is in keeping with the Western emphasis on the individual. When physical death occurs, the soul is liberated from the body. At this point the specific destination of the soul varies to some extent depending on particular theological views. The most familiar vision, however, is of the departed soul receiving divine judgment and then taking its appropriate place in a spiritual realm.

Reincarnation offers a much different version of the human journey through time. We do not come off Nature's assembly line as completely new products. What is most essential – our souls – have already survived many previous existences. It is only the package that is new, and when this package eventually fulfils its biodegradable destiny, our soul will again be on its way to enspirit a new physical form. Survival is not a matter of one soul, one body, one death, one salvation. Survival is one soul journeying from body to body. This soul was not created at our birth nor will it be either destroyed or fixed through eternity at our death.

What do we believe when we believe in reincarnation?

- We already have a rich personal history prior to our birth.
- It may be possible under some circumstances to call upon our 'ancient selves' for knowledge, insight, and inspiration. Certainly, we will from time to time have feelings and memories from our past lives, sometimes taking the form of *déjà vu* experiences.
- Our present situation is not entirely the matter of life and death that it might seem; it is but an episode in a long and still unfurling story.

187

- Our physical being is also not as crucial as it might otherwise seem. We take on many appearances throughout our spiritual journeys, so we cannot be completely identified with any one manifestation.
- Our journey is not a meaningless meandering through time, place, and embodiments. It is a spiritual odyssey, a quest for the highest level of being that it is within our power to attain.

ON BEING A REINCARNATE

It should be clear by now that the meaning of life is different for the believer in reincarnation than for those who adhere to more familiar survival conceptions. Consider these significant differences:

- Reincarnates have a more profound sense of connection to the past and sense of responsibility for the future. One does not just pop in for some few decades, die, and await eternal bliss. Our present selves are shaped for better or worse by the actions of our past selves. It is our responsibility to live in such a way as to prepare our next incarnated self for a higher level of existence. To use Christian rhetoric, we cannot work out our 'salvation' in just one go-around.
- Reincarnates also have a stronger sense of connection to other people. You and I may have been in each other's lives before. If we had a great relationship, then we now have another opportunity to enjoy and enrich it. If we were each other's worse enemies, then now could be the time to turn our relationships around so we both can progress spiritually.
- Reincarnates are also likelier to have a stronger sense of relationship with all of Nature's creatures. Instead of supposing themselves to be standing apart as proud rulers of life forms on earth, the believer in reincarnation feels a kinship with all that swims, crawls, climbs, flies, and ambulates. "Perhaps I was once that creature..." Along with this sense of kinship comes respect and heedfulness for other life forms. "I am not judge, exploiter, and executioner of life on earth; I am but part of Spirit's great journey through Life."
- The reincarnate is less likely to feel like a dependent child who must please its father who art in heaven. Even less is the reincarnate likely to rejoice in the expectation that others will suffer horribly for their failures and sins while he/she basks in the pure light of eternity. The child/sinner concept is replaced by the sense of a spiritual quest. To lock oneself into the identity of child or sinner is to place shackles on continued spiritual development. To picture the divinity as a father figure with a long list of 'dos' and 'don'ts' is to become fixated on an immature image instead of opening oneself up to the spiritual mysteries of the vast universe.

In short, reincarnates may well be more pleasant people to have around: sensitive, responsible, attuned to the larger picture, not consumed by pride and anxiety and not welded to a juvenile conception of deity, and not casually destructive of life on earth.

We move now from the basic conception of reincarnation to some of the major forms it has taken within various societies.

REINCARNATION IN TRADITIONAL (PRE-INDUSTRIAL) SOCIETIES

Throughout much of history people lived in relatively small communities, whether settled or nomadic. In the past century or so there has been a sharp reduction in the number of peoples who continue in their traditional ways, but fortunately there has been the opportunity to learn many of their beliefs and practices before they disappeared under the pressure of industrialization and loss of habitat. What wisdom have these hardy and resourceful people passed on to us? *Reincarnation!*

In North America alone, reincarnation beliefs sustained the Ahts, Algonquins, Dakotas, Denes, Haidas, Hopi, Hurons, Inuits ('Eskimos'), Iroquois, Koloshes, Mohaves, Montagnais, Natchez, Nutkas, Powhatans, Tacullis, and Tlingit. In Central and South America the Abysones, Caribs, Chiriguanos, Icannas, Maya, Patagonians, Peruvians, Popayans, Soutals all recognized that they were on a journey from body to body. This journey was accompanied by respect for all forms of life precisely because of the principle of reincarnation. Among Native Americans of the Northwest, for example, prayers were addressed to the majestic animals they were seeking in their sea-hunts:

> O great and gracious whale, forgive us that we must kill you. But our families are hungry and we must eat. Rest assured that we have no personal grievance against you. In the future time when you are human and we are whales, we will gladly do as much for you.[4]

Although these are but partial lists, they demonstrate the widespread belief in reincarnation among people who did not read books or conduct theological seminars. The idea of reincarnation emerged so forcefully from their own experience that neither elaborate theory nor cultural exchange was necessary. Isolated, self-contained peoples seemed to come up with the reincarnation concept on their own. The same pattern held true for the native peoples of Australia and Pacific islands, e.g., the Anula, Aruntas, Bakongs, Benbenga, Fijians, Indonesians, New Zealanders, Poso-Sandwich Islanders, and Warramunga. A contemporary study of more than a hundred African tribal peoples found that almost all believed in reincarnation.[5]

The Europe of yesteryear also included many who were guided by the vision of reincarnation:

> *In ancient Europe a 'reincarnation belt' covered at least the north of the continent, with outposts in the south, such as the Lombards in Italy. Ancient English and Scottish ballads speak of the souls of men and women passing into animals, birds or plants, and according to British and Breton folklore the spirits of dead fishermen and sailors dwell in the bodies of white seagulls, and those of unbaptised children flutter through the air in the form of birds until Judgement Day. Teutons and even Romans ... carefully tended house-snakes as the incarnations of ancestors or as guardian genii of their homes; as late as 1870 housemaids at the vicarage of St Cleer, Cornwall, refused to kill spiders because they believed that their dead master ... had been reborn in one. There is a Welsh claim that the doctrine of reincarnation began with the Celts far back in pre-history and that it was from them that it found its way to the East to flower in Hinduism and Buddhism.*[6]

Such is the natural affinity of reincarnation to the human mind that this idea has not only flourished throughout the world, but survived even when the official religious establishment opposed this view. Indeed, the re-emergence of reincarnation belief today is also taking place despite uneasiness and criticism from today's religious orthodoxy.

Reincarnation beliefs in pre-industrial or traditional societies were in keeping with prevailing family and community-orientated life-styles. For example, one's own ancestors were generally the most common re-incarnates. The spirit of a deceased elder would become re-embodied within the same family. This often occurred through a birth (which, actually, amounted to a rebirth). It was also possible, however, to return to life as a bird, animals, insect, fish, or even as fruit. The particular form taken did not matter all that much; the principle was the same. At death the spirit was liberated from its existing physical home and sooner or later would find another dwelling. Generally, reincarnation did not include the dimension of continued moral and spiritual development that is salient in Buddhism, Hinduism, and current Western approaches. There are exceptions, however, such as the Zulu creed in which all people are thought to have a spark of the universal spirit that might eventually be fully actualized after many reincarnations to progressively higher levels of being. The belief in reincarnation seems to be equally at home in small, pre-literate communal bands and in societies with sophisticated systems of thought and communication.

SAMSARA AND KARMA: REINCARNATION IN THE GREAT RELIGIONS OF THE EAST

I: HINDUISM

We have seen that reincarnation has never been simply a regional belief of the 'mystical East'. Africans, Australians, Europeans, and inhabitants of Central, North, and South America have also cherished this belief even if they had little or no contact with Eastern thought. It is true, nevertheless, that Eastern religions have long served as the primary reservoir and 'think tank' for reincarnation belief.

The Hindu belief in reincarnation antedates the sacred writings of Judaism, Christianity, and Islam. It can be found in the *Vedas*, which are not only the oldest sacred writings of Hinduism (about 1000 BC), but also "the oldest literary record in the Indo-European languages".[7] Reincarnation is again described in the later *Upanishads*. There is extensive reference to reincarnation in the *Bhagavad-Gita (The Song of the Lord, or Krishna)* that is thought to have been written in the same era as the emergence of Christianity from Judaism. The Bhagavad-Gita itself is a section of the epic Indian story, the *Mahabharata* (which is also the longest poem in the world at more than 100,000 verses).

The doctrine of many deaths and many births is expressed clearly in what might be called the autobiography of Lord Krishna:

> *Whenever there appears*
> *A languishing of Rightness*
> *When Unrighteousness arises*
> *Then I generate Myself ...*
> *Age after age I come into being*

Significantly, Krishna was not presented as the only being who pre-exists birth and post-exists death, but as the only one who seemed to remember these transitions and therefore to maintain a spiritual identity and purpose. We can see a subtle link here between the ancient Hindu sacred writings and the current Western interest in recovering one's own past lives. One can pass from embodiment to embodiment with varying levels of transpersonal awareness.

Reincarnation is not limited to the gods, however. Every person rides the ever-rotating wheel of being, *Samsara*. As the wheel rolls along, we are sometimes in the position of life, sometimes in the position of death. No matter what our position at the moment, one thing is certain: it will change. Life and death are intimately connected, two aspects of the same principles of being and becoming. This concept may be difficult for Euro-Americans to comprehend because of our tendency to believe that death is the negation or enemy of life.

Karma is another concept that until recently was seldom understood in the West. The word itself comes from the ancient Sanskrit language. Its original meaning seems to have been 'act' or 'deed'. Within Hindu thinking, *Karma* refers to the consequences of all the actions that we have taken through our lives. *Karma* is in one sense the outcome of the kind of person (or people) we have been through all our past embodiments as well as our present selves. In another sense it is a force operating through the present into the future because our 'record' is still shaping our destiny. We do not escape the past. We are the past, and we bring this past into the future.

FROM LIFE TO LIFE: REINCARNATION

There is a strong sense of personal responsibility here. We have made ourselves into the people we are today through our past actions. More than that – our intentions and motives have also shaped our present lives even if we never acted on them. For example, those who harbored evil intentions toward others in past embodiments have thereby created spiritual dilemma for themselves in their present lives. *Karma,* therefore is not a blind or random universal force that works its way on us. We get ourselves into our own messes, and must spend life after life trying to reach a level of spiritual purity. Our present character, then, is the result of our own *samskaras,* i.e. the loving or destructive, noble or base thoughts and feelings we experienced in past lives. We inherit ourselves. And to our next self we may pass along an even heavier burden of unworthy thoughts, feelings, and deeds.

Successive rebirths provide the opportunity to free ourselves from this carousel of being. It is a monumentally slow and laborious process, however, with no guarantee of success. One cannot exit simply by putting in time. Sluggish, obtuse, and unrepentant personalities ride the carousel again and again, each time ending up no further along than the previous time. Indeed, one might sink even further and become reincarnated as a lower life form. There must be authentic spiritual development for the individual to at last achieve enlightenment. This transformation requires a purification in which one truly renounces the desire for the satisfactions of the flesh. The unwillingness to give up such trivial pursuits as physical pleasure, material possessions, and power over others all too often stands in the way of spiritual progression.

The wisdom that comprehends the eternal, universal, and spiritual may come with maturity within a given life-course. In old age a person may reach the *Sanyasa* stage of spiritual development where one "is ideally a wandering ascetic who has cut all bonds with family, society, and worldly pleasures. Unlike previous stages where psychological work coupled with artistic activity is prescribed, this period can be one of relative locomotor passivity and life-avoidance: the confrontation of nothingness from which new life will eventually spring".[8] The author, Renaldo Maduro, is speaking here particularly of aged artists in Northern India who personify the cultural mandate for continued spiritual growth through one's life and from one embodied life to the next. All may follow this example, however, and seek *Brahman,* the absolute and universal essence of being.

What is death, then? If by death we mean "the permanent cessation of life/being", then death is an illusion. And so is birth.

As Lord Krishna said to his disciple:
Who thinks that he can be a slayer,
Who thinks that he is slain,
Both these lack knowledge:
He slays not, is not slain.

Never is he born nor dies;
Never did he come to be, nor will he ever come to be again:
Unborn, eternal, everlasting be – primeval…
As a man casts off his worn-out clothes
And takes on new clothes,
So does the embodied soul cast off his worn-out bodies
And enter others new.[9]

II. BUDDHISM

On a recent evening in Tempe, Arizona, the Student Activity Center of Arizona State University was packed with just about as many people as could fit into that commodious facility. Judging by crowd size alone, one might have thought it was the occasion for a major rock concert or a high profile basketball game against our arch-rivals, University of Arizona. We were all there, however, to see a man who did not howl into a microphone while a mega-amplified band blasted away, and did not leap skyward to perform reverse slam-dunks. The gentle, quiet, smiling man was His Holiness Tenzin Gyato, the Dalai Lama. It was the first time I had seen him, but he had been around before. Many times. It is a salient feature of the Buddhist belief system that at his death the Dalai Lama is reincarnated in a child.

The Dalai Lama himself is the incarnation not of Buddha as such, but of a *Bodhisattva*, an emanation from Buddha. (*Bodhisattva* is another word derived from the Sanskrit: an enlightened being). Whenever possible, the search for the next embodiment is aided by the dying Dalai Lama's prediction of the region of Tibet in which the host child will be found. The child who is then identified as the possible re-embodiment is interviewed and questioned about many facts that could only be known to an enlightened being. If the child passes this test, he becomes the next Dalai Lama.

Reincarnation is a core belief for Buddhists just as it is for Hindus, and it can also be traced back to one of the great documents of antiquity. This treatise is most often known as *The Tibetan Book of the Dead*. Scholars have contested the title, however, and I will go with the version offered in a significant new commentary by Tibetan master, Sogyal Rinpoche. *The Tibetan Book of Living and Dying*[10] is the more appropriate title because the association between these two states of being is viewed as inextricable. This is true of the Hindu conception as well, but, as we will see, the Buddhist version differs in significant ways. Rinpoche conveys the essence of Buddhist thought in a concise statement:

*When we say **Buddha**, we naturally think of the Indian prince Gautama Siddhartha who reached enlightenment in the sixth century BC, and who taught the spiritual path followed by millions all over Asia, known today as Buddhism. **Buddha**, however, has a* *much deeper meaning. It means a person, any person, who has completely awakened from ignorance and opened to his or her vast potential of wisdom. A Buddha is one who has brought a final end to suffering and frustration, and discovered a lasting and deathless happiness and peace... It is important to remember always that Buddha was a human being, like you or me. He never claimed divinity; he merely knew he had the buddha nature, the seed of enlightenment, and that everyone else did too. The Buddha nature is simply the birthright of every sentient being...*

Although many people have persisted in regarding Buddha as god, a god, or a close relative of god, that is not how he thought of himself and not part of the vision he offered to humanity. Some people also assume that death is not really important in Buddhism because one goes on to other lives. This assumption is vigorously disputed by Rinpoche and others who live as well as understand the Buddhist way of life. Dying is a crucial experience and death a crucial outcome. The Buddhist credo (though having several alternative versions) does not promise a triumph over death and a happy ever after. What Buddhism does hold as true is a continuity of mind that stretches from the remote past to the distant future. Individuals come into existence, perish, and appear again in altered form. Through all this change the underlying continuity of mind persists. The very nature of the universe includes the principle of change. Nothing endures – at least, not in any one particular form.

It is often especially difficult for followers of other religious traditions to comprehend that both the change and the continuity occur without a deity. There is no god in heaven to plan, supervise, judge, and, perhaps, intervene. As the Dalai Lama expressed it:

... there is no place given to a divine creator, nor to beings who are self-created; rather everything arises as a consequence of causes and conditions. So mind, or consciousness too comes into being as a result of its previous instants. [11]

These 'causes and conditions' are pretty much the same for Buddhists as for Hindus, representing the operation of karma. The concept is expressed well by both faiths in their saying: "If you want to know your past life, look into your present condition; if you want to know your future life, look at your present actions."

The outsider's comprehension is further tested by the Buddhist insight that it is not the self that dies. Not *the* self. Just *a* self. Each existing self is one version of the multiple forms a self can (and does) take through cycles of death and rebirth. Furthermore, one's self is always changing throughout the 'same' life. Are you the same person you were as an infant? As a school child? If you are around to observe your 100th birthday will you be the same self you are now? A credible answer to all these questions is: "Yes... and no." There is a family resemblance among our selves with one life-course and from one incarnation to another. But, along with the rest of the universe, the consciousness that thinks it is a self is always changing.

This Buddhist insight prepares us to understand that reincarnation does not involve popping up again pretty much the way we are (were). The conditions of our being (karma) that we ourselves have helped to fashion, will re-appear in a much altered form. *Personal identity in the usual sense of the term does not survive a death.* The mind that gave rise to personal identity in this life, however, will survive, as it must, and participate in another embodiment.

The brave and open mind accepts not only change but also decay as an intrinsic aspect of reality. This mind does not wait until death come knocking on the door to acknowledge mortality. Rather, this mind lives each day with the awareness of death and with other losses that have something of the character of death (loss of health, loss of social status, etc.). Those who have accepted the whole of life/death reality throughout their daily existence will be at a higher level of spiritual development when they move through the dying process. (Buddhists described stages of dying about fifteen centuries before those presented by psychiatrist Elizabeth Kubler-Ross.[11] The two versions are very different, e.g., the Buddhist stages continue beyond the point of clinical death and culminate in the experience of "the clear light of death".[12]) By contrast, people who have moved through life as though sleepwalkers, unaware of their own nature, will approach their deaths in a confused and fearful way. These people are in danger of having an unfavorable form of rebirth because many Buddhists believe that one's state of being at the time of death influences the next incarnation. The deathbed scene, then, should be populated by family, and friends who offer support and monks who recite scriptures and *mantras* (sayings whose repetition helps people achieve a sense of serenity).

These central concepts must be kept in mind if we are to understand the Buddhist conception of reincarnation on its own terms:

- The self is not a fixed entity that perishes at death and returns to life in another physical form. What we usually think of as the self is fluid, ever-changing. In a meaningful sense of the terms, we are always dying and undergoing rebirth through the course of our lives. In effect, there is no unitary self to die.
- What persists after death is the pattern of consciousness that has been shaped through many previous births, lives, and deaths.

  ... perhaps the most satisfying analogy is that of a motion picture. Just as each frame is similar to, yet slightly different from the one before it, and just as action occurs when the frames change rapidly, Buddhists believe in a moment-to-moment birth and death. Like the unrolling of a film, human life is seen as a continuous process of birth and death, birth and death, in every millionth of a second.[9]

Another useful analogy might be the succession of generations. The child is not the parent born again or cloned. However, the child carries the genetic codes contributed by the parents and the influences of the parents on its mental, emotional, and social development. We inherit our past selves, then, and will pass our own versions of these selves on to the next generation, either in up- or down-graded versions depending on how we have responded to the possibilities of our own lives.

● There is also a quest that persists through all these lives: for *Nirvana*. To achieve nirvana is to become liberated, purified and wise. One no longer desires or suffers. Consciousness of self disappears. Questing itself – including the quest for nirvana – ceases. Nirvana is not a place such as heaven, nor is it a blissful, unending dream. In fact, we cannot really comprehend and articulate the nature of nirvana through language. Our mental operations, both analytic and imaginative, actually stand in the way of experiencing nirvana. *Experience*, though is perhaps as close as words can take us. We will know nirvana only through the direct experience of knowing. After many rebirths and redeaths a person (actually that 'person's' persistent life-stream) may still be locked in ignorance, illusion, and futile desire. Each dying unto death is an ordeal. The person who achieves nirvana in his or her *life* is no longer subject to death. This goal may be approached by learning how to meditate dispassionately on life and death, a process that involves total physical as well as mental and spiritual concentration. Mastery of breathing contributes to this holistic approach.

Buddhism has taken several forms over the centuries. Some forms seem to adhere to the original *dharma* (teachings) of Buddha. Other forms include elements from various other belief systems; the beliefs and practices of villagers may differ in significant ways from those of Buddhist masters. Zen and Tibetan traditions are based on the original dharma but also include additional ideas and practices. Although there are important differences within the Buddhist (as within the Christian) sphere of belief, reincarnation continues to the guiding light, to the clear light of being.

REINCARNATION IN THE EURO-AMERICAN TRADITION

A recent Gallup Poll in the United States[13] found that one person in four now believes in reincarnation (that is, one person out of every four who have any thoughts to share about survival of death). This is a remarkably high incidence when we consider that reincarnation is not part of the official doctrine for Catholics, Protestants, Jews and, for that matter, religions with such variant belief systems as Christian Scientists,

Church of the Latter Day Saints (Mormons), and Seventh Day Adventists. Reincarnation receives little or no attention in either public or religious schools. The millions of people in the U.S. and other Western nations who are finding their way to a belief in reincarnation are doing so despite the exclusion of this life-view from the teachings and preachings of the establishment.

Many clergy are alarmed by this development: people tend to either sever or attenuate their bonds with traditional churches when they become convinced of reincarnation. This belief is often part of a larger world-view. The competitive, aggressive, bureaucratic, materialistic, and alienating machinations of mass society are rejected in favor of a more holistic, natural, relational, and spiritual way of life. Reincarnation with its emphasis on spiritual development and direct personal experience seems preferable to many when compared with a sin-salvation-striving philosophy.

Here we want to pause for just a moment to disabuse ourselves of the idea that reincarnation is new to Euro-American society. There is something significantly new about the rising popularity of reincarnation belief and its alliance with holistic thinking. The idea itself, however, has appealed to many reflective people through the centuries. We might begin with Diogenes of Sinope. You remember him: the fierce old Greek philosopher-dramatist who trudged along holding a lantern, "looking for an honest man". Maybe you *were* Diogenes – or Alexander the Great when he sought out the celebrated thinker and asked if there was anything he could do for him ("You can get out of my way!" is one version of the reply.) Diogenes reported that others long before him had taught the doctrine that the soul moves through a "circle of necessity", being bound at various times to various bodies. During the siege of Troy, when the gods were still the gods, there were warriors who had been incarnated from previous lives.[14] Reincarnation, then, was not exactly news to this tough-minded Greek of the fourth century B.C. Interestingly, he did not reject the reincarnation doctrine although he rejected many of the ideas fashionable in his own time. Diogenes is credited as being the first man to describe himself as "a citizen of the world".[15] Perhaps he saw himself also as a citizen of many lives, many worlds.

History has decided pretty much to ignore the fact that many of its most illustrious and influential thinkers took reincarnation quite seriously. Aristotle was certain that the soul exists prior to birth. His thoughts about reincarnation changed a time or two (we do not have anything like the complete writings of Aristotle). He seemed to settle on the conclusion that the immortal soul may pass through physical embodiments from time to time, although it was better off when not burdened with the ills to which flesh is heir. Although Aristotle had a major impact on many facets of world thought (e.g. logic, scientific classification, ethics, aesthetics), his views on reincarnation did not

197

spark a widespread interest within the Greek-influenced realm. The common people preferred their comfortable old anthropomorphic religions and rituals.

This situation is worth mentioning because the same thing happened when other outstanding thinkers decided in favor of reincarnation in later historical periods. In the Western world, reincarnation was a concept that was worked out and appreciated by the intellectual elite. By and large, it was not breakfast food for the masses. This wrinkle in history suggests that reincarnation, far from being the consolation of impressionable and ill-disciplined minds, has been the conclusion reached by some of the most adroit thinkers in the Western tradition.

Good Christians – indeed, exemplary Christians – also accepted reincarnation. For the first five centuries or so after Christ it was considered reasonable for a person both to be a devout Christian and a believer in reincarnation. This should not come as a surprise because some theologians have interpreted the appearance of Jesus Christ on earth as a reincarnation of a divine essence. Theologians have differed regarding the specific nature of this reincarnation, leading to numerous 'heresies' and, at times, bloody attacks and reprisals among the various partisans. Even today theologians have difficulty explaining the precise relationship between Jesus as man, Jesus as 'son of God', and God. Nevertheless, there was the widely-shared perception that Jesus was the incarnation of a pre-existing soul. Many continue to believe that Jesus will return in the flesh, either as himself or in some other incarnation. And, as was the case with Lord Krishna, if a person partaking in some way of divinity can be reborn, there is the natural inclination to feel that this may also extend to other, if not all people. Even if a 'born again' Christian today does not openly avow belief in reincarnation, this person's intense emotional investment in the sense of spiritual rebirth surely is akin if not identical to the spirit of reincarnation.

Perhaps the greatest thinker in the early history (really, the pre-history) of the Christian church was Origen. He lived until roughly the middle of the third century after Christ, a period that was crucial for the establishment of Christianity as an enduring 'churched' religion with a standard dogma. Origen agreed with Aristotle that the soul was immortal and pre-existent to birth. An immaterial essence, the soul has neither beginning nor end. The soul's final destination is a heavenly state of being, but along the way it occupies several embodiments, seeking the purification needed to be with God.

If venerated philosophers and church fathers saw reincarnation as compatible with Christianity, what happened to expunge this idea? In a word: 'politics'. The Catholic church could not accept every variant opinion on theological matters. It had to articulate – and enforce – a standard version. The process of evaluating and choosing official dogma would go on for centuries, and is still an issue today. A critical factor here was the selection and rejection of acceptable sources. A century after the death of Jesus there was no New Testament as such. Competing factions within Christianity favored various texts and particular versions of those texts. Biblical scholars today – and those in the general public who have sufficient interest – can study some of the major texts that were excluded from the canon although they had strong claims for inclusion. Similarly, philosophical and historical writings that deviated from the 'winning' version of the church dogma were often repressed or destroyed outright.

Reincarnation was given the boot in the middle of the sixth century by Byzantine Emperor Justinian (not one of history's nicest people). He summoned an ecumenical congress to condemn the writings of the illustrious church father who has already been mentioned. Origen was at a disadvantage in defending himself, being dead at the time, and the Emperor held all the cards . Well, no, actually his formidable wife, Theodora did. She wanted to be a kind of god or, at least a reasonable facsimile, and she usually got what she wanted. Her plans to rise at death to the heights of transcendental glory did not match well with the belief in reincarnation. By declaring Origen a no-good and his views anathema, the congress was in effect excommunicating the belief in reincarnation and, by implication, those who might persist in this belief.

The Church did not actually go on to persecute believers in reincarnation with any real passion, probably because it was still accepted by so many respected people. Nevertheless, from this point onward it became more difficult to access early writings favorable to reincarnation or openly discuss the topic. Even when Justinian and Theodora had things their way it was not possible to stir up more than lukewarm interest in expunging reincarnation from Christian doctrine. Over the years, reincarnation has continued to find openings within the minds and hearts of many Christians who are unconcerned with the political infighting of church officials but who are quite taken with the idea that we move from life to life.

Today East and West interact more intensively than ever before. The globalization of commerce, industry, sports, and entertainment has led to many joint ventures and shared experiences. Even more significantly for our purposes, people with a serious interest in understanding humankind and the universe are transcending the traditional East/West boundaries. Particularly exciting developments are occurring in physics and neuroscience. The world-view that is emerging from these branches of science is a sharp departure from the mechanistic-materialistic-deterministic assumptions that once dominated in the West. Reality is no longer taken to consist of fixed objects or states that obey the simple 'laws' of cause-and-effect. Principles of indeterminacy and chaos (non-linear change) are recognized. The Buddhist conception of mind is being affirmed by state-of-the-art neuroscience. Mind is neither a thing nor a conditioned response, but an active force that continually recreates itself through a creative, transformational process. The universe itself is a transformational flow. Familiar categories, including those of time, space, object, and person, no longer suffice to describe or explain. The persistence and transformation of the spirit through various conditions is a concept that is quite at home in the emerging scientific paradigm. Scientists from both the East and West are contributing to this new understanding. Some religious thinkers have also been able to cross over their traditional boundaries to appreciate a shared core of spiritual truth.

Reincarnation once seemed far-out to some people. We can see now that this perception was based on its lack of fit with mechanistic science. Today it is much of advanced science that is likely to strike the uneducated as far-out. Those who have refused to move beyond yesterday's scientific paradigms may still think of reincarnation as a somewhat fantastical idea. Well, the universe itself is rather fantastical, and so are the minds that try to understand the universe (and their own nature). Essentially what has happened is that science is at last catching up with spiritual truths that have been recognized by mature and sensitive thinkers in both the East and the West. Come to think of it, spiritual truths may be the only kind of truths we can have.

EVIDENCE FOR REINCARNATION

We have seen that the doctrine of reincarnation has an excellent pedigree. It comes to us from the world's most ancient sacred writings, has been affirmed by some of the world's greatest thinkers through the centuries, has survived suppression by powerful church establishments, and now is well in accord with the latest developments in neuroscience and physics. Obviously, many people have been persuaded that death ends a life, but not the life-stream. For the benefit of those who are not yet persuaded, and for the demoralization of our official skeptic, I will now turn to evidence for reincarnation.

What types of evidence are available?

First, there is evidence from sacred writings and the writings of renowned authorities. We have already touched on this type of evidence. It meets the evidential needs of people who are strong in faiths that embrace reincarnation, but does not have the same value for outsiders. We will say no more about scripture and authority as sources of evidence because we want to offer information that goes beyond particular belief systems.

Secondly, there are personal experiences that convince people that they have had previous lives. One's own immediate experience is a source of evidence that cannot be dismissed or contradicted by what others happen to believe. "I know what I felt. I know what I experienced – you don't!" Nevertheless, the incontrovertible nature of personal experience also can be a limiting factor. How can we go from one person's experience to another's? This is one of the questions that philosophers have been trying to answer for centuries, and there still is no consensus. Obviously, we do want to consider reports of personal experiences, but it would be useful to have evidence from other perspectives as well.

This is where 'thirdly' and 'fourthly' come in. We have not only reports from individuals who have experienced their prior existences, but also from (thirdly) past life regression therapists and (fourthly) behavioral scientists who have examined cases suggestive of reincarnation from an objective standpoint.

We begin with the objective scientific approach because it is the one that is most likely to meet the undecided and the skeptic on their own terms. One does not have to hold any particular belief system to consider the evidence and draw the appropriate conclusion.

CASES SUGGESTIVE OF REINCARNATION: THE WORK OF IAN STEVENSON

The foremost researcher in this field is Ian Stevenson, M.D., Carlson Professor of Psychiatry and Director, Division of Personality Studies, in the Department of Psychiatric Medicine at the University of Virginia (Charlottesville). As his title suggests, Stevenson is in the mainstream of professional education and research. He had already earned a reputation as an expert in the art of clinical interviewing before he became interested in paranormal phenomena. Although reincarnation has been the primary focus of his studies for many years, Stevenson also has investigated near-death experiences, telepathy, speaking in tongues and related phenomena.

He introduced the cautious term 'cases suggestive of reincarnation', and has been reporting such cases in depth for two decades. His study, *Twenty Cases Suggestive of Reincarnation*[16] opened many eyes and minds. Further reports continued to appear in scientific journals and books, including *Children Who Remember Previous Lives.*[17] Stevenson has been exceptional in the systematic way he conducts his studies and the detail in which they are reported. Put simply, those who have not read Stevenson's studies are in no position to have a credible opinion on the evidential basis for reincarnation.

THE STEVENSON INTERVIEW

Stevenson kindly consented to an interview in which I had the opportunity to ask some of the questions that perhaps you would also have liked to raise. Excerpts from this interview will help us to see very quickly what it is that Stevenson does, how he does it, what he finds, and what it means.

The typical case is one in which a young child has spoken of having had a previous life, mentioning a number of details that might be checked against objective fact. About 2600 cases have come to Stevenson's attention; he has investigated about 500 of them himself, and has taken part in the investigation of about another 100 in collaboration with other researchers. Now let's hear directly from Stevenson.[18]

> We start an interview with an invitation to the informant to tell what he or she knows about the case from his or her own observations. Questions come after the informant's spontaneous flow has stopped. Our notes record the questions we ask as well as the answer (or spontaneous comment) of the informant...
>
> Tape recorders have been overrated as aids to interviewing in the field. They pick up a lot of irrelevant material and they miss most of the extremely important non-verbal elements of an informant's communications. I learned to make notes rapidly, using my own peculiar abbreviations as needed. In India, I preferred to have two interpreters, and was often able to arrange this. One interpreter would take notes in Hindi, while I made mine in English. Back at the hotel at night, we would compare our notes and learn what one or the other might have missed or misunderstood. This helped us also to notice what we had all overlooked, so that we could go back later and ask more questions to obtain missing information or resolve discrepancies...
>
> Readers of my case reports will know that I favor having multiple informants whenever possible. I also like to have repeated interviews and follow-up interviews when these are possible. At the first interviews the families are sometimes a little shy and even wary.
>
> At the second and later interviews they become less guarded and usually talk freely.
>
> Every interview has to include an assessment of the person being interviewed... We often found that the simplest peasants could say, 'I don't know,' whereas a scientist may not have this gift.

One of the most difficult methodological problems is to determine if "the subject could not have learned normally about the deceased person." For example, perhaps the parents had spoken of the deceased person that the child speaks of as his or her own previous self. Much of the investigative effort is put into the effort to establish or rule out the possibility of communication through normal means. In some cases "a crack of doubt remains. Skeptics could drive a wedge into this if they wish; but they cannot say that I ever concealed such weaknesses."

What type of cases have been most convincing to Stevenson himself? There *are* cases with high evidential value, but these are but a fraction of the total he and his colleagues have investigated.

> A child may state many details, but if it does not mention sufficient and adequately specific names – of places and people – we cannot find any family corresponding to its statements. For years we had little

success in this endeavor. In the last eight years, however, our luck has changed. In Sri Lanka my associates and I have identified some ten cases of this type for which we first made a written record of the child's statements and then succeeded in tracing a family having a deceased member whose life fitted them. Even so, the total number of such cases in our whole series is still under thirty, which is only a little more than one per cent of all the cases in the series.

Reflect a moment on Stevenson's report. He has applied such high standards for evidence that relatively few cases have met these standards. Does this mean that most of the cases are not authentic? No – it means only that cases which meet Stevenson's exacting evidential standards are difficult to come by. We are talking evidence here, not anecdotes, and one thoroughly verified case is worth a thousand stories.

In his quest for documentation and verification Stevenson has

concentrated attention on the cases whose subjects have birthmarks and birth defects that correspond to wounds or other marks on the deceased person of whose life the child will speak when able to do so. I find these cases of great interest and importance.

We have been able to photograph the birthmarks and the birth defects... In addition, we have obtained numerous medical documents, usually post-mortem reports, that describe the location and appearance of the concerned deceased person's wounds.

These photographs and medical documents raise the level of testimony above that of informants drawing on fallible memories. Up to the present, the medical documents show a correspondence between the congenital abnormalities (birth marks or birth defects) and wounds in forty-three of forty-nine cases (87 per cent).

Stevenson identifies several cases in which the documentation is particularly strong:

- A boy was born in India with the fingers of his right hand being almost entirely absent. This is a very rare type of birth defect. As soon as he was old enough to speak, the boy talked about another boy who had lived in a village about five miles away. He said this boy had accidentally put his right hands into the blades of a fodder-chopping machine that his father was operating, instantly severing the fingers. The injured boy recovered, but died a year later from an unrelated ailment. Stevenson found documentary and photographic evidence for the injury described by the boy who had been (re)born with the missing fingers.
- A Turkish boy was born with only the stump of his right ear. This boy "remembered the life of a farmer from a village not far away who had gone to sleep in a field at the end of a long day of work. A neighbor, out hunting in the twilight, had mistaken the sleeping man for a rabbit and had shot him at point-blank range with a shotgun.

The wounded man died in a hospital six days later of brain damage from the shotgun pellets that had penetrated the right side of the skull." Stevenson was able to obtain a copy of hospital records that confirmed the major details of the boy's story.

● A teacher in Thailand was riding his bicycle to work when he was shot in the head. "The bullet entered at the back of his head and exited near the left eye. After this man's death, a boy was born in the same area who had at the back of his head a small round birthmark (a hairless puckered area). At the front of his head, above the left eye, he had a larger irregularly shaped birthmark, which was also a puckered hairless area. These correspond to the bullet wounds of entry and exit on the murdered teacher (of whose life the boy later had detailed memories)." This was not just a general match-up between the school teacher's fatal wound and the newborn's birthmarks. Entry and exit gun shot wounds have very specific characteristics, and these characteristics matched the unusual birthmarks. Stevenson adds, "We have found similar correspondences in size between the birthmarks and the wounds of entry and exit in eight other cases where the deceased person died of a gunshot wound."

We have gone well beyond personal experiences and stories, then. Stevenson and his colleagues have been able to find official documents and photographic evidence that matches up with the previous life reports given by young children. If this is not evidence for reincarnation, then what is it? And what kind of proof would a reasonable person require? This is good evidence, remarkable evidence, considering all the difficulties involved in field research.

At this point I raised a question that might have been on the skeptics list: if some people reincarnate, why doesn't everybody? As usual, Stevenson has a thoughtful response that again reflects his cautious and responsible approach to this challenging topic.

This question reminds me of a heated discussion between two informants in Turkey that I once listened to with awe at the vehemence of the speakers.

One of them asserted that only murdered persons reincarnate. The other dismissed him as an ignorant clown and insisted that everyone reincarnates, but only murdered persons remember their previous lives! This debate was apposite for Turkey where 75 per cent of the deaths of the previous personalities occurred violently, most of them in murders. The cases of other cultures (besides Turkey) all show a higher incidence of violent death in the previous lives remembered – an incidence far higher than that of the general population. It appears, therefore, that a violent death may somehow fix memories and, if reincarnation occurs, may make it more likely that a life ending in violence would be remembered more than one that ended naturally. As a man being led to execution once remarked: 'This is going to be a great lesson to me.' Yet we also do have many cases in which the presumed previous life ended naturally.

To come to the point, I cannot answer this question. Although pleased that we now have data on some 2600 cases, these are as nothing compared with the billions of persons who have lived and died. What can we say about so many persons who have seemingly disappeared without trace? I think that if everyone reincarnates this would require more revision of Western thought than the alternative possibility that only some persons reincarnate.

Opinions and beliefs are notoriously resistant to change. This is certainly true of scientists and teachers who clutch their precious theories to their breasts and are loath to let go. The possibility of universal reincarnation (with and without memory) would shake many defenders of the establishment to their core. Nevertheless, the pressure of evidence – good evidence – makes it increasingly difficult to dismiss reincarnation.

ADDITIONAL FINDINGS FROM STEVENSON'S RESEARCH

We turn now from the interview to some other valuable findings contributed by Stevenson and his colleagues.

What is the typical case that is suggestive of reincarnation?

The child starts talking about his or her previous life somewhere between the ages of two and four. These statements often are accompanied by behavior "which is unusual in the child's family, but which harmonizes with the statements he is making. ... For example, if the child claims to remember a previous life as a wealthy man with many servants, he is likely to refuse to do any household chores or other menial work, no matter how poor his family is."[19] It is also common for the child to ask to be taken to the place he or she identified as their residence in the previous life. When the child has provided enough specific information and the parents have the means to do so, the search for the previous family "is nearly always successful".

The child's reports of a previous life usually fade around age five or so, along with the behaviors that went along with these memories. Some children seem to keep their previous-life memories but seldom speak of them again. In general, the children develop normally through adolescence and into adulthood even if the memories remain.

Is there anything unusual about the fears experienced by children who seem to recall previous lives?

Yes. Their phobias (fears) "nearly always corresponded to the mode of death in the life of the deceased person the child claimed to remember ... and sometimes the child showed the phobia in early infancy before it had begun to speak about a previous life"[20] These fears could not be explained by traumatic experiences since their (re)birth, nor by imitating other members of the family. In a sample of 387 children who claimed to remember a previous life there were 141 (36 per cent) who exhibited such phobias. The phobias varied in their intensity from mild to extreme. The findings are consistent with the previously mentioned fact that most children who claim previous lives report that they had died in a violent manner. The phobias discovered in this study were most frequently associated with violent deaths. The relationship between type of phobia and type of death can be illustrated by the 47 cases in which a child remembered having drowned. Thirty of these children were afraid of being in water.

Where do cases suggestive of reincarnation turn up?

The largest concentration of reported cases comes from northern India; Sri Lanka; Burma; Thailand; Vietnam; western Asia, especially south-central Turkey, Lebanon, and Syria; and Native Americans of the north-west. However, there are also many cases throughout Europe and North America and these cases are similar in their main features to those from areas in which reincarnation belief is more prevalent. Stevenson acknowledges that cultural beliefs play a role in the ease with which people communicate about reincarnation, but rightfully holds that one must examine the evidential value of individual cases and not draw conclusions based on generalizations about cultural influences. He also presents evidence indicating that it may be the report of such cases and not their actual incidence that is lower in the United States as compared with societies that have a strong tradition of reincarnation belief.[21]

REINCARNATION AND BIOLOGY

The world will soon have the opportunity to review Stevenson's evidence for reincarnation at great length and in impressive detail. *Reincarnation and Biology*[22] offers almost 4000 pages of case reports and documentation. There has been nothing of this magnitude before. Even more impressive than the extent of the material, however, is the quality of the evidence. Stevenson provides photographic and documentary evidence for birth marks and birth defects that support the individual's claim to have had a previous existence and to have died in a particular way.

Most of the birthmarks investigated here are different from ordinary birthmarks. Stevenson notes that ordinary birthmarks are patches of altered coloration that are caused by the presence of a more than usual concentration of pigmentation or superficial blood vessels. These birthmarks are at the same level as the surrounding tissue. By contrast, birthmarks associated with reincarnation reports are three-dimensional forms that are puckered, elevated, or depressed as compared with the surrounding skin and which may have a variety of coloration.

Some appear indistinguishable from the healed scars of acquired wounds. Furthermore, most of the birthmarks that I describe here are much larger than the ordinary birthmarks that everyone has... The second distinguishing feature... is that someone attributes them to a wound or other mark that the subject had in a previous life... it has been possible to show in most cases that the subject's birthmark (or perhaps birth defect) corresponds in location and other features to a wound or other mark on the deceased person whose life the subject remembers or with whom he is identified.

Stevenson rightfully emphasizes that these correspondences contribute much to the evidence and interpretation of cases suggestive of reincarnation. Not all cases have such birthmarks or defects, and not all cases with birthmarks or defects can be matched and documented. Nevertheless, enough cases have been investigated in which documentation has been discovered to make up a set of two very large volumes.

Critics can say what they like about a person's verbal reports of a previous existence – but what can they say about the undeniable physical evidence?

Several of the many cases in Stevenson's soon-to-be-published book have been described briefly in an article he published in the *Journal of Scientific Exploration*.[23] These included examples of individuals who had not just one but several physical markers that correlated with their childhood reports of a specific previous life. A Burmese girl, for example, recalled the life of a girl who had been run over by a train. There were eyewitnesses to this accident. They reported that the train first severed the girl's right leg and then crushed her body. The young girl who spoke of the deceased girl's life had herself been born without a lower right leg. According to Stevenson, this is an extremely rare condition. An Indian boy recalled the life of a man who had been killed by a shotgun blast at close range. The fatal wounds were recorded by a pathologist. The location of these wounds matched the birthmarks on the boy's chest. Overall, there was almost 90 per cent concordance between wounds suffered by the deceased person and birthmarks in cases where it was possible to obtain medical and photographic documentation. At least some children seem to be remarkably accurate in their reincarnation memories.

There is usually more than one way to interpret clinical and scientific data. When a controversial topic is involved one must expect alternative interpretations as a matter of course. One might therefore search feverishly for explanations other than reincarnation when confronted with the impressive data compiled by Stevenson, especially as presented in his latest book. Stevenson himself identifies the most likely alternatives, e.g. chance or telepathy, and finds that they do not explain the hard facts of the case, i.e. the documented, observed, and photographed correspondences between physical marks on the deceased person and the child with memories of a previous existence.

Stevenson and his colleagues have provided high quality objective data for 'cases suggestive of reincarnation'. Furthermore, other qualified investigators can conduct their own studies to confirm and extend his findings. It is no longer credible to maintain that reincarnation cannot be studied scientifically. Facts are replacing idle opinions and assumptions. Doubters – do your own studies and see that you keep up the high standards set by Stevenson and his colleagues!

PAST-LIFE RECALL

Many people have been persuaded of reincarnation through their own personal experience. Memories of previous lives may come back to us when we are in a receptive mental state. Such a receptive state can be produced by a variety of means. Hypnosis was used in some of the instances that first brought this phenomenon to the fore, and it is still in use. Others report equal success through guided imagery or direct instructions and suggestions. I think the simpler the better, so we will use the neutral term, *past-life recall* instead of the jargonesque 'past-life regression'.

We will take for our example the approach employed by one of the most respected and influential practitioners of past-life recall as therapy. Brian L. Weiss is a psychiatrist with a distinguished reputation as both psychotherapist and researcher. Before his first encounter with past-life recall he had been, by self-description, "left-brained, obsessive compulsive, and completely skeptical of 'unscientific' fields such as parapsychology. I knew nothing about the concept of past lives or reincarnation, nor did I want to." Weiss had published about 40 papers in scientific journals and a technical book. He is now much better known to the general public for his books on reincarnation, *Many Lives, Many Masters*[24] and *Through Time into Healing.*[25] (The case of Catherine is reported in detail in *Many Lives...;* the other information excerpted here is given in *Through Time...*)

How did this establishment-type psychiatrist become a leader in the exploration of past lives? One of his clients was still suffering from anxiety attacks, depression, and recurrent nightmares despite a year of psychotherapy. Catherine was a hospital laboratory technician, intelligent, insightful, and secure in her Catholic belief system. Although some childhood traumas, including sexual molestation, had been recalled under hypnosis, Catherine had not made the expected progress. Weiss was puzzled and disappointed. He figured that there must be some other traumatic childhood experiences that had not yet come to light. He decided to try hypnosis again.

For some reason that Weiss does not or cannot explain, he gave the deeply hypnotized woman an instruction that was more open-ended and vague than the usual: "Go back to the time from which your symptoms arise." He expected her to go back to early childhood again. Instead, Catherine spoke of being a very different person – a woman who had lived in the near-East about four thousand years ago. Catherine spoke in detail of this supposed previous existence, giving details of the environment, the clothes she wore and other everyday items. She even described her death, and in detail. It was a dramatic event in which she drowned in a flood or tidal wave with her baby torn from her arms by the force of the water. According to her report, Catherine's former self had floated above her body at the time of death. (Catherine had never heard of near-death experiences.)

As we might expect, Weiss was even more puzzled than before. He became more upset as Catherine reported two other life-times (a Greek woman two centuries after the mid-Eastern incarnation, and an eighteenth-century Spanish prostitute) and all within the same hypnotic session! Weiss was an experienced hypnotist, but had never run across anything like this. Because he had come to know Catherine so well, Weiss quickly ruled out the possibilities of psychosis, multiple personality, substance abuse, or extreme suggestibility. What then? Well, her so-called memories must have been some kind of dream or fantasy material that had become ready for release.

But – hold on! Catherine's distressing symptoms now started to disappear, and quite rapidly. Weiss knew that bringing out dream-like material would not produce such a quick and complete improvement. As Weiss and Catherine continued their hypnotic sessions she recalled even more past lives. Within a few months she was entirely free of her symptoms and without the use of medicines.

If this was all that happened, it would have been enough to arouse Weiss' curiosity and need to reflect on his own belief systems. But something else did happen. Catherine had been reliving another previous existence and was in a state of transition between lifetimes. Suddenly she started to tell Weiss some things about his own life that she would have had no way of knowing. One of her statements left the psychiatrist "in an awed silence" and "completely changed the rest of my life". Catherine said:

> Your father is here, and your son, who is a small child. Your father says you will know him because his name is Avrom, and your daughter is named after him. Also, his death was due to his heart. Your son's heart was also important, for it was backward, like a chicken's. He made a great sacrifice for you out of his love. His soul is very advanced... his death satisfied his parent's debts. Also he wanted to show you that medicine could only go so far, that its scope is very limited.

In these words Catherine had penetrated deeply into Weiss's family life and in unbelievably accurate detail. For example, their firstborn son, Adam, had died in infancy because of an "extremely, extremely rare" anomaly: the pulmonary veins entered from the wrong side (the backward heart). One detail after another struck home, and not just idle details but facts and events that were at the core of the therapist's own life experiences. As Weiss recalls his response:

> a deafening cascade of hidden, secret truths was pouring upon me... Catherine could not possibly know this information. There was no place even to look it up.

Weiss tried to look it up, that is, look up what observations others might have made. He discovered Stevenson's work and a few published studies of clinicians who had used past-life recall. To learn more, he would have to continue along this pathway himself. And he has come a long way in a relatively short time. Weiss has since found that many other people can also report past lives – and also receive significant therapeutic benefit from the experience.

We touched on the case of Betty at the beginning of this chapter. Unlike Catherine who disliked taking medication of any kind, Betty had become dependent on several substances prescribed for her allergies and asthma. Weiss recalls that "She seemed destined to live out the rest of her life plagued by these terrible bouts of asthma, dependent on medicines just to breathe."

It was during a past-life recall episode in therapy that Betty had a fit of choking and gasping for air. She told Weiss that she was being burned at the stake. Betty then floated out of her body and observed her death in the smoke and flames.

Goodbye, asthma! Farewell, fears! Take a hike, drugs! Betty's physical symptoms and anxieties vanished almost immediately after recalling and relating this previous existence and its catastrophic ending.

After helping a number of other people through past-life recall, Weiss has concluded that physical afflictions sometimes have their origins in suffering that was experienced in a previous life. Rediscovering that experience and working it through emotionally seems to have a powerful healing effect.

To help make this healing experience available to a larger number of people Weiss has provided instructions for those who would like to induce their own reincarnation experiences. He offers a script to serve as a guide in making one's own relaxation tape that can lead into past-life experiences.[25] This is a convenient and effective technique for some people; others may find that they need the assistance of another person. Weiss notes that "Most people handle and integrate the memories without difficulty." It is basically a self-healing procedure. If the problem does not resolve or if the experience is accompanied by anxiety or guilt, then it would be a good idea to see a therapist. Weiss also recommends the use of dream-journals as a way of getting in touch with past selves.

We see that there may be many techniques that enable a person to discover previous lives. These techniques do not require the use of drugs or other physical interventions, nor do they require a lot of props and special doings. Many people, then, can be their own therapists, educators, and researchers. It is extremely valuable to have researchers such as Stevenson who will travel half way around the world to document cases suggestive of reincarnation, but it is also heartening to know that we can make adventures of personal discovery in our own living room.

BRIDEY MURPHY: BELEAGUERED BUT TRIUMPHANT

These have been only a mere sample of the reincarnation experiences that have been reported by people of intelligence and integrity, many of whom were skeptical about anything that smacked of the paranormal until they had their own encounters. Once again we must step aside for the impatient critic. First, though, we wish to pay tribute to Ruth Simmons and Bridey Murphy who were, you might say, two and the same person. Simmons had accepted the offer of Morey Bernstein, a gifted amateur hypnotist, to re-experience her childhood (age-regression hypnosis). She surprised herself and the hypnotist by discovering a previous version of herself. This prior incarnation was Bridey Murphy, a woman who she said lived in Ireland from her birth (1798) to her death (1864). Her full name, after marriage, was Bridget Kathleen Murphy MacCarthy. Through the course of several additional sessions, Simmons/Murphy provided an extensive, detail-filled account of the past life.

The Search for Bridey Murphy[26] became a sensation when it was published nearly half a century ago. In seeking out this book it would be wise to obtain a later edition that includes valuable additional material by William J. Parker, the investigative reporter who most systematically compared the story with available information about Bridey Murphy's Ireland. Millions of people learned of past lives for the first time. The seeds were planted in the 1950s for what would ripen into a broadening acceptance of reincarnation today.

There are now so many accounts of past lives that Bridey Murphy's story may not have the impact it did at the time it appeared. But the reaction of the establishment to this account should not be forgotten. As Parker noted, "Bridey is an underdog almost without parallel, beleaguered by ancient dogma on one front, conservative science on another... and the inevitably skeptical press to which 'exposé' is synonymous with 'bread and butter.'" Bridey's story was repeatedly distorted and misrepresented by those who felt threatened by the possibility that reincarnation might be authentic. It would not be an exaggeration to say that there was a vendetta against this rather pleasant and ordinary Irish woman who had been in her grave for almost a century. Many clergy, scientists, and reporters played so loose with the facts that they brought dishonor on their callings. (See, for example, Parker's two chapters in *The Search...*).

Bridey, we hope you are somehow in contact with the current scene and can appreciate how the truth you shared with Ruth Simmons has now been accepted by a great many other people.

Not, of course, by our all-too-punctual critic who is ready to do his best (or worst) to undermine a belief that is supported by remarkable objective data, personal experiences, and the assent of thinking people from ancient times to this very day.

THE CRITIC'S RESPONSE

Let us take a moment to open the doors and windows. Ahhh, that feels good! The temple of incense vapors conjured at such length by the advocate will soon dissipate in the freshened air. For an instant or so one might be reluctant to surrender the seductive visions of life after life, just as one lingers in the theater after viewing an enjoyable cinematic fantasy. Sooner or later, though, we must come home to reality. And the sooner the better.

A POPULAR GAME: MAKE YOUR OWN VERSION OF REINCARNATION

The increased popularity of reincarnation belief in some Western nations has been made possible by a convenient process of selection, avoidance, and outright ignorance. It seems to offer something that is in short supply in postmodern societies – a personal sense of connection, purpose, and hope. We utilize the products and services made possible by science, technology, industry, and commerce, but at the same time we are put off by the accompanying pressures, demands, and impersonality. The religious establishment does not seem to provide shelter and inspiration for all those who are struggling in the postmodern stream, and that tradition of monumental heroic stupidity – hypernationalism – continues to pile up corpses without contributing much in the way of consolation. Many people were ready for something. And, for many, this something turned out to be reincarnation.

But not 'real reincarnation'.

The new believers have fashioned their own version. It bears about the same relationship to the faith that has sustained untold millions of Asians and Africans over the centuries as a Disney World adventure does to an actual adventure. The difference is so fundamental that advocates of the new, improved reincarnation concept are not entitled to turn to the ancient belief systems for support. A person of any intellectual integrity just cannot have it both ways: claiming the respect that might be accorded to a venerable tradition while having substituted for this tradition a diluted, sweetened, cosmeticized version. "Oh, isn't reincarnation simply precious! Does it come in pastels? Shall we hang it over the electric fire place, and invite our friends over? We can serve them herbal tea, and listen to New Age music while we celebrate the blessings of reincarnation."

The synthetic construction that often passes for reincarnation belief in the West lacks the grit, depth, and passion of the real thing. New Agers (who mostly hate to be called New Agers) seldom demonstrate awareness of the conditions from which the ancient reincarnation traditions emerged and survived. Most of all, they miss the sorrow, pain, and resigned acceptance that is at the core of reincarnation in its great Hindu and Buddhist manifestations.

What should we understand, then? We should understand that life was experienced as nearly unremitting misery by many people. Babies were born. Babies died and, all too often, their mothers along with them. Newborns were at double jeopardy – first, from untreated disease or birth defects, and then from (mostly female) infanticide. So precarious were the conditions of life that almost all societies practiced infanticide in order to reduce the competition for food and other resources. Famine and drought were also recurring facts of life. Periodic epidemics decimated the population. Accidents and acts of violence were commonplace. People labored to survive another day – and must have often asked themselves, "Why?" Hard-earned accomplishments could be wiped out by illness, violence or natural catastrophe. Those who did not perish young were often doomed to a life of hardship, frustration, and loss. Furthermore, humans were pretty much their own worst enemies (sounds familiar, doesn't it?). At the very dawn of what came to be known as the Hindu faith, Lord Krishna reported sadly that on the decline in virtue and the resurrection of vice and injustice: that's why he had to come back, a precursor of the later caped crusaders of comic book and animated cartoon fame. We suffered from our own wickedness as well as all the sorrows to which flesh is heir.

People who lived under such circumstances often developed a fatalistic attitude. What will be, will be. There's nothing much we can do, so why fight it, and why compound our misery by outbursts of sorrow and rage? Fate is our master. And when Fate has had its fling with us, out we go. There is no point in shedding a single tear. Omar Khayyam (courtesy of Edward Fitzgerald) expressed this theme more elegantly than most:

> The Moving Finger writes; and, having writ,
> Moves on: nor all your Piety nor Wit
> Shall lure it back to cancel half a Line,
> Nor all your Tears wash out a Word of it. [27]

Why have ambitions? Why strive mightily? Why try to overcome our fate? To do so would be a futile and depressing endeavor. The Will Be that Will Be has already been determined and will not alter its design for the likes of us:

> With Earth's first Clay They did the Last Man knead,
> And there of the Last Harvest sow'd the Seed:
> And the first Morning of Creation wrote
> What the Last Dawn of Reckoning shall read.

The world that Omar Khayyam experienced in 11th century Persia was already ancient. There were lingering memories of great cities that had risen and fallen, of ardent heroes, beautiful maidens, wise counselors, and sly scoundrels stretching back to the times beyond memory. And all, all, all had perished. There was a lesson in this. Life was a gift quickly and often unexpectedly taken back. Fate mocks at our ambitions and pretensions. Even the mightiest rulers soon are dust.

Here now is the essence of the world-view that fostered and sustained reincarnation belief:

- We suffer in this life. We see others suffer. We contribute to the suffering of others.
- We cannot change the external conditions of this life.
- Unfortunately, our misery does not come to an end with death. We must ride the sad carousel of life again and again. And we must die our sad deaths again and again.
- Our only hope is to escape both life and death. This, at best, is a long and arduous process. There is no guarantee that we will ever break through the centrifugal force that keeps us in rotational motion.
- As we go through our present existence we can reduce the pain by accepting that which cannot be changed, renouncing futile ambitions and desires, and freeing ourselves from illusions of meaning and comfort.

How does this prospectus strike you? Does it make you want to join the ranks of Western converts to reincarnation belief? Most converts prefer to distance themselves from this founding conception. This is not the kind of journey from life to life that they had in mind.

Try selling this severe conception to those who fancy themselves as believers in reincarnation! Wait – let's adds this significant feature of the Hindu version: the caste system. People are sorted out according to their place in the scheme of things. This place is determined before birth. The infant born into a low caste was meant to go through life as a second, third, or fourth class person, entitled to little respect or opportunity. You there, New Ager sipping your herbal tea to numbingly banal music – is it acceptable to you that millions of people must experience the stress and indignity of being 'Untouchables'? Would you accept this status for yourself? Not bloody likely!

The most popular current version of reincarnation in polite Western society is a fabrication produced by middle-class escapism. It goes more or less like this:

● Our souls exist prior to our birth. Where? Some nifty spiritual zone or astral plane.
● Crafty little devils – or angels – that they are, the souls wait for just the right opportunity to enter the mortal scene. That means just the right parents at just the right time.
● The soul brings with it a spiritual work list and educational curriculum. It must try to accomplish certain things in this new life, such as getting out of spiritual debt from a previous incarnation. It must also try to learn its necessary lessons and further its spiritual education. This particular existence, then, is like a semester at school through which one hopes to move to a higher grade.
● What actually happens in this life – including the death that concludes it – is not as important as the small but useful role this particular life plays in our overall journey.

Stoic expectation of suffering is not part of this view, nor is passive acceptance of external circumstances that threaten one's happiness. New Age believers in reincarnation are often go-getters who solve problems in the real world in a determined and aggressive Western style. If their physicians tell them something they don't want to hear, they will get – or create – a second opinion. This applies to the whole spectrum of action in the world. Their faith in reincarnation does not emanate from a weary, pessimistic-to-the-bones philosophy of almost infinite misery. Indeed, many are perky, up-and-at-'em people. This is not just a temperamental difference from traditional reincarnation believers; it is also a difference in how they construe their place in the universe:

● The universe serves primarily as the setting within which individual development occurs. It's therefore mighty convenient to have a universe handy. The process of spiritual development is glorious, transcendent, ineffable, ecstatic, and other words to the same effect. We are not only on our way to the Light of Lights and the Boundless Beyond of Infinite Wisdom, but we should be singing and dancing as we go. It is misery that is illusion. It is pain that is unreal. And death? Dear old death is just a door opening up to another passage-way in our portable spiritual picnic. You bring the eats; I'll bring the drinks.

Here's what it comes down to: reincarnation belief – Western revised version – serves as a refuge from the impersonality and pressures of mass, technologically-driven society. It also serves as an alternative from establishment churches whose dogmas and practices seem (to some) to be out of touch with that society. Many converts to New Age/reincarnation were raised to be church-goers. This version of reincarnation is not grounded in the deeply embedded experiences of many generations. It is not the last hope for release from the sad carousel. It's just an extra, a bonus. Most Western converts to reincarnation want to frolic here and now. They are not desperate for release from the coils and toils of misery-laden life. They will take their satisfactions here *and* there, now *and* later. Let the good times continue to roll...

"I want more of *this* life! I want to cruise more channels on a larger television set with my remote control! I want more conveniences, more kicks, more pleasure. And, oh, yes, I want even more and better the next time around!" This is not the song of Omar Khayyam, Lord Krishna, or the Buddha.

New style reincarnates are willing to work for their spiritual gains. They will meditate. They will exercise. They will be careful about what they eat and drink (and almost certainly will not smoke, unless already trapped in a severe nicotine addiction). They will be pleasant and helpful to others, given a chance. In all, their plan for this life has much to recommend it. But their concept of life after death is a hodge-podge, a thrown together, ill-matched combination of elements plucked out of other people's belief systems, scraps of popularized science, and a lot of wishful thinking. Few would accept reincarnation as part of the whole Hindu or Buddha package. Few would renounce the conveniences and pleasures of a technologically advanced society. Few would feel at home in the world view that bred the major conceptions of reincarnation.

There has been a fascinating exchange between East and West that somehow has not received the attention it deserves. The patient, enduring, philosophical East has picked up on Western technology with a vengeance. Zen masters may still be revered by the culture elite, but computer experts are more in demand. Meanwhile, the West has inhaled the tantalizing vapors of mysticism from the East. Computerized industry and commerce for the East, reincarnation for the West. Fair enough! But the East did not degrade technology originating in the West; instead Asian scientists and industrialists have become among the leaders. By contrast, the West has misunderstood, degraded, and trivialized the dominant reincarnation traditions.

This exchange is making reincarnation less necessary in the East. There have already been several generations of modernists in India, Japan, China, Korea and other Asian nations. These people have demonstrated that fate may not hold all the cards after all. People do not have to adhere so firmly to reincarnation for escape from the miseries of life when it becomes possible to alleviate some of these miseries through effective action in the world. Odd, isn't it? Well-to-do people in the United States are drifting away from their indigenous beliefs and institutions in favor of a distorted version of reincarnation, while the homelands of reincarnation are a-buzz with efforts to replace the sad carousel with the dizzying roller-coaster of physical joys and material achievements.

The case for reincarnation is falling apart even before we come to the question of evidence. Reincarnation belief was a response to the burdens, miseries, and tragedies of human existence before we could protect ourselves and meet our needs by action in the world. It will remain the belief of choice for some intellectuals who are enticed by the mind-games one can play with reincarnation theory. It will also remain at least a temporary refuge for those who are retreating from mainstream life. They might prefer their fantasies on the sidelines to trying – and losing again – in the competitive scrimmage of daily life. Otherwise, the future of reincarnation is in doubt. As already noted, the East is rapidly losing the need to maintain this colorful but outmoded faith, and the West has concocted a flimsy substitute version that cannot long prove satisfactory.

The advocate has already emphasized that in the sophisticated Buddhist version of reincarnation: *personal identity in the usual sense of the term does not survive a death.* There is also not a divine creator whose plan is being fulfilled. And there is not an eternity of bliss awaiting. When sober reflection eventually sets in, the drop-outs from Christianity are likely to acknowledge that reincarnation is not quite what their hearts desire. They will show up in church again on Sunday, wearing their finest, or they will go on seeking an even more extravagant fantasy of survival.

EVIDENCE, WHAT EVIDENCE?

Oh, yes, the evidence. We must not forget the evidence. What evidence? Much like a rumour that is too tasty to relinquish, the reincarnation scenario has been self-perpetuating. When we focus on evidence we are taking the road less travelled. Evidence doesn't have much to do with the popularity of this belief. To be sure, a smattering of putative evidence is comforting for those who harbor some doubts or who fear that others might think them odd for believing in reincarnation. By and large, though, these people are not concerned with evidence as such, but simply with the legitimization of a belief that they feel good about. The prevalence of this casual attitude toward critical examination and verification is the reason why this section started by exploring the knowledge base and attitudes of Western converts to reincarnation. A handful of researchers and several handfuls of scholars do concern themselves systematically with the truth value of reincarnation belief, but most people are satisfied with beguiling stories. We have the right and perhaps the obligation to ask: how do these stories stand up?

TRIPPING TO OTHER LIVES

Have you seen Marie Antoinette lately? Hélène Smith did, about a hundred years ago. Actually, Smith *was* Antoinette. She was also, in the fourteenth century, Simandini, the eleventh wife of Prince Sivrouka

Nakaya. Smith/Simandini and the prince had a passionate relationship that remained hot to the end: she was burned alive on his grave. She was quite a few other people as well. Ms Smith certainly got around. These recollections usually were shared during seances, her verbal report being accompanied by pencil drawings as she went along. During the seances she would sometimes *become* a previous self again. One could hardly ask for more impressive verification of reincarnation, right? At times the evidence was quite extensive. For example, in what appeared to be a somnambulistic trance (i.e. sleep walking), she played out the scene of her fiery death in pantomime for the better part of an hour. An eyewitness reports on this performance:

> She goes slowly around the room, as if resisting and carried away in spite of herself, by turns supplicating and struggling fiercely with these fictitious men who are bearing her to death. All at once, standing on tiptoe, she seems to ascend the pile, hides, with affright, her face in her hands, recoils in terror, then advances anew as though pushed from behind. Finally she falls on her knees before a soft couch, in which she buries her face covered by her clasped hands. She sobs violently. By means of her little finger, visible between her cheek and the cushion of the couch, Leopold (her primary spirit guide) continues to reply very clearly by yes and no to my questions.
>
> It is the moment at which she again passes through her agony on the funeral pile: her cries cease little by little; her respiration becomes more and more panting, then suddenly stops and remains suspended during some seconds which seem interminable. It is the end![28]

Bravo! Bravissimo! Professor Theodore Flournoy, the distinguished philosopher and psychologist who studied Hélène Smith (a pseudonym) closely, was pleased to add that "Her pulse is fortunately strong, though a little irregular."

Not only did she have exciting past lives, but also an exceptional travel itinerary. Long before the first man set foot on the moon, Hélène Smith had visited Mars. Repeatedly. She even spoke and wrote the Martian language fluently. Would you like to brush up on your Martian? Here is a transcription of one of her trance conversations (October 24, 1897):

> *Sike' e'vai divine' ze' nike' crizi capri ne' ame' orie' antech e' eze' carimi ni ezi e'rie' e' nie pavine'e hed le' sadri de' ze' ve'chir tizine Matemi misaime' ka le' ame'z essate' Arva ti ezine' udanitz ames' t'es uri ames' sandine' ten ti si 'e'val divine'e. Rome' va ne' Sike' atrizi ten te' tamech epizi.*
>
> *Sike', be happy! The little black bird came yesterday rapping at my window, and my soul was joyful; he sange to me: Thou wilt see him tomorrow. Matemi, flower which makes me live, sun of my dreams,*

come this evening; come for a long time to me; be happy! – Rome',
where is Sike'? – Yonder, near the "tameche" rose.

Furthermore, she was able to provide hard data for her planetary excursions: she painted landscapes of Mars, and seeing is believing as we all know.

Smith's 'evidence' was as electrifying in her times (not so very long ago) as any of the 'evidence' presented today. She was more adventurous and evidential than many of those among us who commune with past lives. The trips to Mars were extra added attractions. With her entranced performances, drawings, and fluency in an extra-terrestrial language, she ran circles around those who merely talk about past lives.

Flournoy's book was titled, *From India to The Planet Mars. A Study of a Case of Somnambulism with Glossolalia* (speaking in tongues). He observed and analyzed Smith's communications with an open but disciplined mind. Conclusion?

> *As far as Hélène's mediumistic phenomena are concerned, their careful analysis has not revealed to me in them any evident vestige of the other world, not even traces of a telepathic transmission on the part of the living. I have only succeeded in perceiving in them very beautiful and instructive examples of the well-known tendency of the subliminal imagination to reconstruct the deceased and to feign their presence, especially when the favorable suggestions of the surrounding environment incites them to do so. (pp. 424-425)*

Hélène and Leopold were able to provide no verifiable information when in either the reincarnation mode or the more customary mediumistic communication with discarnate spirits. The performances accorded best with the actions of a personality that could move with relative ease from one dissociated self to another. Each of these alternative selves held its own store of memory and fantasy. They took turns in pouring their mixture of miscellaneous facts, impressions, and imaginings into the presiding voice of Hélène Smith, but they could not discourse credibly on past lives when the discourse was asked specific question and when their messages subjected to careful analysis. She knew nothing remarkably true about Antoinette, and history tells us nothing of Prince Sivrouka Nakaya, his eleven wives, or the kingdom he supposedly ruled. Smith's trips, whether backward in time or outward in space, all occurred within her mind. Make that *minds*.

We all have some capacity for dissociation. Multiple personality, so-called, results from the inability to integrate conflicting impulses into a dominant and capable presiding personality. Other people with a high degree of dissociation may avoid the pathological consequences, but experience the dissociated self-systems as though independent entities. This should sound familiar. We encountered the same dynamics in medium/channeling phenomena. From the standpoint of personality dynamics, it does not much matter whether one interprets the self-to-self message as coming from a spirit guide or a past life. 'Spirit communication' often consists of memories and imaginings that operate free from critical scrutiny and come to the surface as situations warrant. Fraud accounts for much as well, as does suggestibility whether induced through hypnosis, guided imagery, or spontaneously through one's own needs.

The case of Hélène Smith is important here because it was a high profile example of apparent reincarnation that came to the systematic attention of a qualified investigator. His explanation made sense then, and makes even more sense now in the light of modern neuro-psychology.[29, 30] Memory and fantasy are closely related functions, anatomically as well as psychologically. This is one of the reasons why the testimony of witnesses often proves to be unreliable in court, and why several people may have several different recollections of the 'same' event. Our minds are quite capable of constructing vivid and, as Flournoy notes, 'beautiful' scenarios, whether in the form of con-sciously created art, so-called near-death experiences, or visitations with past selves.

Especially worth attention were her supposed visitations to Mars and her fluency in that (rather French-accented) language as well as her recitations from ancient Persia and other remote lands.

Speaking in tongues often impresses the impressionable. It is taken as evidence that the speaker has special powers or connections. A fluent stream of glossolalic verbalizations can induce others to believe almost anything the speaker cares to inflict on them. This suggestibility phenomenon frequently operates even when the listeners cannot really make head or tail of what supposedly was said. Glossolalia has been with us since at least the early days of Christianity. Many seem to have forgotten Saul's/St Paul's admonition that speaking in tongues has no value unless the messages could be interpreted in a clear and reliable manner. Speaking in tongues was in itself not very impressive. Interpreting the message was the hard part. St Paul would have had his doubts about a message that is attributed not to God, but to a child deceased for half a millennia and whose alleged content cannot be verified. If we believe reincarnation can be proved by relying on pseudo-languages that can be 'translated' only by the speaker and which convey no verifiable information, then we are indeed wonderfully capable of believing anything.

Now – about those excursions to Mars! Hélène Smith's version of Mars bears no resemblance to the barren planet that has now been studied by many scientists. Too bad – her version is a lot more interesting. It is unfortunate that there are no Martians to speak their own language. Flournoy was right, of course, about the origin of the Mars reports in Smith's own dissociated imaginings.

And these imaginings are just what we might expect when criteria for evidence are disregarded and people are willing to believe practically anything. *The attempt to prove reincarnation by encounters with 'past selves' is seriously undermined by its frequent association with claims for absolutely ridiculous phenomena.* Were I a believer in one of the traditional reincarnation doctrines I would be distressed to see this belief associated with such nonsense. Claiming to be the reincarnation of an ancient princess one day and a visitor to Mars the next, Hélène Smith has trivialized one of the major belief systems of humankind and invited its ridicule.

It would be hard to think of a more foolish – wait! It's not hard at all. The next (il)logical step has already been taken. You like past selves? Fine. Can I interest you now in future selves? Some reincarnationists (again, not those holding to tradition) claim that to be in contact with their future selves as well. Of those who have written about 'future-life progression', perhaps the most responsible person is Helen Wambach, a psychologist who had earlier published two interesting books on past-life regression.[31, 32] Those books offered case histories that were presented as examples of communication with past selves. In a more recent book,[33] Wambach and C. B. Snow report on what they call *future-life progressions*. Most of these reports come from workshops in which the participants were guided to their future lives. Not all were delighted:

> *I definitely did not like the man who was going to become my husband (in 2100 AD). I had married him following some sort of order. It was an awful experience! (p. 136)*

Imagining oneself in the future can be a stimulating mental experiment, and is used for this purpose in a number of educational settings. For example, when teaching a course on ageing and communication I often guide the university students to imagined interactions with their selves-to-be (say, at age 80). They are sometimes asked to take the role of their aged self to gain perspective on who they are now and who they would like to become. The material presented by Snow and Wambach is also useful when considered as products of the imagination. It is quite another thing, however, to drop the role-pretend framework and claim that a future incarnation of one's self already exists and is available at short notice.

It is difficult to accept reincarnation doctrines; facts and logic keep getting in the way. However, one can at least think seriously about past selves because they *are* past. The human race has a history. We know this history incompletely and with varying accuracy, but there is no doubt that others have lived and died before we appeared on the scene. It's a different story with future selves. Are we to believe the future already exists? That tomorrow is here today? This is a theme that has already been well worked over in science fiction, where it rightfully belongs. There is also a place for alternative views of time in mathematics and physics. But no, no, no, it is asking way too much of our intellectual flexibility when we are expected to believe in specific pre-incarnated selves humming along in socio-environmental settings that have yet to develop.

No empirical proof is offered, yet whatever fantasies the time voyagers come up with, there is no way to disprove them either. Like the performances of Hélène Smith and other parlor variety reincarnationists, there is no verifiable substance. There is no explanation offered, either. Why should we suddenly abandon reason and experience to accept the reality of pre-incarnated selves simply because some people are able to imagine them? What would we *not* believe? Perhaps just the sensible conclusion that each of us has one life and one death!

PAST-LIFE REGRESSION
(EMPHASIS ON 'REGRESSION')

Much of the current hoo-hah about reincarnation has been aroused by reports of past-life regression. The advocate tried to stay away from the term 'regression' as being too technical and off-putting. Nevertheless, it is the term most in use and 'regression' nicely captures the intellectual and emotional level at which so-called past-life evidence is celebrated.

There are few researchers available to investigate the many claims. This was true as well in the days when tables were being rapped, mystic trumpets sounding, and ectoplasm floating about with the celestial fragrance of goats' bladder (which some of them were). There is also a parallel in the findings. When qualified researchers do have the opportunity to examine past-life regression under controlled conditions, the claimed phenomena fail to make the grade.

Melvin Harris[34] has reviewed investigations of apparent past life regressions. Here is a sampling of what happened to reincarnation stories when subjected to careful study:

● University students were hypnotized and instructed to remember past existences. They did so, and quite convincingly. Next, they were asked to listen to the tape-recordings of their past life regressions. All were surprised and said they had no knowledge of these previous lives. So far, so good for the reincarnationists! But another step was taken. The students were hypnotized again and inquiries made into the sources of their mystical knowledge. And the sources were reported! All of the supposed past-lives were "nothing but a mixture of remembered tales and strong symbolically colored emotions."

● A Finnish school girl proved adept at recalling past lives under hypnosis; she had about eight of them, most in the remote past and in faraway places. However, one of these previous existences had run its course in London until, as 'Karin Bergstrom', she had died in an air raid.

She was able to supply an address for her old home, and she knew the names and occupations of her former parents. Inquiries showed that indeed there had been an air raid on the exact date she had given. What is more, the addresses she had given had been hit. But the population records showed that neither a real Karin Bergstrom nor her relatives had died in the raid. (p. 135)

Did this discrepancy represent only a near miss in an otherwise impressive past life recall? Not really. The girl was hypnotized again and asked to report when she had first heard of Karin Bergstrom. It turned out that she had read about the air raid and seen a photo of a woman and her seven-year-old daughter who had been killed. Like so many others, the girl who reported previous existences had stored memories that she had not had occasion to retrieve until requested to provide past-life regressions. These memory bits were then supplemented by invention – with all of this taking place outside of her normal-state awareness.

- The Bloxham Tapes were a sensation of the 1970s that were brought to the attention of the public through a BBC television documentary. The tapes had been made by Arnall Bloxham, a hypnotherapist who had practised for many years in Cardiff. There were about 400 tapes in which people seemed to be reporting on their previous lives. Hot stuff! The television producer, Jeffrey Iverson, selected the two best cases for special attention. Graham Huxtable reported having served aboard a Royal Navy frigate in action against the French two hundred years previously. Jane Evans came up with six past lives that were filled with enormous detail. Harris' investigation found that neither Huxtable's ship or any ship answering to its description existed in the Royal Navy at that time. Because extensive information is available regarding this period of British military history it was possible to demonstrate that this 'past life' differed from the known facts and provided no information that school children could not have learned in the course of their readings.

One of Jane Evans' lives was based, passage after passage, on an historical novel. The other lives also came unravelled as their sources in available information were discovered. Her impressive description of the life of a fifteenth-century French merchant prince was found to be based on another historical novel, augmented by a book of photographs. It turned out she knew those details that the novel (C.B. Costain's, *The Moneyman*) had mentioned, and not some important facts about the merchant prince that the author omitted because they were irrelevant to his story. For example, as a serving girl for Jacques Coeur, Jane correctly recalled that he had an Egyptian slave, but did not know that he was married and had five children. The slave was mentioned by Costain; the family was not.

And so it goes... We have been able to give only snippets of the findings that discredit claims of past lives in these cases. In all likelihood, the people who made these reports did so in the belief that they were recalling real personal experiences from previous existences. Many people joined them in this belief. But no matter how sincere the reporter and how multitudinous the believers, claims of past lives do not withstand competent critical inquiry.

Even that sentimental favorite, Bridey Murphy, has not escaped this fate. It is true, as Barker laments, that some critics attacked her story with more vehemence than probity. Both sides of the controversy were caught up in their emotions. Objectivity and logic suffered. Open-minded readers found it difficult to come to a firm conclusion as half-baked claims and criticisms proliferated. Today, cooler judgment prevails. Bridey's most impressive memories now have been traced to information that had been accessible to Ruth Simmons (her present incarnation). For example, an Irish village had been constructed for the World Columbian Exposition in Chicago (1893). This village included an enormous relief map of Ireland, daily performances of songs, sales of books and other merchandise, and a replica of the famous Blarney Stone. Many of Simmon's relatives and some of her friends had in all probability visited the Exposition and come away with their heads full of Irish lore: about three and a half million people had done so. Those supporting claims for Bridey Murphy's reincarnation story seemed never to have said a word about the Exposition, nor about a copycat Irish village that was presented at the St Louis World Fair of 1904. The Irish village attractions were real. The stories were, well, just stories. Reincarnation tales associated with Edgar Cayce still circulate widely, but they are of even less evidential value than the one we have reviewed here. Their documentation hardly deserves this term, but I guess we're not supposed to notice that.

I have observed another phenomenon that should be mentioned before we close the book on past-life fantasies as supposed proofs for reincarnation. For want of a better term, I am calling it the *co-creation of discarnate spirits*. In a previous chapter we noted the circus of self-deception and other-deception that surrounded a Canadian group's attempt to manufacture Philip, the Ghost. It is probable that many other claimed communications with the dead also involve a process of co-creation, but on a more sincere and subtle level.

The *interpersonal* nature of spirit communication has yet to be given its due. I must admit that as a critic I share in the blame. We have been emphasizing the ways in which such communications are constructed by our internal mental/neurophysiological processes. Memories and imaginings are blended into stories which are then projected upon what is itself a construction, whether conceived as a discarnate spirit or a past self. It is time to remind ourselves that everyday communications are transactions that are shaped by all of the participants. We construct messages and scenarios not only in our heads, but also in the course of our interactions.

Consider this example. Two people are engaged in an intense and prolonged communicational episode. There is something at stake for them emotionally. A dialogue is taking place – yet each person is also carrying out an inner dialogue, a conversation or confrontation between one's own thoughts and feelings. The outer dialogue is significant. Each participant's internal dialogue may be even more significant. Now one person's verbal and non-verbal communication combine to make a very strong impression on the other person. What this person said and how it was said penetrates the inner dialogue that has been building within the other person. On a conscious level, the receiver of this message is not aware of its undertones and its impact on his or her own state of mind.

Still following? Good! Here is what happens next. The individual who has been ignited by the partially masked communication now has an intensified state of mind in which thoughts are rising to the surface without an obvious source. These thoughts are being constructed through the interaction of the speaker's message and his or her inner dialogue. The message had a component that resonated emotionally and symbolically with something that was already going on (unaware) within the listener.

This deep communicative interaction took place with so little awareness that the recipient cannot identify its source (which, as we have seen, is partially in the semantic harmonics of the message, and partially in the listener's own stirred-up state). "What's happening? Where did these thoughts come from?" Uncertainty arouses anxiety. Coming up with an answer (even if fallacious) reduces anxiety.

"Ah, I know what is going on! Remarkable! This person has a mysterious knowledge of my life. It must be that this person has paranormal powers. In fact, the best explanation – the only explanation – is that this person has information gleaned from the dead, because only the dead would have known all of this and spoken to me in such a way."

This is an example of mistaken attribution. Uncertainty and emotional involvement often lead us to attribute statements, actions, and motivations to the wrong person. Or the wrong spirit entity. In the type of situation that has just been described, the listener is misattributing his own thoughts and knowledge to the other person. If the speaker has made just one statement that conveys compelling information to the listener, this can be sufficient to produce the mental equivalent of a nuclear chain reaction. "She and the spirits know everything and they are giving me a powerful message," thinks the listener, instead of "My memories and fantasies have created a compelling story that is responsive to my urgent needs of the moment."

Catherine's and Weiss's response fit this pattern well. Whether not this is what happened in that instance cannot be determined without a careful investigation and, perhaps, not even then. By self-report, Weiss had much on his mind regarding his own personal life.

He was also frustrated and puzzled as his attempt to relieve Catherine's symptoms failed to produce results during the course of a long and frustrating therapeutic process. A personal insight, a revelation, a transformation is just what he needed. The co-creation hypothesis is based on established principles of communicative interaction. Past-life regression is based on no established scientific principles. As long as a viable alternative exists and has not been ruled out, we should hestitate to embrace the extravagant claim of previous lives.

"CASES SUGGESTIVE OF REINCARNATION": BUT ONLY SUGGESTIVE

The last hope for reincarnation evidence rests with the studies of Ian Stevenson and his colleagues. He has certainly done more than his share not only in the sheer number of cases investigated, but also in improving the quality of case investigation and interpretation. Despite his labors, however, 'cases suggestive of reincarnation' remain, at best, suggestive.

Philosopher Paul Edwards[35] remind us that "Reincarnation... presupposes an extreme form of dualism." One must accept the proposition that mind/spirit and body are separate or separable. Furthermore, the body must be regarded as somehow the property of mind/spirit. It is not only an extreme dualism but one that treats one level of reality as somehow higher or more real than the other.

Extreme dualism has been rejected by science and by most Western philosophers. It is too big and consequential a belief to accept merely through its assertion. Those who continue to assert extreme dualism must offer strong evidence. This has not been done, and it is not fair to expect Stevenson and his cases to carry all the burden of proof. Evidence for the independence and superiority of mind/spirit should have been provided from many quarters. All that we do have – and it is significant on its own terms – is evidence that what we commonly call 'mind' and what we commonly call 'body' have mutual influences. For example, a person who has just heard some very bad news is likely to feel bodily distress in consequence. But: mind without body? This remains the question, not the answer.

Every case investigated by Stevenson (or anybody else) is up against the whole tissue of scientific knowledge and thought. It is not enough just to have some interesting observations. We need proof that is of a quality one can seldom verify by the case history method. Consider, for example, the most significant cases in the early history of psychoanalysis. Sigmund Freud was not attempting to prove anything as far-out as reincarnation or communication with the dead. He was just trying to discover the origin of his patient's symptoms (and his own, since his self-analysis was perhaps the most illuminating case). And yet the meaning of these cases remains controversial to this day, despite his relatively modest goal and despite his gifts as observer, narrator, and interpreter. It is just in the nature of case histories that various interpretations are possible and that one cannot be entirely sure that all the relevant information is on hand and that the information that is on hand is completely accurate.

Stevenson himself is quite aware of these limitations. He has set aside a number of cases for insufficient information. Other cases have been rejected because it was possible that the person who claimed previous lives might have obtained the information through normal channels. Stevenson has noticed that some informants "improved" upon the reports and others seemed to be engaging in outright deception. He has therefore done quite a bit of the critic's work by winnowing the cases down to those that most deserve serious consideration.

Even the best cases pose difficulties, however. The time lag between the original report and the investigation is a major problem and it is one that exists for all or nearly all the cases. Stevenson has to wait until he is informed about the case, and then he has to find the time (and perhaps the funding) to start his investigation. In the meantime, the original statements may have been modified by the memories and retellings of various people, and the child itself may have been subjected to the opinions, expectations, and ideas of others. Furthermore, typically there is no adequate record of precisely what was said and within what kind of setting. By the time Stevenson arrives on the scene he must do what he can with the memories of various informants and with whatever objective data might be available.

Given the opportunity, Stevenson no doubt would want to be on the scene *before* all of this happens. He could then observe the total situation, and observe and record for himself all that takes place. Unfortunately, this is an unlikely scenario. In doing what he can when he finally has access to the child and other informants, Stevenson has offered some observations that are worth pondering. 'This...just... could...be...the...real...thing'. But honest doubt always remains. As an expert interviewer, Stevenson knows that verbal reports are subject to modification over time. Reincarnation proof may therefore hinge upon small but crucial details whose accuracy can be doubted. If this person did not say precisely what we think this person said, then we cannot with confidence evaluate its possible correspondence with what is known about claimed past selves.

There are numerous other methodological problems that Stevenson did not create, but which he has little or no means of overcoming. Take, for example, the high proportion of violent deaths among the past lives recalled in various cultures. Why should this be the case? The simplest explanation is that violent deaths make more impact on the survivors and the general public. You can confirm this fact for yourself by monitoring the coverage of violent and non-violent deaths by newspapers, radio, and television. People talk more about violent deaths, and they talk with greater intensity. This means that there is more information about violent deaths flowing through normal channels of communication. If cases suggestive of reincarnation actually involve crypto-amnesia (hidden memories) of information obtained through normal means, then the preponderance of violent deaths in claimed past lives is just what we should expect.

This simple explanation may or may not be the correct explanation. Nevertheless, this simple, naturalistic explanation must be favored unless it can be overcome by supplementary facts and analyses. For example, a research team might possibly demonstrate that there was little or no talk about the violent deaths that are later the subject of reincarnation claims. This is easier to say than do, however, especially when investigators are few and funds are limited. What it comes down to is that in this regard and in some others, Stevenson has not had the opportunity to rule out simpler alternative explanations.

Here is another fairly simple explanation and, in this case, it is an explanation for a phenomenon for which no existing credible explanation seems to exist. Stevenson reports that, typically, the children started talking about reincarnation just about as soon as they start talking. A few years later, though, these children stop or significantly reduce this line of conversation and often (though not invariably) seem to have forgotten the past life. Why? Many children have imaginary companions. This is a normal feature of childhood, although not present in all. What people in reincarnation-saturated societies interpret as discourse about a previous life might be only the local version of the imaginary companion. After all, there are many types of imaginary companion a child might invent. If one's culture provides a lot of cues for reincarnation, then one might naturally enough select one's own self – in a previous incarnation – as an imaginary companion. Most children outgrow their imaginary companions in a few years, just as the child-informants in Stevenson's studies tend to cease their talk of previous lives.

Again, it is not necessary for me to assert that this is the definitive explanation. It is, however, a reasonable explanation and one that does not violate what we know about child development. Over and again, we find that simpler explanations are at least competitive with the huge claim that these observations prove reincarnation.

A SHORT WALK ON THE WILD SIDE

In previous chapters I occasionally relaxed the critic's position to consider possibilities that are somewhere between complete acceptance and complete rejection of a claim. Because Stevenson's work deserves respect and does raise a number of questions, let's take just a short walk on the wild side.

Return for a moment to the preponderance of sudden and violent deaths in the reports compiled by Stevenson. This preponderance seems to be a well established fact. At first I suggested an explanation that would obviate the need to believe that the information about past lives and deaths was obtained through paranormal means. Here is another kind of explanation: sudden and violent deaths exercise a disrupting effect on life-streams. *Life-streams?* Sure, why not? Let us take one of the central propositions of traditional reincarnation beliefs: the continuity of mind or consciousness. This is not a preposterous idea; it is just an idea that is mighty difficult to verify. It is also an idea that is difficult to reconcile with mainstream science and philosophy. Difficult, not impossible.

Think of life-streams as bio-energy forms. They are not pure consciousness or spirit. They are not pure physical matter. Life-streams show characteristics of mind and/or matter depending on how they are observed and the circumstances in which they are observed. This conception is well within the bounds of present day philosophy of science. It also does away with the need to assume an extreme dualism. We have learned to take very seriously the relationship between observer and observed, and to accept limits to the accuracy of our observations (as demonstrated in various ways in Heisenberg's Principle of Uncertainty, and Chaos Theory, each of which hold that it is not even theoretically possible to know everything from one set of observations).

I would suggest that life-streams are different when perceived from the inside and the outside. And I would quickly admit that the inside/outside distinction itself is a crude one that needs further thought and refinement. For sake of discussion, let us further suppose that life-streams do not necessarily conform to our usual conceptions of personal identity. And, while we are at it, let us suppose that our usual conceptions of 'alive' and 'dead' do not apply either, i.e., do not describe precisely the continuities and transformations of life-streams. What we have, then, is a kind of flow through the universe which is itself a kind of flow. (There are alternative ways of saying this, some of which may be more heuristic, but this formulation will do for the present purpose.)

The flow of life-streams is not identical with separate 'lives', 'deaths', and 'identities' because these familiar concepts are too heavily saturated with our conventions of language and thought. There is an ongoingness, however. Furthermore, there are resonances or influences among life-streams. These interactions should not hastily be interpreted as 'causes' and 'effects', which are utilitarian categories that have a limited range of effective application.

What we have, then, are flowing streams of bio-energy (or something of that nature) that are responsive to each other in ways that we do not yet understand. Now: a violent death. This is a shuddering event that resonates through and across life-streams. It is something we might roughly describe as a threat or challenge. There is a 'sympathetic' response from other life-streams, perhaps like the reverberation of a second set of strings when the primary strings are sounded on some musical instruments of the past. Should we construe the *life-stream as the music of bio-energy* we might be on our way to an even better way of presenting this phenomenon to our minds.

Because the life-stream integrates mind and matter, it may on some occasions respond to violent deaths as themes to seize upon and develop, perhaps in order to keep the streams flowing. The correspondences that Stevenson offers between physical marks of death and (re)birth might follow naturally within this scenario.

As wild as all of this may sound, it is within hailing distance of the observations that have emerged from reincarnation research and yet does not ignore or thumb its nose at the mainstream philosophic/ scientific enterprise. It is certainly a 'stretch' as an explanation, but a stretch may be just what we need now and then to maintain our vigor in the quest for understanding.

8

SOULS ON ICE: WHO NEEDS AN AFTERLIFE?

Most of us now breathing have a good chance of physical life after death – a sober, scientific probability of revival and rejuvenation of our frozen bodies. – R.C.W. Ettinger

This challenging assertion was made by the founder of the cryonics movement as it first came to attention three decades ago. *The Prospect of Immortality*[1] contended that a human body could be maintained at a very low temperature over long periods of time. This was the basic plan:

- Do not burn or bury that corpse.
- Preserve the body in a hypothermic (cold, cold, cold) state so that little or no further damage will occur.
- Wait.
- Keep waiting.
- It's a good thing we did keep waiting, because now an effective treatment has been developed for what ailed our friend or relation.
- Resuscitate the soul on ice.
- Apply the new treatment.
- Have a party! (Perhaps a Rebirthday Party, as Ettinger has suggested).

The Prospect of Immortality was a best-seller and has been kept in print. Stimulated by this book, some visionaries formed organizations to educate the public, encourage research, and develop the services specified by Ettinger. Things started to happen. Cryonicists can point to some achievements and to the promise of further achievements. The promise has not been entirely fulfilled, however. In 1968 Robert F. Nelson published a book entitled *We Froze the First Man*.[2] Nobody has yet come up with a factual sequel:

We Thawed the First Man.

Will the cryonic vision ever be actualized? Will it become commonplace to recover from 'fatal' illness after hypothermic storage? And *should* this technology be used if it does become available?

These questions are well worth our consideration today. Cryonic resuscitation cannot be judged a failure. There is general agreement that the technology has not reached the point where a resuscitation should be attempted. Whether or not it ever will is the big question and it deserves to be examined in some detail.

Technology apart, the cryonic vision introduces a radically new approach to the survival of death. This alternative could be unsettling both to believers and non-believers in a life after death. Believers are accustomed to thinking that a parting of the ways occurs between spirit and flesh. "Ashes to ashes, dust to dust" is the fate of the body, but not of the spirit, soul, or essence. Whether or not the spirit later is provided with another physical frame is a divisive but secondary consideration among believers. Non-believers hold that one body and one life is all that each person has to work with. Mind is a function or aspect of body and must share its fate.

The cryonic movement has the potential to unnerve us, then, by contending that we do not have to take leave of our bodies. We can survive our deaths and pick up where we left off. Neither 'death' nor 'survival' answer to their traditional meanings.

With the stage now set, it is time to turn loose our believer and disbeliever.

THE ADVOCATE'S CASE: REPLACING DEATH WITH REANIMATION

There is no point in offering immortality to people whose minds are dead set against it. I am speaking of real, honest, right-here-on-earth immortality, not spiritual pie in the sky. Although people in general are not fond of dying and death, neither are they ready to accept the prospect of immortality when it is presented on a (frozen) silver platter. We need a moment, then, to blink a few times and rub the sleep out of our eyes.

BEING DEAD IS A BAD HABIT

Most of us are creatures of habit. Which shoe did you put on first this morning? Perhaps you are not sure of the answer. It's such a habit. Chances are very good that if you put on the left shoe first today, you did so also the day before and the day before the day before. Habits make life more comfortable for us. But habits can also take over our lives. Every day we meet people who seem to be sleepwalking. They manage to perform their jobs, more or less, and to slide through perfunctory social interactions. What they don't do is to observe their immediate realities through fresh eyes, recognize possibilities and incongruities, or identify new problems and solutions.

Physical habits are not so bad. After all, what difference does it make if you put your left or right shoe on first? Mental habits are what drag us down. The habit of burying or burning our dead is one of the worst. This thoughtless indiscretion leads to an equally unfortunate habit: being dead and staying dead. Like many other habits, burying, burning, and staying dead had justifiable origins. Something had to be done with the inanimate remains of a person. Cannibalism was an attractive option, providing nutrition and obviating the need to dispose of the body by more laborious and expensive means. Less sensible customs prevailed, however, and for centuries societies have enslaved themselves to the habit of burying, burning, or simply abandoning the remains of their fallen brethren.

To be sure, there was also a persistent theme of optimism – or desperation – that attempted to revivify the dead. Spells, prayers, rituals were given a whirl. Alchemists and magicians engaged in both silly and ingenious efforts to set dead bones to dancing again. The dead stubbornly stayed dead, however. Nice try – but they just didn't have the right technology!

Give our ancestors credit: through all the failures, many retained the hope and even the conviction that dead today did not have to be dead tomorrow. This intuition could not be supported by results, so many lapsed into a kind of 'consolation prize' mentality. They allowed themselves to believe that people survive in a wispy sort of way – wandering souls, dream-visions and so forth.

Am I saying what you think I am saying? Indeed! Ghost-sightings, channelings and the like are merely the poor substitutes for direct, palpable evidence that death is not fatal. These poor substitutes constitute an extra layer of crust over habit-dulled thought. These two assumptions – (a) death is fatal; (b) there is an escape hatch for an invisible, unverifiable, soul-vapor – conspire against recognizing a real opportunity when it presents itself.

And today we do have that real opportunity, the opportunity that was sought by the most passionate and life-loving of our ancestors. How ironic it would be to ignore this opportunity because we allowed such bad habits to rule our thinking about survival of death. I will now tell you just why these assumptions do not stand up to the facts. It is up to you, however, to free your mind from its shackles long enough to engage with the emergent reality of cryonic resuscitation.

KEEPING OUR COOL

It is not that complicated. Our bodies function within a relatively narrow temperature range. Changes in the temperature of the environment are compensated by our homeostatic mechanisms to preserve a constant internal temperature. Both heat and chill act as stressors. Our personal temperature may deviate from its normal level when the external temperature is extreme and prolonged or when our

233

health is impaired. A slight rise in temperature – less than two degrees – and we have spiked a fever. A few degrees higher and we are in serious difficulty. Less familiar in daily life is a drop in temperature below the somewhat mythic standard of 98.6°. Health-care professionals will suspect that the circulatory system is in difficulty when a person is cold to the touch (and characteristically bluish as well).

There is a critical difference between too hot and too cold. Overheating taxes physiological systems beyond their capacity. It destroys tissues. It literally burns us up. Cold slows down and eventually shuts down body processes. The structure remains essentially intact, however. Biological time is nearly suspended. An organism in a total hypothermic state does not grow up and does not grow old. This victory over clock and calendar has its price, of course. The organism does not interact with its environment nor carry out any of its usual functions. It is still alive, however, waiting for its next opportunity.

The cure for death, then, begins with lowering body temperature to the sub-zero range. This prevents decomposition. When you really think about it, becoming dead is not nearly as bad as what comes after. A person may be structurally intact at the time a physician decides to reach for the death certificate. For example, before people knew about the Heimlich maneuver there was many a casualty from choking on food, even so innocuous an item as the watercress sandwich that almost did in the mayor of New York City. The deceased sometimes was in excellent health except for the unfortunate fact of his or her sudden death. But the deceased did not long remain in excellent health as post-mortem processes worked their way with the corpse.

The intact corpse may not be exactly alive, but neither is it exactly dead. Neither of these familiar terms is completely accurate in characterizing this transitional state. We need to get over the idea that a person is alive one moment and dead, dead, dead forever at the next moment. We will be coming back to this idea later.

We have to careful about this freezing business. The temperature must be lowered quickly enough to prevent decomposition, but slowly enough to protect tissues from ice damage. Along with regulating the rate of freezing, it is necessary to use glycerol or some other cryoprotective agent.

What, precisely, are we protecting against? Ice does not do its damage by forming inside individual cells and then bursting their membranes. Instead, ice forms between cells and removes the crucial elements that exist normally within the cellular fluid as solutes. Individual cells dehydrate as their water flows through their membranes toward the higher concentration solutions produced by the freezing fluid outside the cell. It is more like a persistent series of leaks in the wall of a dam than a shattering rupture. The cells then shrink to a much reduced size. Think of a tiny ice cube in which what is left of cellular material is imbedded.

SOULS ON ICE: WHO NEEDS AN AFTERLIFE?

This kind of damage can be held to a bare minimum through a controlled freezing process and the use of cryoprotective agents. The principle is similar to the proven effectiveness of anti-freeze compounds that are added to the radiators of motor vehicles in cold weather. As a matter of fact, glycerol is a common anti-freeze additive. Careful motorists who take good care of their faithful engines during the frigid blasts of winter are more likely to be rewarded by continued reliable performance. Why not take as good care of our own body when we have been inconvenienced by so-called death?

Bear in mind that we are not being theoretical. Lowered temperatures do slow down biological processes and much lowered temperatures do preserve living tissue for extended periods of time.

In your friendly neighborhood hospital there are surgeons cooling the sector of the body they will be operating on. There are refrigerators and freezers in abundance to prolong the shelf life of a great variety of organic materials. Organs that are intended for transplantation are kept at lowered temperatures as they are rushed from one unit to the next, or even across continents on a jet.

And what kind of sperm bank would it be that had no cooling system? Society has quickly accustomed itself to the reality of sperm banks. Although people have various attitudes toward the use of frozen sperm, this is an option that is being used every day, e.g., by couples who are unable to have a baby through the old-fashioned, pre-modern method. To repeat: there is nothing theoretical here: new lives have come into being through a not-very-complex technology that relies on the well demonstrated effectiveness of keeping cool. So: why not freeze the sperm donor and the sperm recipient as well when the need arises? All we need is reasonable care and larger refrigerators!

Actually, it is not refrigerators that are used, but stainless steel cylinders that are filled with liquid nitrogen. These vessels (also known as *dewars*) resemble oversized thermos bottles. With a little imagination, they also resemble space capsules, waiting instructions to soar off into the heavens. The vessels consist of two layers of stainless steel that are welded together. There is space between the inner and outer walls that is filled with multiple layers of foil and paper. This improves the insulating properties and eliminates heat leaks. The dewars that are used by cryonic societies today are so well insulated that only about 13 litres of liquid nitrogen are lost per day – that's 13 litres out of the 1600 litres in a storage vessel that holds four patients. The liquid nitrogen supply inside the dewar is replenished about once every 10 days. There is no electric power involved, therefore nothing to worry about from malfunction of electrical equipment or a loss of electric service.

How cold is it inside these vessels? About 196°C below zero. That's cold! At this temperature a person can be maintained for centuries (and probably millennia) with very little change. Time is effectively denied its opportunity to turn us into dust.

HOW TO CHOOSE LIFE OVER DEATH

Religious doctrines have asserted various claims about survival of death. Most religions are rather vague, however, when it come to the how-to-do-it part. Perhaps the most detailed guide comes from Buddhists who offer their version both of the dying process and of the early stages of being dead.[31] Success, however, is deemed possible only for the most spiritually enlightened individuals, and even then, the grand prize is not survival but a kind of benign oblivion. The person who wants to live and live well after death will find little guidance in the – sorry to use this word again – vague reassurances that increasingly fail to reassure even the clergy people who utter them.

Cryonic suspension breaks radically with this dulled and ineffective tradition. How to choose life over death? Follow these steps:

- Contact a cryonic society. If there is no cryonic society in your locality, contact one of the sources listed in the chapter notes for further information. If you are a resourceful and determined person, you might gather up some like-minded people and form your own society.
- Investigate carefully the entire picture, for example, financial arrangements, legal and regulatory issues, and the facilities, services, and track record of the organization you have contacted.
- If you choose the option of renewed life over death, discuss your wishes with your family, friends, and medical care providers. Misunderstandings and disagreements can make it difficult or even impossible to assure that cryonic suspension will be carried out.

I know very well that at the present time there is a rather limited availability of cryonic suspension services. It could be a frustrating experience to locate such a service as well as to persuade others to accept your decision. The only way these circumstances will change, however, is to have an increasing number of upright citizens such as yourself who are determined to remain upright after a horizontal episode!

We will suppose for the moment that there are no insurmountable practical obstacles to your choice of the cryonic option. This is what you will do and what will be done for you:

- You will sign an agreement with a responsible cryonic society. This agreement will include a financial arrangement that covers the services provided after death as well as maintenance and resuscitation. Ettinger[4] recently told me that his Cryonics Institute does the job for about $28,000, but this seems to be lower than the usual cost. You might have to figure on an investment of $50,000-$60,000 or even a bit more to assure your survival. How would you pay for it? In the United States this is generally accomplished by designating the required amount from the death benefits of a life insurance policy.

- You go on living, loving, learning, doing whatever it is that brings you satisfaction in this, your first life episode.
- Finally, many years later (or so we would hope), the end of this life is coming into view. You deal with end-of-life issues in a confident and competent manner. There are arrangements to be made and people from whom leave must be taken. This separation process may not be easy, but it will not be nearly as traumatic and depressing as for those who believe they will never again walk on this earth.
- You die. (Sorry about that – but delighted that I can show you how to overcome this inconvenience.)
- A physician decides that this is the moment to pronounce you dead. You are not breathing. Your heart is not beating. Even in this day of high-tech medicine, the absence of respiratory and cardiac activity is usually enough to convince the physician.
- Right by your side are emergency response technicians from the cryonics society. These people immediately start the process that will protect against tissue damage both in the short and the long term. In fact, with the permission of the medical team and hospital, they will have already reduced your body temperature through the use of ice packs.
- Now the technicians carry out a procedure that is crucial for your survival of death. A cryoprotective fluid is introduced into your body. This solution contains glycerol and several other ingredients that have been dissolved in water. Over a period of several hours this protective fluid will gradually replace body water. The purpose of this procedure is to prepare your body to withstand the liquid nitrogen freezing that is to follow. Again, there is a reasonable, though, of course, imperfect comparison with adding anti-freeze to our motor vehicles as winter approaches.
- It is necessary to transport this protective fluid throughout your body. How is this accomplished? By the same method that fluids and their nutrients are transported in your body today – through your circulation system. It is true that the circulation system shuts down at the time of your death, but it's all there, just requiring a little outside help to continue to do its job. This help is provided by a heart-lung machine, the same device that is used effectively in open heart surgery. Perfusion (as it is called) of the cryoprotective fluid can begin as soon as the heart-lung machine is operative.
- The technicians will be monitoring the procedure every step of the way to make sure that it is working properly. They will also be making notes on your condition to serve as a guide for those who will be resuscitating and treating you at a later time. Their observations will include direct observation of your brain through a scalp incision.
- You did very well. Those small incisions in your scalp and chest have been closed, but not before a temperature monitoring device has

been placed on the surface of your brain to provide information as additional procedures are carried out.

- Now you are ready for a deep cooling bath. You wear a plastic, double-layered bathing suit that is not entirely fashionable but which facilitates a safe and effective cool-down. The bathing fluid is silicone oil that is chilled to the desired temperature and adjusted as necessary through a pump system. You will remain in this bath until your temperature has been reduced to -79°C. This procedure usually takes between 36 and 48 hours.[5] If you want to take your rubber ducky with you into the tub you will have to make special arrangements; most find a new home for their faithful bath toys before matters reach this stage.

- After this refreshing bath has been completed you are quickly placed into a nest of two pre-cooled sleeping bags. You and your wraps are then placed inside an aluminum pod which is lowered into a cooldown vessel. If you thought it was cold before, think again: nitrogen vapor will now lower your temperature all the way down to -196°C. This is a slow procedure, but time is no longer a critical problem. You don't have to get up early and go to work on Monday. After about five days you and the liquid nitrogen will be at about the same temperature.

- After all these post-mortem activities it is time to rest. This you will do in the liquid nitrogen-filled storage vessel that you share with three other companionable souls. Fortunately, you will not be obliged to make small talk and listen to their little complaints about this and that. Instead you will wait without discomfort until the day that you return as a living, breathing, rejoicing survivor of your own 'death'.

This is only the beginning of the story. It is enough, however, to assure the open-minded reader that we do not have to enter the oven or the grave when a state of 'deadness' interrupts life. Present technology, based on well established bio-physical principles, can keep us ready for renewed life. I would like to continue with this scenario, but the rules of engagement require that we pause to give our wordy – I mean, worthy – skeptic an opportunity to make another fool of himself.

THE CRITIC'S RESPONSE: REPLACING REALITY WITH FANTASY

I enjoy fantasy as much as the next person. Through the centuries storytellers have been scaring people out of their wits with horror stories and charming each of them with beguiling tales in which hero and heroine live happily ever after. Technology has not changed things as much as it might seem. We are still being frightened or charmed by stories that are not much different in basic plot and characters from the folk tales that have been invented in many societies at many times. We just think they are different because science and technology (very loosely interpreted) have replaced ogres, witches, wizards, and incantations. Actually, if we look closely enough we can still see those demonic and droll characters peering at us through their high-tech disguises. Yesterday's evil magician became today's mad scientist without losing a beat.

SLEEPING BEAUTIES, ONE AND ALL

Fantasies must fulfil some universal human needs because we keep demanding and producing them. So be it. There are occasions, however, when we must put away childish things. There are occasions when we must think and act like adults. We are confronting one of those occasions now. The cryonic fantasy attempts to replace the reality of one life and one death with a variation on the sleeping beauty theme. Those who mistake this fantasy for reality are in danger of trivializing both this one life that we do have and the finality and inevitability of the one death that concludes this life.

The passing moments of our lives bring us all that we will experience as joy, sorrow, hope, fear, and insight. Many people already devise strategies for escaping the responsibility of being. These are people who choose to evade the opportunities and dangers of the moment by drinking themselves blotto, merging their personalities with the characters that flicker across the television tube hour after hour, and in many other ways try to subdue the pangs of being a mortal who is living and dying at this moment among other mortals.

The new version of sleeping beauty is well designed to appeal to people who, in one way or another, are already sleeping through their lives. I prefer the old version with its core of psychological reality and its surface of romantic yearnings and fulfilment. When the developmental clock reaches the appointed hour, young females may indeed awaken from their suspension in innocent dreams to the reality of love and sexual fulfilment. Until that time arrives, it is safer to remain locked in a dream world. Prince Charming also has roots in reality. Young males have long been expected to go out into the world to prove themselves and, unless their fathers wore crowns, to make their fortunes.

The cryonic version speaks of alienation rather than romance, adventure and fulfilment. The real-life parallels are of a depressing sort: coma, persistent vegetative state, catatonic stupor, dementia, and the like. The awakening – if there were an awakening – would not be a rebirth or transfiguration in any meaningful sense of the terms. A selfish, routined, frustrated, dreary person would emerge (if at all) as the same selfish-routined, frustrated person, ready to make life miserable again for others as well as himself. None of these defrosted beauties would return to the world with the freshness, innocence, and potential of a baby. None would be greeted by a Prince or Princess Charming with a castle on the distant hill and the promise of a transfigured life. The defrostee would have to settle for a squad of technicians, to be followed by battalions of doctors, nurses, lawyers, tax collectors, and feuding bureaucrats with their endless supply of forms and procedures. One look at this crew and sleeping beauty might well decide to nap for another few centuries!

And what a gift to bequeath to future generations! In Gulliver's visit to the land of the Luggnaggians[6] he learned that every now and then an immortal is born in their midst. Soon he learned that these blessed immortals, the Struldbrugs, were

> not only opinionative, peevish, covetous, morose, vain, talkative, but uncapable of friendship, and dead to all natural affection ... they were despised and hated by all sorts of people. (p. 233)

It would not be a very sporting proposition to burden posterity with hold-overs from previous generations who were self-centered enough to insist on another boring life after their original boring life.

There is nothing in the universal human condition that resonates with the preservation and (supposed) resuscitation of a person who has already had a life. All the traditional alternatives have a more authentic grip on some facet of the psyche. *Return to the earth after enjoying the miracle of life?* That makes sense, and certainly corresponds to our observations of Nature's way. *Move on to a transcendental new realm of being that some call heaven?* That idea is certainly close to the hearts of many people. *Return to life in a different form as part of a vast cosmic cycle?* Here is an idea that has been found so appealing by many Westerners, that it can no longer be considered the exclusive property of Asian believers.

By contrast, cryonic suspension is a contrived scenario and a really, really bad scenario at that. It is suitable for science-fantasy movies, but hardly for real people in their real lives.

THE COLD TRUTH ABOUT SURVIVAL THROUGH CRYONICS

Nobody has been resuscitated from the liquid nitrogen freezer. And nobody ever will. The movement had an early rallying cry: "Freeze – wait – reanimate!" We are still waiting. We might as well be waiting for the equestrian statue in the public park to snort, kick up its heels, and gallop off to its next adventure.

The cryonic scenario has been promulgated for some time now. An entire generation has popped into the world and reached adulthood since Ettinger's best-seller appeared. Every now and then the media rediscovers cryonics and does a video or print piece on it. People involved in the cryonic movement have been more than willing to provide information and offer their services if desired.

SOULS ON ICE: WHO NEEDS AN AFTERLIFE?

So what has actually happened? About 50 people have been placed in cryonic suspension.[4] Only 50! Millions and millions of people have died since the prospect of immortality was described. Many of these people knew that they did not have long to live. And many could have well afforded the financial investment. The late Jack Benny had a characteristic reply to the cliché, "You can't take it with you." "Hmmm – then I won't go!" Wealthy people should have welcomed this opportunity to keep their fortune by transforming death into a mere interlude. The cost of cryonic suspension – perhaps even with one's very own storage chamber, not to be shared with ordinary riff-raff – would be less than they might spend on a party or lose at the gaming table. Furthermore, with sound investments, think how much money would accumulate between the freeze and the reanimation! Never would the concept of cold, hard cash have been so literally realized!

The superwealthy, the wealthy, and the pretty-damn-well-off could have chosen the cryonic alternative in droves. It might have become just the thing to do among the elite and fashionable. "Yes, my dear. Last year we (yawn) went around the world again. Now we are making plans to go someplace else. Everybody's doing it – care to come along?"

Some of the more significant developments are those that do not happen. Why have so many people chosen to survive their deaths when there was no financial barrier to doing so? This question takes on a broader dimension when we remind ourselves that a great many people have gone to extremes to save their lives by other means. These stories are often quite sad. The father of one of my friends rejected further medical treatment when the doctor could not promise that he would recover from the cancer that had reached an advanced stage. He went off by himself to an island 'clinic' whose brochures promised complete healing, and without surgery or other unpleasant treatments. After a brief period of feeling better, he became violently ill, suffered great pain, and died far from home. In the process he essentially bankrupted the family by spending every dollar he could draw upon or borrow. Unfortunately, this is not an unusual story. I mention it here to emphasize how remarkable it is that cryonic suspension has failed to attract a sizeable number of customers. People who were desperate to try anything did not try cyronics. People who grasped at a slight hope of survival did not sign up for a procedure that has been presented as the sound application of proven scientific principles. If the cryonic movement has been unable to persuade those who are in most peril for their lives, who most intensely seek a way to avoid death, and who can well afford the investment – well, who can it persuade?

Most people know that the cryonic promise cannot be fulfilled. They recognize it for what it is: a fantasy based on a little clinical experience, a little science, and a lot of wishful thinking.

Scientists, too. If there were anything to cryonic preservation and resuscitation, why, we would have to beat scientists off with a stick.

What fame! What fortune! What power! Why would scientists muddle around with routine projects if there were a chance – just a chance – that they might make a crucial contribution to survival of death! Furthermore, how easy it should be to cadge money out of philanthropists and foundations to support their research! People have thrown money at dubious projects before – and, occasionally, with success. Despite years of slim results, researchers into ESP and related hokey-pokey have attracted funding. Scientists with strong credentials could develop project proposals that would require serious consideration by funding sources – if these scientists believed that cryonic preservation and resuscitation had a reasonable chance of proving out.

This has not happened. Relatively few scientists have aligned themselves with the cryonic cause. I have not been able to find any long-term, systematic research projects conducted by qualified scientists and devoted to the testing of the cryonic scenario. One can only conclude that members of the various scientific disciplines that bear on cryonic preservation and resuscitation do not believe it is worth their time and efforts.

A FEW FACTS, STRETCHED INTO A FABLE

The cryonic scenario does build on the uncontested fact that temperature has an effect on biological processes. Lower temperatures do slow the rate of the organism's electro-chemical processes and retard the growth of micro-organisms. In some circumstances and within limits a hypothermic state can help organisms to survive. There are documented cases of humans and various animals who were revived after being found chilled and unresponsive, e.g. caught in a snow drift. Alert physicians are careful not to pronounce a person dead prematurely if this person has been found in a hypothermic state. We do not want to forget, though, that some of these recovered victims would not have been in such peril in the first place had they not been exposed to excessive cold! Hypothermia is a well-known stress factor and, overall, probably does a lot more harm than good to flora and fauna.

It is also a fact that we place meats and some other organic perishables in a low temperature environment such as a refrigerator or freezer. This practice does retard deterioration. We do not ask nearly as much from a frozen sausage, however, as we do from a sleeping beauty in the liquid nitrogen dewar. The sausage only has to look fresh and taste good. We do not expect it to recall childhood memories, learn new information, engage in complex conversations, and so forth. Still less do we expect the sausage to reconstitute itself as its original ingredients: a pig and a cow, or, more exotically, the combination pig-cow it had become by the time it reached the grinder.

From the defrosted person we expect a nervous system that has been exquisitely preserved – a nervous system that can wriggle its left big toe when it intends to do so, decode incoming verbal information, distinguish between dream and reality, and calculate the size of tip to leave on the restaurant table. Freezing will keep a sausage a sausage. It will also preserve a sleeping beauty for some time, but as a sausage-brain. Everyday life poses challenges enough for the incredibly complex yet highly vulnerable human nervous system. Sleep deprivation, noise, and medication side-effects are only a few of the circumstances that can interfere with the brain's ability to cope with internal and external affairs. Sleeping beauty might still have a well-turned ankle, but not a functioning brain that can hear music and set feet to dancing.

What proof do we have that brain structure and function is preserved at extremely low temperatures for even a minute, let alone for many years? And what proof do we have that vital structures are not destroyed both before and during the freezing process? And – excuse the repetition – what proof do we have that the attempted resuscitation will not inflict further damage?

Preservation of souls on ice happens occasionally in novels and films. My favorite example was provided by the celebrated illusionist and escape artist, Harry Houdini. He revived from his entombment in a block of ice to experience further adventures. Unfortunately, this happened not in the midst of his actual adventurous life, but in his awkward (1922) silent movie, *The Man from Beyond*. The master of illusion and escape, like today's scientists, and most other thinking people, knew very well that only in fantasy can we awaken from frozen death to passionate life.

THE ADVOCATE

Our skeptic has come through again with another dismal performance. He may be pathetic in his arguments, but, at least, he is reliably pathetic. It is possible that he did have a thought in there some place, all but obscured by the ranting and rhapsodizing. I think – and don't you agree? – that he was asking for more information. This I will be happy to provide. Beyond what we have already covered, there is evidence to support the thesis of survival through cryonic preservation and resuscitation. Indeed, there is much more evidence than can be reported here. Here are some examples cited by Gregory M. Fahy, Ph.D., an internationally renowned researcher in the area of mammalian cryobiology.[7]

● Researchers have found that golden hamsters can make full neurological recoveries after 60 per cent of the water in their brains has been frozen. Hamsters are mammals, of course, and so are we.

243

SOULS ON ICE: WHO NEEDS AN AFTERLIFE?

- Cat brains have been perfused with glycerol – the cryoprotective agent and then slowly frozen and kept in storage for up to 203 days. After thawing, these brains regained spontaneous electrical activity and individual cells and tissues functioned in a vigorous manner. The electroencephalic (EEG) readings showed a strong though somewhat slowed pattern. The brains looked to be viable in both structure and function. Needless to say, but perhaps we need to say this anyhow: dead brains do not produce EEG patterns other than the flatline.

- Follow-up studies with cat brains confirmed that preservation occurred when temperatures were dropped to the dry ice level (-79°C). Tissues in the cerebral cortex (the brainiest part of the brain) seemed to be intact, as was the case with other central nervous system structures such as the hippocampus.

- The brain shrinks when it is frozen, but this does not cause structural damage. In addition to evidence from animal studies, Fahey cites his own observations of the glycerol-perfused brain of an adult woman, Mrs Dora Kent. Her brain tissues were found to be intact despite their shrinkage.

- Neurosurgeons sometimes have to remove small sections of the brain in order to reach tumors. What would happen if we froze these sections of cerebral cortex, taken from living people? Such studies have been done. Furthermore, the investigators also obtained samples of rat brains to freeze and thaw for comparison purposes. After thawing, the brain tissue was analyzed with particular attention to the preservation of synaptic function. As you probably know, synapses are crucial to the transmission of electrochemical impulses from one cell to the next. Synaptic integrity is required for communication within the brain and throughout the body. Substantial synaptic function was detected in the brain tissue of both humans and rats. For example, in the human brain tissue, oxygen uptake was 78 per cent and 91 per cent of the protein was recovered. Human brains generally did better than rat brains in demonstrating continued ability to function. These results were even more impressive because an inferior cryoprotectant (sucrose) had been used. Does brain function survive freezing? It does.

- Brain banks are now an important resource for neuroscientists. Fahey[7] notes that: "Sections or sub-regions of post-mortem human brains, frozen rapidly several hours after death, are sent to medical researchers who analyze these brains for neurotransmitters, proteins, enzyme activity, lipids, nucleic acids, and even histology. There would be no reason for such banks if no molecular or structural preservation were achieved by freezing."

Here, then, is evidence that speaks for itself. And Fahey speaks for the evidence:

The scientific literature allows no conclusion other than that brain structure and even many brain functions are likely to be reasonably well preserved by freezing in the presence of cryoprotective agents, especially glycerol in high concentrations. Thus, cryonics' premise of preservation would seem to be well supported by existing cryobiological knowledge. (p. 13)

FROM PRESERVATION TO RESUSCITATION: WELCOME NANOTECHNOLOGY!

Now let us anticipate the skeptic's next grumble by discussing the second step in survival of death. Bodies survive freezing very well, thank you, especially when protected by glycerol. It is not only possible but probable that even more effective cryoprotective agents will be developed in the future. The brain is not the weakest but the hardiest organ. It is made to survive. The findings we have just surveyed are very much in keeping with general advances in understanding brain function. The more that neuroscientists learn about the brain, the more they stand in wonder at its resourcefulness, versatility, and self-protective strategies. A good brain is hard to keep down.

Can the preserved body with its preserved brain be restored to full functioning? Yes, it can. We have already seen that human and other mammalian brain tissue retain function after freezing and thawing. It is for a very good reason, however, that there has been no rush to thaw out the first cryonically preserved man or woman. The 50 or so bold 'souls on ice' are there because something went wrong. They were felled by a cardiovascular condition, aggressive cancer, or one of the other common causes of death. There is no point in simply putting them through resuscitation procedures: it would be going back to square one without having accomplished anything of real value.

The goal is not to prove that structure and function can be preserved through long-term cryonic storage and resuscitation. The goal is to escort a person through the so-called state of death to vital and healthy life. The real task, then, is to devise techniques for fixing what went wrong in the first place.

It is one of the (all too few) glories of the modern era that people have been given reprieves from death by new treatment modalities. Lest we forget, many conditions that are now relieved by routine surgery were considered inoperable. A muscular surgeon might hack off a diseased limb quickly enough to save the patient's life, but taking the scalpel to the chest or abdomen was a gilt-edged invitation to fatal infections. Hormone replacement therapy, pacemakers and a growing arsenal of new medications are among other treatment modalities that save lives every day. Modern medicine is sometimes chastised as being overly aggressive, as well as overly expensive. This aggressiveness, though, has led to significant advances throughout a broad spectrum of life-threatening conditions. These advances will continue independent of the cryonic movement, but will also continue to provide more 'fix-its' for those who are awaiting resuscitation.

Year after year there will further progress in curing what ails – and kills – us. This means that year after year more people in cryostasis will be eligible for treatment. But that's only part of the story. We are on the verge of a major breakthrough in repairing defective bodies. This breakthrough goes by the name of *nanotechnology*. Although the potentials are huge, we should be thinking small, very small. A *micro*circuit (known more popularly as a microcomputer) is plenty small. Its components are measured in millionths of a meter. These tiny devices are still revolutionizing communication, education, production, distribution, and virtually every corner of modern life. Next to *nano*technology, however, the microcircuit looks like a behemoth. Nanotechnology operates on a scale a thousand times smaller than a millionth of a meter. We would not want to lose one ("Dear, did you see my nanocircuit? I put it down some place...")

Nanotechnology exists today and is rapidly developing along many fronts. Its most profound realm of application will be within our own bodies. Nanotech units have been described as mini-factories or machines. They can be placed inside blood vessels and other structures. Through their sophisticated computer intelligence capabilities, the nanounits locate and repair obstructions, ruptures and other defects. Nanotech units are not necessarily machines, however, in the usual sense of the term. They may also be organic material that has been 'taught' how to make house calls on ailing body structures. A complete toolbox of nanotechnology will include both miniature machines and organic agents such as protein molecules and enzymes. Biochemical engineers are already hard at work in creating the nanomachines that will make even more sophisticated nanomachines.

K. Eric Drexler has been educating the public on nanotechnology through his pioneering book, *Engines of Creation*[8] and other writings. He points out that genetic engineers have already "programmed bacteria to make proteins ranging from human growth hormone to rennin, an enzyme used in making cheese. The pharmaceutical company, Eli Lilly is now marketing Humulin, human insulin molecules made by bacteria." It may be difficult to get used to the idea that "bacteria are our friends," but this is the coming reality.

In devising nanotechnology, scientists have an excellent model to consult: nature. Protein machines directed by RNA programs are what keep us going now. Scientists have learned a lot more about nature's own nanotechnology in recent years. This information will make it possible to do some things that nature never quite got around to – including the repair of life-threatening defects and damage. Nano-machines will remove arterial blockages, restore injured cell membranes, deactivate viruses, and destroy cancerous growths without harming healthy tissue ... and so forth. Because these are computer-guided machines they will be well instructed and focused in carrying out their tasks, therefore holding undesired side-effects to a minimum. As you know, most existing treatment procedures have side-effects, some of which can be very serious. The risk of side-effects will be much smaller with those clever little nanotech units on the job.

Drexler again, and reporting on what has already been accomplished:

> *Nanomachines floating in sterile test tubes, free of cells, have been made to perform all the basic sorts of activities that they perform inside living cells... Life is special in structure, in behavior, and in what it feels like from the inside to be alive, yet the laws of nature that govern the machinery of life also govern the rest of the universe. (p. 17)*

Drexler asks us to imagine a person who has been placed in a prolonged state of inanimation (his term for this is *biostasis*). A physician who is not versed in nanotechnology would quickly determine to his or her satisfaction that this is a corpse, not a person. Bad things would then happen. The competent physician, however, will check to see if this is the right time to begin resuscitation. Perhaps, for example, this person has been placed in biostasis in preparation for a space voyage of many light-years and therefore should be maintained in the present condition until the destination has been reached. When it is time for resuscitation:

> *Repair machines enter the patient's tissues... repair any damaged molecules and structures, and restore normal concentrations of salts, blood sugar, and so forth... The interrupted metabolic processes resume, the patient yawns, stretches, sits up, thanks the doctor, checks the date, and walks out the door. (p.112)*

Nanotechnology will continue to advance because its potential is so great in many spheres of application. Biomedical applications are already in process. Cryonicists do not have to plead with scientists to explore this exciting frontier, nor come up with the funding. Basic research in biomedical nanotechnology has a strong momentum that will provide much of the knowledge and equipment needed for resuscitation from cryostasis. (I use this term, cryostasis, because it refers to the specific form of biostasis that we are dealing with here. Theoretically, one might develop any number of techniques for suspending biological processes; cryonic preservation is an existing technology that has already proven itself.)

We will need research and training projects to apply bionano-technology effectively in the resuscitation of people from cryostasis. It would be irresponsible to begin the resuscitation phase until all the technology is in place and adequate testing and training has been carried out. When we come *that* close to thawing out the first man or woman, you can be sure that there will be widespread public interest and all the funding that is needed!

There is a kind of psychological switch that needs to be turned before the general public and even the general scientific enterprise realizes the potential of the cryonic alternative. Few people know the facts that I have summarized for you here: these facts are not taught in our schools, even to people in the allied health fields. The popularity of cryonics in fiction and films has led many to believe that it is just a script writer's invention, like cone-headed aliens from outer space.

This switch-on will probably also require the participation of a few highly visible people. Admit it or not, most people are afraid to depart from their accustomed ways. Almost every technological innovation, even the most modest ones, had to make it through a period of fear, doubt, and resentment. People are also very stubborn (not you and I, of course... *other* people!). This unwillingness to change attitudes and behaviors extends to life-and-death matters. Consider, for example, buckling up the seat belt in the car or truck, or wearing a helmet when riding a motorcycle. In the United States there have been both public information campaigns and legislation intended to reduce accident fatalities by persuading people to apply these simple safety measures. And every day hospitals and morgues receive the bodies of those who had remained unpersuaded. If so many people decide against protecting their lives through such simple means, then think of how many more also recoil from the less familiar option of cryostasis.

This herd mentality exercises an inhibiting influence over those who take a real interest in the possibility. "What would people think? Will I be ridiculed? Will my friends and family be uncomfortable with this idea?" These are not unrealistic fears. People do tend to think that other people are 'weird' when they pick up on a new idea. Furthermore, most people continue to avoid as much as possible the anxiety of thinking about dying and death. The person who talks seriously about cryonic preservation and resuscitation is likely to raise their listeners' anxiety level. "Don't talk about such things! What are you trying to do – remind me that I'm mortal, that one day I will be shovelled into the ground or cooked in an oven? It's not just that I don't want to think about cryonics: I don't want to think about any of that stuff!"

This reluctance to try something new and this determination to ignore good advice can vanish like a puff of smoke when the public is awed by celebrity models. Celebrity emulation – or worship – has both its positive and negative aspects. A confused and depressed person who already has suicidal thoughts might take lethal action after the well-publicized suicide of another confused and depressed person who happened to be a celebrity. Millions of people took up cigarette smoking because it was such a cool and sexy thing to do – like the stars do in the movies. Getting high on drugs also became more of an

SOULS ON ICE: WHO NEEDS AN AFTERLIFE?

attraction as it became known that some celebrities were making this a way of life (and, all too often, their way of death as well).

Celebrities can also be positive models. For example, celebrities who have devoted themselves to preserving the earth's environment and resources have attracted others to these worthy causes. The celebrity athletes and actors who first spoke openly of their alcohol or drug addictions and entered rehabilitation programs were positive models for others who had been reluctant to deal with their similar problems.

Walt Disney's name is often mentioned in connection with cryonics. People who know very little about cryonics will ask, "Say, didn't Disney get himself frozen?" This question is asked with genuine interest. You can bet that there would be an excited response if I could reply: "Yes, he did, and we expect to resuscitate him to direct *Fantasia II*." This would not be an accurate reply, however. The great animator did think seriously about reanimation. It did not work out for a variety of reasons, including opposition by many of the people in Disney's life. Too bad, don't you think? What cinematic wonders might be in store for future generations if his experience and imagination could have been applied to the new technologies.

What we most want to notice, though, is the curiosity and excitement that has been aroused merely by the rumor that one celebrity has been placed in cryostasis! Other celebrities have also considered the idea but also have encountered opposition from family and friends and the medical profession. For every person who has entered cryostasis there are many others who were headed in that direction but frustrated, sometimes at the last moment, by the unwillingness of physicians or hospital officials to participate. This situation will change and will change radically when a few famous and respected people enter cryostasis with full media coverage. These people will earn fame well beyond their present celebrity status as the brave souls who showed the way to survival.

Shucks all get-out, pardner: if John Wayne had done it, wanna-be cowboys and cowgirls would have been standing in line at the old cryonics corral, asking if they can take their hats and spurs along with them when they hit that long trail to forever. He might even have favored us with a little song:

Oh, bury me not on the lone prairie
Where the squirrels scowl
And the bumble-bee
And not in a mall
With a stone on my head
Heck, don't bury me at all,
Cause I ain't dead!

Well, pardner, time to mosey down to the bunkhouse for a little grub and shut-eye while that shifty-eyed varmint has his next say.

THE CRITIC

Has he really gone? Is it safe again to have a little intelligent conversation around here? I would characterize his arguments as half-baked, but perhaps half-thawed would be more appropriate. What he lacked in substance was more than compensated by length. We will be brief because we will deal only in basic facts. And we promise: no stupid songs.

- *Few are frozen; none are revived.* All our cryonicist's antics and speculations have not altered these basic facts. There is absolutely no evidence that a human can be placed in cryostasis and return as a human.
- *The laboratory studies have used only a few animals of a few species and have numerous flaws and limitations.* This statement is not intended to discredit the researchers whose work is repeatedly cited by cryonicists. They have made a reasonable beginning. However, the available data are neither as broad nor as deep as cryonicists would like us to believe. The 'star' document appears to be the literature review presented by Fahey, whose credentials we will not challenge. Let us read again one of his key statements, and then go on to his very next sentence:

  > *Thus, cryonics' premise of preservation would seem to be well supported by existing cryobiological knowledge. This is not to say that cryonics may work. (p.13)*

  Fahey's caution is well taken. Cryonic preservation to the extent required for resuscitation of an intact human being has not been proven, nor are the available findings anywhere close to establishing the case.
- *Nanotechnology is positioned to generate unpredictable and catastrophic outcomes.* It is an exciting line of development and no doubt eventually will have many positive uses. We would be exceedingly naive, though, to suppose that it will not also introduce many problems of its own. We have already had enough experience with computer-driven processes to recognize the dangers. I recall seeing nearly a hundred students on the verge of heat exhaustion – and nearly melting myself – when the *heating* system came on. I should explain that this was during an Arizona summer in which temperatures were soaring about 110°F on the outside. It turned out that a new and improved computer program had just been installed, and this new and improved program decided that what we needed was more heat instead of cooling. No doubt you can add your own close encounters of a frustrating kind with the wonderful world of computers. Nanotechnology may prove to be even more wonderful, and, therefore, a source of even more wonderful stress, chaos, and catastrophe.

SOULS ON ICE: WHO NEEDS AN AFTERLIFE?

One small example: the ventilator has become a familiar device in hospitals. It supports respiration when patients are unable to breathe for themselves and, as such, can be very useful. One of its drawbacks, however, is that ventilator support can suppress the person's own respiratory impulses. A person who is kept too long on a ventilator loses the ability to breathe spontaneously. This fact is well known by nurses and physicians. Multiply this known fact by the many unknown of nanotechnological invasion. How and how drastically will those clever little machines disrupt the body's – and the mind's – ability to do things its own way? Nobody has the answer to this question and few have even thought about it.

- *Cryonic preservation cannot begin until the person is dead.* 'dead' as in 'not alive'. That is the law. That is the law that prevails in all jurisdictions. To disobey that law is to expose oneself to a homicide indictment. The odds against revival of an intact human from cold storage are increased by the damage that occurs during the final phase of life and during the interval between death and freezing. In practice, this may be a considerable interval – not the immediate response scenario that has been described to us. People have to die in the right place at the right time. There needs to be perfect communication among all the professionals and family members involved in the process. And – sorry to bring this up – if an autopsy is conducted, you canpretty well forget about that fabled day when the patient "yawns, stretches, sits up, thanks the doctor, checks the date, and walks out the door." Autopsies are mandatory under some circumstances of death, and may be requested at any death.

Such are the facts, to cite only the most obvious. Let us now consider, again very briefly, some of the reasons why cryonic preservation and resuscitation would be a really bad idea even if it did work.

First, this venture would not lead to survival of death. At most, it would lead to temporary survival of one death. What is to be done when our sleeping beauty dies again? Go through all that nonsense again? We would have either one encore post-mortem appearance or a repeating cycle. It is very likely that the cryostasis and nanotech trick can be performed only once per customer. If so, people should not be too quick to throw away their prayer books and abandon their traditional faiths. They are not paying for immortality or even for an extended return engagement: just another lifetime, and a lifetime that already has some mileage on it. John Wayne would not spring out of the freezer as a robust young dude, but struggle out painfully as the grizzled elder he had become. We would be better off enjoying the re-runs of his films rather than the expensive re-run of a rapidly aging defrostee.

Given the most favorable attitudinal and financial climate, there will be a limit to how much of this nonsense society will tolerate. Let's not deceive ourselves into supposing that people will be thawed out *ad infinitum, ad nauseam.* Wouldn't you think twice even about putting that thawed sausage back into the freezer?

Next, we must factor in the ugly effects of discrimination. I will speak only for the United States, but I am well aware that fear and hatred divides the citizens of many other nations. No country has the monopoly on racism, sexism, as well as religious bigotry and persecution. Universally, the Haves consider themselves morally superior to the Have Not's and are determined to keep the good life for themselves. In the medical field we can already see the conflict between the principles of democracy and compassion on the one hand and discrimination and elitism on the other. Who is to receive the opportunity to have their health restored through an expensive treatment procedure? Not everybody. Usually: only 'the right kind of people', i.e. white-faced upper class. Cryonic preservation and resuscitation would add another dimension to this conflict. Every time a fancy up-town person is given the opportunity for another ride on the merry-go-round there will be anguish and rage among the folks who live down-town and do not receive adequate resources to protect their health and well-being in their one and only life. I don't think we need one more way to oppress and enrage the good people who do not happen to live on easy street.

Now consider, if you will, the overall impact on global population. Experts have been telling us for years that we are on course for catastrophe: too many people, not enough resources. The world's forests have already been seriously depleted. Arable land has been abused and now longer provides sustenance. The overpopulation issue has been well documented and is a major concern for international bodies such as the United Nations. Unless effective measures are taken, the quality of life will decline precipitously for everybody. The toys that amuse people in high-tech societies and the higher attainments of culture and enlightenment will perish under global stress and hunger.

And to this alarming situation we are asked to add people who should have been dead and buried! Are we to have a new war between generations, literally, a war for survival? Are we that greedy for life? Are we determined to be the first generation in history that refuses to relinquish its place to future generations? Let there be no mistake about it: there is already fierce competition for resources, including food, water, energy, health care, and desirable habitat. Cryonic resuscitation would be a nightmare of corpses risen from their ice chambers like a legion of vampires to suck nourishment that belongs to the living. *And for what?* What is so wonderful about the present generation? What have we accomplished as individuals and as a generation that deserves perpetuation beyond the normal span of life?

The more promises, the greater the improbability and the more hideous the nightmare. Tell us, friend, about your freeze-dried shrunken heads and your hyperfantasy of perpetual youth. Tell us the rest of the story and see how many people are willing to suspend their good common-sense to convert to the cryonic cause.

It was natural for Walt Disney to be fascinated by cryonic preservation and resuscitation. He was responsive to fantasy themes. But he also knew the difference between fantasy and reality. Disney was right to consider cryonics, and he was right to reconsider and to allow his life's work rather than a frozen corpse to survive as his gift to posterity.

A LITTLE HONESTY AND A LITTLE COURAGE WILL GO A LONG WAY

Our skeptic is probably a great success in scaring children around a campfire. This tactic will not work, though, for people who, along with their critical intelligence, possess a full quota of honesty and courage. Moral cowardice prevents many people from admitting to desires that are natural to all living creatures. Life has the urge to continue. Life abhors death. Administer truth serum, and the same people would admit: "I want to live in a healthy and vigorous condition for as long as I can. If it were possible to continue to live in this condition indefinitely, of course I would prefer that to having but a few decades to enjoy, and those decades increasingly afflicted by the ageing process."

There is no theme more ancient and universal than the quest for prolonged or renewed youth and freedom from the death sentence.[9] The quest that started with rituals and invocations and continued with alchemists is now on its way to actualization through the sophisticated research of geneticists and gerontologists. Should we tell scientists to abandon their laboratories because we do not want to extend our lives? And because we would rather continue to grow old than to live in youthful health and well-being? Science is closer than ever to gaining control over the aging process. Isn't it about time to admit that this is precisely what we want? A little honesty and a little courage can go a long way.

Who complained when public health and medical advances conquered such scourges of childhood as scarlet fever, small pox, and diphtheria? Who argued that it is wrong to prevent deaths from malaria, tuberculosis, and polio? We have accepted medical victories and asked for more. Why stop now? Why suddenly twist ourselves into knots with so-called moral questions that we have not raised in a thousand other circumstances? A little honesty. R.C.W. Ettinger, the person with whom the cryonic movement is most identified, puts it this way:

> On the personal level – the only one that really counts – most of us will choose to save our lives and those of our families, and worry about consequences later. Suppose your daughter has a fever. The physician says she has a potentially fatal infection, but an antibiotic will take care of it. Then he stands there. You ask him what he is waiting for.

SOULS ON ICE: WHO NEEDS AN AFTERLIFE?

*He replies that you must consider the consequences of saving this child.
Her survival would add to population pressures in this crowded city,
increase the drain on limited resources, etc. Just about this time, you
hit him with a blunt instrument and give the child the antibiotic
yourself!* [4]

Ettinger also points out that cryonics will be a minor factor in
population pressures. Lifespans are already increasing throughout
much of the world and adaptations have started to take place. He cites
the example of the Japanese sharply reducing their birth rate within a
single generation. Furthermore, technological solutions will be found
for many of the world's problems. In light of all the scientific and
technical advances being made across the board, this is a particularly
foolish time to be pessimistic. A little courage.

Yes, we are envisioning more than survival of one death. We are
envisioning people emerging from cryonic preservation not only with
their 'fatal' illnesses cured, but with nanogenetic engineering that will
restore and preserve youthful, healthy functioning. This is one of the
reasons why there is no rush toward resuscitation. Why settle for just
one more go-around with life when we will be able to take advantage of
scientific advances to return as new and improved models? Bear in
mind that research to prevent and reverse aging is a high priority today
and would continue to be so even without the cryonics option. Aging
will be defeated, and the 'sleeping beauties' will then indeed awaken
more beautiful than ever from a spectacularly refreshing sleep.

Freeze-dried shrunken heads? I have good news for our faithful
skeptic. He is a particularly well qualified candidate for this procedure
because he is obviously functioning with a head that is already pre-
shrunken (perhaps through all that cold, rigorous logic).

Neurosuspension, as it is called, is a reality. The head of Mrs Dora
Kent (previously mentioned) is now in cryostasis, prepared by her
cryonicist son. Preservation and storage of the head is less expensive
than full body preservation and, of course, takes less space as well.
Some cryonic societies offer the neurosuspension option; others have
been reluctant to do so because they fear adverse public reaction. Those
who are in head-only cryostasis will have to wait a little longer for
resuscitation. Scientists have already learned how to encourage nature
to replicate organic living material by use of genetically programmed
instructions. Further research will make it possible to replicate the
entire body. Preservation of the brain with its individual memory store
and personality will make it possible to provide the self with a brand
new body. People who are not willing to wait for the perfection of this
biotechnology will probably want to settle for good old-fashioned
resuscitation of brain and body together. As more people embrace one
or the other form of cryonic suspension, the legal, medical, and other
difficulties encountered today will dissipate.

At the very least, cryonic revival and rejuvenation is an authentic possibility that has secure roots in scientific knowledge and technology. Being dead and staying dead does not offer much of an alternative for those who are willing to risk a little for the potential of enormous gain.

Stay cool. See you thawsday!

ALL TOGETHER NOW

Advocate and skeptic take this occasion to share in the following thought. *The very idea of cryonic preservation and resuscitation challenges our fundamental values.* What is it that we really want and what is it that we really deserve from an afterlife? And from this life? Would continued survival on earth be preferable to an eternity in heaven, hell, or other territories unknown? If there is a transcendental afterlife awaiting us, would it then be a mistake to prolong our existence here? And is it probable that we would only screw up prolonged and regenerated life on earth? Some people hope fervently for survival of death in order to make up somehow for their failures and foibles in their present lives. Wouldn't this same attitude also dominate cryonic-style survival?

Dr James H. Bedford, the first human placed in cryostasis under controlled conditions, may or may not return to the golf course to work on his putting. Dora Kent's head may or may not preside over a vigorous young body for which she must find the latest fashions. Nevertheless, the prospect of virtual immortality right here on earth is altering our view of what we really want and what price we are willing to pay for it.

9

A NEW DAWN

Perhaps you are as ready as I am to set aside the advocate, the critic, and their strenuous contentions. They did their jobs. We now have a better command of the evidence and arguments that can be brought to bear on both sides of the survival question. What we need at this point is not another round of controversies to keep us in doubt, but a way of thinking about death that will help us to move through our lives as whole and confident people. Here are some thoughts to consider.

ON THE GOODNESS OF THE GOOD LIFE

The value of a life does not depend on its duration. A long life is not experienced as a better life if it is beset by regrets, bitterness, and suffering. A short life can be aglow with excitement and radiate its beauty to others. Even the longest life is lived one moment at a time.

Imaginative literature and mythology have given us powerful examples of those who were unable to feel content with the mortal lives they had been given. One after another, they fell into despair, became caricatures of themselves, or monsters to others.[1] For example, Dorian Gray became a thing of evil, repulsive to himself and unable to enjoy his wished-for perpetual youth.

With this perspective in mind, we can see that goodness in life does not require the guarantee of a life after death. It is quite within our capacity to appreciate what life has to offer each day... the majesty and unanswerability of a sudden storm... the delicacy with which a cat grooms itself... the warm smile from a person who understands you before you have said what you thought you needed to say...

It is the same with morality. Is my 'goodness' only the fear of punishment for transgression? Does it take the promise of eternal bliss and the fear of eternal suffering to get me to behave like a responsible person? I certainly hope not! What are we to say of those who believe that we need the belief in an afterlife to be good little boys and girls while we are here? Perhaps the kindest thing we can say is that they lack faith in their own religion and in their own moral strength.

Furthermore, the promise of a happy ever after has itself contributed to some of the most vicious behavior ever seen on this planet, while failing to serve as a safeguard against still other atrocities. This is continuing to happen even as these words are written. It has been estimated that about one and a half million children have died in warfare during the past decade. A great many more have suffered developmental anomalies, injuries, stress, and parental absence. Most of the killers were people who believed in their respective religions and who believe in some form of survival after death. Spiritual beliefs should not be held responsible for those who abuse them, but it is abundantly clear that doctrines of survival by no means guarantee moral behavior.

It is not a fast-breaking news story to report that the goodness of a good life depends on what we make of it rather than on our subscription to a particular doctrine. All the great spiritual leaders have known this truth and have tried to convey it to us.

We do not need to resolve or to come to the same conclusion about survival of death in order to appreciate this life and conduct ourselves with good-will, mutual respect, and integrity.

ON THE HARDINESS OF SURVIVAL BELIEF

The persistence of survival belief is a matter of historical record. It is also likely to be a part of humankind's future as well. This is not just because many people hope for a life after death. Scientific logic also works in its favor. Survival can never be disproved. All that we can say in our most critical moods is that the available evidence is not entirely convincing. Science is not making a special concession for the survival hypothesis. It comes down to the inability to disprove the negative instance or *null hypothesis*.

"There could be a ghost in this room."

"Could not!"

"How do you know?"

"Because I don't see or hear or feel or smell a ghost."

"So what? This could just mean that you are not much good at seeing, hearing, feeling, or smelling ghosts. It could also mean that ghosts like to hide from you because you're such a twerp. And it could also mean that there was a ghost here just a moment ago, or that there will be a ghost here a moment from now."

"You're just being infuriating!"

"You're just being stupid! The fact that you have not been able to detect something does not mean that it is absent or unreal. You are entitled to your opinion, but you cannot claim to have disproved the null hypothesis. Perhaps I cannot prove the presence of a ghost in this room – today – but you can never, ever disprove the possibility that it might exist."

The most telling criticisms presented in this book come down to the proposition that not enough solid evidence has been brought forward to justify acceptance of the survival hypothesis within the frame of reference favored by mainstream science and logic. This is different from asserting that the survival hypothesis has been found to be false.

Each of us can decide for ourselves how we want to proceed when there is not conclusive evidence. Many people are in this situation all of the time. In my days as a service provider and health-care administrator I often had to make decisions and take actions without sure knowledge of all the major facts. As a researcher, I continue to hold some ideas as 'working hypotheses' until they can be confirmed or rejected by appropriate studies, if, indeed, a clear outcome is ever reached. What I could not and what I cannot do is wait around until everything is perfectly clear and settled. And so it is with the survival hypothesis. As William James averred in a famous essay,[2] we are entitled to believe when a belief is necessary to cope with real, live, consequential situations. If you believe in survival, you might have difficulty in convincing skeptics on the basis of available evidence, but they would be demonstrating a weak hold on the logic of science if they insist that your belief has been shown to be mistaken.

ONE EXAMPLE SHOULD DO IT.

There is an even more positive side to this. It should take only one undeniable positive instance to prove survival of death. Much of contemporary science involves number-crunching. I am most personally familiar with the socio-behavioral sciences. We usually express our results in terms of probabilities. We hesitate to say, "This is what happened." Instead, we say, "the results were significant beyond the .01 level of confidence." Our devotion to probability theory carries with it the need to accumulate as many respondents, incidents, and observations as possible, and then to test our findings on other samples if we should actually happen to find anything of interest.

Many of us seem to have forgotten that one really good observation can demonstrate the authenticity of a phenomenon. Perhaps we are also too chicken to come to our colleagues with data based on only a few sets of observation. In many circumstances there is ample reason for this caution. But there are some compelling phenomena in which a single set of observations could demonstrate a phenomenon. For example, drowning victims who had no respiration or pulse were considered to be dead, dead, dead until the Royal Humane Society fished one person out of the Thames and resuscitated him. One person and the 'drowned is dead' assumption was history. Of course, we would want more than one instance and we would do our best to follow-up on the first set of observations. Nevertheless, reason tells us that one fully evidenced case should be sufficient to prove survival of death.

Some people think we already have such cases; others don't. However, nobody can say that an even better (more evidential case) is out of the question. When that better case does come along, we will all be put to the test: can we accept survival of death if this conclusion is clearly supported by a single strong example?

ON DEATH AND SURVIVAL AS DIMENSIONS OF THE COSMIC SCENARIO

It may seem presumptuous to talk of the cosmic scenario. Who are we? What do we know? Well, we may not know much, but we do not have to apologize for having curiosity (one of humankind's better traits) and for attempting to use the knowledge that has been acquired.

The name-brand theories of cosmic creation (The Big Bang is still the most popular, but facing some opposition) do not have life coming on the scene until a lot else has happened. I will assume this to be true on the grounds that astrophysicists know more about their field than I do. We begin, then, with the reasonable inference that there was no death for quite some time because there was no life. No life. No death. No survival question.

Somewhere along the line our own planet came into being. Eventually there appeared the makings of life or, if you prefer, the prototypes of life forms to come. The 'primal soup' had a stage in which it was neither exactly organic or inorganic. Could this soup be destroyed? Yes, presumably so. Would this destruction amount to its death? We see immediately that 'deathness' cannot be defined without reference to the type of life or proto-life with which it is associated.

Not only our planetary home but the entire cosmos has continued to change. Each change has had its implications for the conditions of life and, therefore, the conditions of death as well. At certain points within the cosmic saga it would not have been meaningful to speak of life, death, and survival. It would be naive to suppose that the present arrangement of life in the universe will hold steady in the future: this seems to be the least likely possibility.

As the place of life changes within the changing universe, so will the meanings of death and survival.

This cosmic process, operating on a time scale beyond easy imagining, places our usual assumptions in a new perspective. 'Life,' 'death,' and 'survival' comprise a rather crude and primitive vocabulary with which to think about the future of (well, here we go again), life, death, and survival. This new perspective will take some getting used to, so we might as well start now.

I had been wondering if I was the only person who was trying to relate the nature and meanings of life-death survival to the changing cosmos. I guess not: a promising new book seems likely to contribute to this discussion. I have not yet read *The Physics of Immortality* [3] because its publication was announced just as this book had to meet its pressing appointment. From the publisher's advance information, however, it appears that mathematical physicist Frank J. Tipler has offered a prediction of the fate of all lives when the universe reaches what he calls its *Omega Point*. It sounds like a wild, daring, scary theory with a surprisingly wonderful ending. If Tipler is right, we will become our own future selves after greater cosmic adventures than Héléne Smith could imagine in her 'visits' to Mars. Is Tipler right? Who knows? It is not his particular theory that should concern us so much as the legitimate enterprise of conceiving of life, death, and survival within the space-time frame of all that exists. To put it the other way, how foolish it would be to ponder the survival question while neglecting the entire universe in which we live and die.

FLOWING WITH THE LIFE-STREAM

Is the universe 'matter'? Yes, kind of.
Is the universe 'energy'? Yes, kind of.
Is the universe 'idea' or 'spirit' Yes, kind of.

The universal flow is variously matter, energy, and spirit depending on our own frames and circumstances of observation. It is also, in a deep sense, music. Were we able to experience the flow of universe in a direct, encompassing, and profound manner, we would probably be experiencing the music to which all music relates and aspires. Music, we might remind ourselves, is by no means inferior to matter, energy, and idea/spirit as a construction of reality. It is both familiar and mysterious, a *melos* through which life and cosmos express themselves. Our life-streams partake of this 'music of the spheres'. Music has its rests and silence, without which melody could not be shaped. Themes emerge, develop, and transform themselves as though being improvised through all time by a Johann Sebastian Bach or a John Coltrane.

This music existed before we did. It will continue when we are no longer in our present form. In a sense, however, we have always been part of this flow of cosmic music and always will be. It hardly matters what beliefs we hold and what we require as evidence. What does matter is whether or not we will free ourselves to make a joyful music as we travel this life.

The Navajo have known this for a long time. As they, since the time of the ancients, have blessed the traveller, may we also be blessed:

Then go on as one who has long life.
Go on as one who is happy.
Go with blessing before you.
Go with blessing behind you.

A NEW DAWN

Go with blessing above you.
Go with blessing below you.
Go with blessing around you.
Go with blessing in your speech.
Go with happiness and long life.
Go mysteriously.

REFERENCES

Chapter 1. There and Back: The Near-Death Experience
1. Moody, R., Jr., *Life After Life*. Covington, Georgia, Mockingbird Books, 1975.
2. Ritchie, George G., *Return to Tomorrow*. Old Tappan: Fleming Revell, 1978.
3. Roszell, C., *The Near-Death Experience*. Hudson, New York, Anthrosophic Press.
4. Holck, F. H., "Life Revisited (Parallels in Death Experiences)", *Omega, Journal of Death and Dying*, 1978, *9*, 1-12.
5. Sabom, M. B., and Kreutziger, S., "Near-Death Experiences", *New England Journal of Medicine*, 1977, *297*, 1071.
6. Sabom, M. B., and Kreutziger, S., "The Experience of Near Death". *Death Education*, 1977, *1*, 195-203.
7. Sabom. M. B., "The Near-Death Experience: Myth or Reality? A Methodological Approach". *Anabiosis*, 1981, *1*, 44-56.
8. Greyson, B. and Stevenson, I., "The Phenomenology of Near-Death Experiences", *American Journal of Psychiatry*, 1980, *137*, 1193-1196.
9. Garfield, C. A., "The Dying Patient's Concern with Life After Death" in R. Kastenbaum (ed.), *Between Life and Death*, New York, Springer Publishing Co., 1979, pp. 45-60.
10. Noyes, R., Jr, "The Experience of Dying," *Psychiatry*, 1972, *35*, 174-183.
11. Noyes, R., Jr, and Kletti, R., "Depersonalization in the Face of Life-Threatening Danger: A Description", *Psychiatry*, 1976, *39*, 19-27.
12. Noyes, R., Jr, and Kletti, R., "Depersonalization in the Face of Life-Threatening Danger: An Interpretation", *Omega, Journal of Death and Dying*, 1976, *7*, 103-114.
13. Noyes, R., Jr, and Kletti, R., "Depersonalization in Response to Life-Threatening Danger", *Comprehensive Psychiatry*, 1977, *18*, 375-384.

REFERENCES

14. Noyes, R., Jr, and Kletti, R., "Panoramic Memory: A Response to the Threat of Death", *Omega, Journal of Death and Dying*, 1977, *8*, 181-194.
15. Noyes, R., Jr, Hoenk, P. R., Kuperman, S., and Slymen, D. J., "Depersonalization in Accident Victims and Psychiatry Patients", *Journal of Nervous and Mental Disorders*, 1977, *164*, 401-407.
16. Noyes, R., Jr, & Slymen, D. J., "The Subjective Response to Life-Threatening Danger", *Omega, Journal of Death and Dying*, 1978-1979, *9*, 313-321.
17. Ring, K., *Life at Death: A Scientific Investigation of the Near-Death Experience*, New York, Coward, McCann & Geoghegan, 1980.
18. Ring, K. *Heading Toward Omega*, New York, William Morrow, 1984.
19. Pribham, K. H., *Languages of the Brain*, Englewood Cliffs, New Jersey, Prentice-Hall, 1971.
20. Pribham, K. H., "Holonomy and Structure in the Organization of Perception" in U. M. Nicholas (ed.), *Images, Perception and Knowledge*, Dordrecht, D. Reidel, 1977.
21. Grof, S., *The Holotropic Mind*, San Francisco, Harper Collins, 1993.
22. Zaleski, C., *Otherworld Journeys*, New York, Oxford, Oxford University Press, 1987.
23. Morse, M., *Closer to the Light*, New York, Villard Books, 1990.
24. Morse, M., Venecia, D., Jr, and Milstein, J. "Near-Death Experiences: A Neurophysiological Explanatory Model", *Journal of Near-Death Studies*, 1989, *8*, 45-54.
25. Morse, M., with Perry, P., *Transformed by the Light*. New York: Villard Books, 1992.
26. Dobson, M., Tattersfield, A. E., and Adler, M. W., "Attitudes and Long-Term Adjustment of Patients Surviving Cardiac Arrest", *British Medical Journal*, 1971, *3*, 207-212.
27. Schoenbeck, S. B., and Hocutt, G. D., "Near-Death Experiences in Patients Undergoing Cardiopulmonary Resuscitation", *Journal of Near-Death Experiences*, 1991, *9*, 211-218.
28. Holden, J. M., "Rationale and Considerations for Proposed Near-Death Research in the Hospital Setting". *Journal of Near-Death Experiences*, 1988, *7*, 19-31.
29. Greyson, B., Editor's Foreword. *Journal of Near-Death Studies*, 1994, *13*, 3-4.
30. Ring, K., "Solving the Riddle of Frightening Near-Death Experiences: Some Testable Hypotheses and a Perspective Based on A Course in Miracles". *Journal of Near-Death Experience*, 1994, *13*, 5-24.
31. Siegel, R. K., *"The Psychology of Life After Death"*, American Psychologist, 1980, *35*, 911-931.
32. Osis, K., and Mitchell, J. L., "Psychological Correlates of

Reported Out-of-the-Body Experiences", *Journal of the Society for Psychical Research*, 1977, *49*, 525-536.

33. Brent, S. B., "Deliberately Induced, Premortem Out-of-Body Experiences: An Experimental and Theoretical Approach". In R. Kastenbaum (ed.), *Between Life and Death*, New York, Springer, 1979, pp. 89-123.

34. Gazzaniga, M. S., *The Social Brain*, New York, Basic Books.

35. Ruderman, S. A., "Personal Encounter with Death and Some Consequences" in R. Kastenbaum (ed.), *Between Life and Death*, New York, Springer, 1979, pp. 1-14.

36. Roth, M., and Harper, M., "Temporal Lobe Epilepsy and the Phobic Anxiety-Depersonalization Syndrome, Part II: Practical and Theoretical Considerations", *Comprehensive Psychiatry*, 1962, *3*, 215-226.

37. Lilly, J. C., *The Deep Self*, New York, Simon & Schuster, 1977.

38. Winters, W. D., "The Continuum of CNS Excitatory States" in R. K. Siegel & L. J. West (eds.), *Hallucinations: Behavior, Experience, and Theory*, New York, Wiley, 1975.

39. Domino, E. F., and Luby, E. D., "Abnormal Mental States induced by PCP as a Model for Schizophrenia" in J. O. Cole, A. M. Freedman, and A. J. Friedhoff (eds.), *Psychopathology and Psychopharmacology*, Baltimore, Maryland, Johns Hopkins University Press, 1973.

40. Jung, C. G., *The Portable Jung*. (J. Campbell, ed.), London and New York, Penguin Books, 1962.

41. Lundahl, C. R., "The Perceived Other World in Mormon Near-Death Experiences: A Social and Physical Description", *Omega, Journal of Death and Dying*, 1961, *12*, 319-328.

42. Kellehear, A., "Near-Death Experiences and the Pursuit of the Ideal Society", *Journal of Near-Death Studies*, 1991, *10*, 79-96.

43. Counts, D. A., "Near-Death and Out-of-Body Experiences in a Melanesian Society", *Journal of Near-Death Studies*, 1983, *3*, 115-135.

44. Blackmore, S. J., and Troscianko, T. S., "The Physiology of the Tunnel", *Journal of Near-Death Studies*, 1989, *8*, 15-28.

45. Blackmore, S. J., *Dying to Live*, New York, Prometheus Books, 1993.

Chapter 2. Safe Conduct: Angel Escorts Across the Border?

1. Kastenbaum, R., *The Psychology of Death*. Second Edition. New York: Springer Publishing Company, 1992.

2. Turner, P., "The Grey Lady": A Study of Psychic Phenomena in the Dying, *Journal of the Society for Psychical Research*, 1959, *40*, 124-129.

3. Barrett, W. F., *Death-Bed Visions*. Northampshire: The Aquarian Press, 1986 (first published in 1926).

4. Burnham, S., *A Book of Angels*. New York: Ballantine Books, 1990.
5. Daniel, A., Wyllie, T., & Ramer, A., *Ask Your Angels*. New York: Ballantine Books, 1992.
6. Osis, K., & Haraldsson, E., *At the Hour of Death*. New York: Avon, 1977.
7. Haraldsson, E., "Apparitions of the Dead. Analysis of a New Collection of 350 Reports". Presented at a parapsychological research convention, Heidelberg, August, 1991.
8. Glaser, B. G., & Strauss, A. L., *Awareness of Dying*. Chicago: Aldine, 1966.
9. Becker, E., *The Denial of Death*. New York: Free Press.
10. Kastenbaum, R., *Death, Society, and Human Experience*. Fifth Edition. Needham, MA: Allyn & Bacon.
11. Sacks, O., *A Leg to Stand On*. New York: Harper & Row, 1987.

Chapter 3. Do the Dead Stay in Touch? And Do They do It with Mirrors?

1. Baudrillard, J., *Symbolic Exchange and Death*. (Translated by I. H. Grant). London: Sage Publications Ltd., 1993.
2. Gurney, E., Myers, F.W.:H., and Podmore, F., *Phantasms of the Living,* 2 vols, London, Trubner, 1886, pp. 247, 249, 256.
3. Berger, A., "Quoth the Raven: Bereavement and the Paranormal", *Omega, Journal of Death and Dying,* in press.
4. Haraldsson, E., "Apparitions of the Dead, Analysis of a New Collection of 350 Reports", Presented at Parapsychological Association conference, Heidelberg, August, 1991.
5. Hansel, C. E. M., *ESP: A Scientific Evaluation,* second edition, Buffalo, New York, Prometheus Books, 1980.
6. Kurtz, P., (ed.), *A Skeptic's Handbook of Parapsychology*, Buffalo, New York, Prometheus Books, 1985.
7. Randi, J., *Flim-Flam, Psychics, ESP, Unicorns and Other Delusions,* Buffalo, New York, Prometheus Books, 1987.
8. LeShan, L., *Clairvoyant Reality,* Wellingborough, Northamptonshire, 1982.
9. Morse, M., Venecia, D., Jr, and Milstein, J., "Near-Death Experiences: A Neurophysiological Explanatory Model", *Journal of Near-Death Studies,* 1989, *8,* 45-54.
10. Moody, R., A., Jr, *Life After Life, Part II*. To be published.
11. Chosen, S. M., Cambridge, Massachusetts & London, England, The MITT Press, 1994.

Chapter 4. The Spirit Survives: Case Histories

1. In G. Appellation, (ed.), *The Oxford Book of Prayer*, Oxford, Oxford University Press, p. 1066.
2. In G. Appellation, (ed.), *The Oxford Book of Prayer,* Oxford, Oxford University Press, 1987, p. 311.

3. Osis, K., and McCormick, D., "A Poltergeist Case Without an Identifiable Living Agent", *Journal of the American Society for Psychical Research*, 1982,76, 23-52.
4. Richest, C., *Thirty Years of Psychical Research*, (translated by S. de Breath), London, Collins, 1923.
5. Mull Holland, J., *Beware Familiar Spirits*, New York, Charles Scriber's Sons, 1938 (reprinted New York, Aran Press, 1975, p. 312.
6. Myers, F. W. H., *Human Personality and Its Survival of Bodily Death*, London, Longmans, Green, 1903, vol. two (reprinted New York, Aran Press, 1975), pp. 5, 28, 46.
7. Hart, H., *The Enigma of Survival*, Springfield, Illinois, Charles C. Thomas, 1959, pp. 178-179.
8. Calico, R. A., and Reynolds, D. K., "Phenomenological Reality and Post-Death Contact", *Journal for the Scientific Study of Religion*, 1973, *12*, 209-221.
9. Kastenbaum, R., "Two-Way Traffic on the River Styx", presented to annual meeting of the American Psychological Association, Washington, DC, 1971.
10. Editors of *USA Weekend*, "I Never Believed in Ghosts Until … 100 Real-Life Encounters", New York, Barnes & Noble Books, 1992, pp. 133-135, 139-141, 147-148.
11. Kozak, D., "Dying Badly: Violent Death and Religious Change Among the Tohono O'Odham", *Omega, Journal of Death and Dying*, *29*, 207-216, 1991.
12. Emmons, C. F., *Chinese Ghosts and ESP*, Methuchen, N. J., The Scarecrow Press, 1982, p. 155.
13. Rogo, D. S., *An Experience of Phantoms*, New York, Taplinger, 1974, pp. 60, 79.

Chapter 5. No Chance of a Ghost

1. Doyle, A. C., "Lot No. 249", in E. F. Beiler (ed.), *The Best Supernatural Tales of Arthur Conan Doyle*, New York, Dover Publications, Inc., 1979, pp. 74-111.
2. Collins, W., "The Dream Woman". in *Classic Ghost Stories*, New York, Dover Publications, Inc., 1975, pp. 183-206.
3. Coates, J., *Photographing the Invisible*, London, Fowler, 1911.
4. Myers, F. W. H., *Human Personality and Its Survival of Bodily Death*, London, Longmans, Green, 1903, vol. two (reprinted New York, Arno, 1975), pp. 5, 32-33.
5. Mulholland, J., *Beware Familiar Spirits*, New York, Charles Scribner's Sons, 1938 (reprinted New York, Arno Press, 1975).
6. Podmore, F., *Modern Spiritualism: A History and a Criticism*, London, Methuen, 1902 (2 vols).

REFERENCES

7. Rinn, J. R., *Sixty Years of Psychical Research*, New York, The Truth Seeker Company, 1950.

8. Roll, R. G., "Poltergeists", in B. B. Wolman (ed.), *Handbook of Parapsychology*, New York, Van Nostrand Reinhold, 1977, pp. 382-413.

9. Hart, H., *The Enigma of Survival*, Springfield, Illinois, Charles C. Thomas, 1959.

10. Gauld, A. O., "Discarnate Survival", in B. B. Wolman (ed.), *Handbook of Parapsychology*, New York, Van Nostrand Reinhold, 1977, pp. 577-630.

11. Tyrrell, G. N. M., *Apparitions*, New York, Macmillan, 1962.

12. Stevenson, I., "The Contribution of Apparitions to the Evidence for Survival", *Journal of the American Society for Psychical Research*, 1982, *76*, 341-358.

13. Wolman, B. B. (ed)., *Handbook of Parapsychology*, New York, Van Nostrand Reinhold,. 1977.

14. Owen, I. M., and Sparrow, M., *Conjuring up Philip*, Toronto, Fitzhery & Whitseely, 1976.

15. Osis, K., and McCormick, D., "A Poltergeist Case Without an Identifiable Living Agent", *Journal of the American Society for Psychical Research*, 1982, *76*, 23-52.

16. Baudrillard, J., *Symbolic Exchange and Death*, (Translated by I. H. Grant), London: Sage Publications Ltd, 1993.

Chapter 6. How Spirits have Their Say: From Mediums to Channelers

1. Podmore, F., *The Newer Spiritualism*, London, Fisher Unwin, 1910 (reprinted New York, Arno Press, 1975).

2. Besterman, T. (ed.), *Collected Papers on the Paranormal*, New York, Garrett Publications, 1968.

3. Angoff, A., *Eileen Garrett and the World Beyond the Senses*, New York, William Morrow & Co., Inc., 1974.

4. Garrett, E. J., *My Life as a Search for the Meaning of Mediumship*, London, Rider, 1939.

5. Garrett, E. J., *Many Voices: The Autobiography of a Medium*, New York, G. P. Putnam's Sons, 1968.

6. Stemman, R., *Spirits and Spirit Worlds*, London, Aldus Books, 1975

7. Smith, S., *The Mediumship of Mrs Leonard*, New York, University Books, 1964.

8. Lodge, Sir Oliver, *Raymond*, London, Methuen, 1916.

9. Myers, F. W. H., *Human Personality and Its Survival of Bodily Death*, London, Longmans, Green, 1903, vol. two (reprinted New York, Arno Press, 1975).

10. Munthe, A., *The Story of San Michele*, New York, Dutton, 1953, pp. 370-372.

11. Saltmarsh, H. F., *Evidence of Personal Survival from Cross Correspondences*, London, Bell, 1938 (reprinted New York, Arno Press, 1975), pp. 149-150.

12. Cummins, G., *Swan on a Black Sea: A Study in Automatic Writing: The Cummins-Willett Scripts*. London: Routledge & Kegan Paul, 1965.

13. Ravaldini, S., Biondi, M., and Stevenson, I., "The Case of Giuseppe Riccardi: An Unusual Drop-In Communication in Italy", *Journal of the Society for Psychical Research*, 56, 1990, 257-265.

14. Haraldsson, E., and Stevenson, I., "An Experiment with the Icelandic Medium Hafsteinn Bjornsson", *Journal of the American Society for Psychical Research*, 1975, 69, 192-202.

15. Reed, H., *Edgar Cayce on Channeling Your Higher Self*, New York, Warner Books, 1989.

16. Tietze, T. R., *Margery*, New York, Harper & Row, 1973.

17. Dodds, E. R., "Why I Do Not Believe in Survival", *Proceedings of the Society for Psychical Research*, 1934, 42, 142-168.

18. Sidgwick, E. M., "Discussion of the Trance Phenomena of Mrs. Piper", *Proceedings of the Society for Psychical Research*, 1900, 15, 16-38.

19. Sidgwick, E. M., "A Contribution to the Study of the Psychology of Mrs. Piper's Trance Phenomena", *Proceedings of the Society for Psychical Research*, 1915, 28.

20. Ian Stevenson on secondary personalities of mediums.

21. Campbell, J. (ed)., *The Portable Jung*, New York, Penguin, 1976.

Chapter 7. From Life to Life: Reincarnation

1. Wordsworth, W., "Intimations of Immortality" from *Recollections of Childhood*, Quoted in J. Head & S. L. Cranston (eds), *Reincarnation, An East-West Anthology*, Madras & London, 1985, p. 126.

2. Rolland, R. Quoted in J. Head & S. L. Cranston (eds.), *Reincarnation, An East-West Anthology*, Madras & London, 1985, p. 210.

3. Weiss, B. L., *Through Time into Healing*, New York, Simon & Schuster, 1992, p. 69.

4. Hall, M. P., *Reincarnation, The Cycle of Necessity*, Los Angeles, The Philosopher's Press, 1939, p. 11.

5. Besterman, T., *Collected Papers on the Paranormal*, New York, Garrett Publications, 1968.

6. Murray, D. C., *Reincarnation, Ancient Beliefs and Modern Evidence*, Dorset, England, Prism Press, and Garden City, New York, Unity Press, 1988, p. 17.

REFERENCES

7. Parrinder, G., *Avatar and Incarnation, A Comparison of Indian and Christian Beliefs*, New York, Oxford University Press, 1982, p. 15.
8. Maduro, R., "The Old Man as Creative Artist in India", in R. Kastenbaum (ed.), *Old Age on the New Scene*, New York, Springer Publishing Co., 1981, pp. 77-78.
9. Kramer, K., *The Sacred Art of Dying*, Mahwah, New York, Paulist Press, 1988, p. 32.
10. Rinpoche, S., *The Tibetan Book of Living and Dying*, San Francisco, HarperCollins Publishers, 1992, pp. 47-48.
11. Kubler-Ross, E., *On Death and Dying*, New York, Macmillan, 1969.
12. Kastenbaum, R., *Death, Society, and Human Experience*, 5th edition, Boston, Allyn & Bacon, 1995.
13. Gallup, G., Gallup Poll, *Fear of Dying*, 1991.
14. Martin, E., *Reincarnation, The Ring of Return*, New Hyde Park, New York, University Books, 1963.
15. Kidd, I. G., "Diogenes of Sinope", in P. Edwards (ed.), *The Encyclopedia of Philosophy*, volume 2, New York, Collier-Macmillan, 1972, pp. 409-410.
16. Stevenson, I., *Twenty Cases Suggestive of Reincarnation*, Second revised edition, Charlottesville, University Press of Virginia, 1974.
17. Stevenson, I., *Children Who Remember Previous Lives*, Charlottesville, University Press of Virginia, 1987.
18. Kastenbaum, R., Stevenson, I. An *Omega* Interview, *Omega, Journal of Death and Dying, 28*: 165-182, 1993-94.
19. Stevenson, I., "The Explanatory Value of the Idea of Reincarnation," *Journal of Nervous and Mental Disease, 264*: 305-326, 1977.
20. Stevenson, I., "Phobias in Children Who Claim to Remember Previous Lives," *Journal of Scientific Explorations, 4*: 243-254, 1990.
21. Stevenson, I., American Children Who Claim to Remember Previous Lives, *Journal of Nervous and Mental Disease, 171*: 742-748., 1983.
22. Stevenson, I. *Reincarnation and Biology*, New York, Praeger, in press.
23. Stevenson, I., "Birthmarks and Birth Defects Corresponding to Wounds on Deceased Persons," *Journal of Scientific Exploration, 7*: 403-410, 1993.
24. Weiss, B. L., *Many Lives, Many Masters*, New York, Simon & Schuster, 1990.
25. Weiss, B. L., *Through Time into Healing*, New York, Simon & Schuster, 1992.
26. Bernstein, M., *The Search for Bridey Murphy*, Garden City, New York, Doubleday, 1985.
27. Fitzgerald, E., *The Rubaiyat of Omar Khayyam*, New York, Dover, 1990.

28. Flournoy, T., *From India to the Planet Mars. A Case of Multiple Personality with Imaginary Languages*, New York, Harpers, 1900, p. 285. (For a currently available edition: Princeton, N.J., Princeton University Press, 1994, with introductory comments by S. Shamdasani.)

29. Hacking, I., *Rewriting the Soul, Multiple Personality and the Sciences of Memory*, Princeton, N. J., Prince University Press, 1995.

30. Hobson, J. A., *The Dreaming Brain*, New York, Basic Books, 1988.

31. Wambach, H., *Life Before Life*, New York, Bantam, 1979.

32. Wambach, H., *Reliving Past Lives*, New York, Harper & Row, 1978.

33. Snow, C. P., & Wambach, H., *Mass Dreams of the Future*, New York, McGraw-Hill, 1989.

34. Harris, M., "Past-Life Regression: The Grand Illusion", in R. Basil, (ed.), *Not Necessarily the New Age*, Buffalo, New York, Prometheus Books, 1988, pp. 130-144.

35. Edwards, P., The Case Against Karma and Reincarnation, in R. Basil, (ed.), *Not Necessarily the New Age*, Buffalo, New York, Prometheus Books, 1988, pp.87-129.

Chapter 8. Souls on Ice: Who Needs an Afterlife?

1. Ettinger, R.C.W., *The Prospect of Immortality*. New York: Doubleday, 1964.

2. Nelson, R. F., with Stanley, S., *We Froze the First Man*. New York: Dell.

3. Gyatos, Tenzin, the 14th Dalai Lama, *Kindness, Charity, and Insight*. Ithaca, New York: Snow Lions, 1985.

4. Kastenbaum, R., "Cryonic Suspension: An *Omega* Interview with R.C.W. Ettinger." *Omega, Journal of Death and Dying*, in press.

5. Alcor Life Extension Foundation. *Cryonics. Reaching for Tomorrow.* Fourth edition. Scottsdale, Arizona: Alcor Foundation, 1993.

6. Swift, J., *Gulliver's Travels*. Boston: Beacon Press, 1963.

7. Fahey, G., *Affadavit: Montgomery County, State of Maryland.* Oak Park: Michigan: Cryonics Institute, 1988.

8. Drexler, K. E., *Engines of Creation*. New York: Doubleday, 1986.

9. Kastenbaum, R., *Dorian, Graying: Is Youth the Only Thing Worth Having?* New York: Baywood, 1995.

Information on cryonics can be obtained by contacting:

Alcor Foundation.
7895 E. Acoma Drive #110
Scottsdale, AZ 85260-6916
USA

Immortalist Society
24443 Roanoke
Oak Park, Michigan 48237
USA

SUGGESTED READING

General introductory books

Auerbach, L., *ESP, Hauntings, and Poltergeists: A Parapsychologist's Handbook*, New York, Warner Books, 1986.

Basil, R., (ed.), *Not Necessarily the New Age*, Buffalo, New York, Prometheus Press, 1988.

Bernstein, M., *The Search for Bridey Murphy*, revised edition, New York, Avon, 1975.

Cavendish, R., (ed.), *Encyclopedia of the Unexplained*, New York, McGraw-Hill, 1974.

Douglas, A. *Extrasensory Powers, A Century of Psychical Research*, Woodstock, New York, The Overlook Press, 1977.

Gardner, M., *The New Age, Notes of a Fringe Watcher*, Buffalo, New York, Prometheus Books, 1988.

Gauld, A., *The Founders of Psychical Research*, London, Routledge & Kegan Paul, 1968.

Gyatso, Tenzin, His Holiness the Fourteenth Dalai Lama, *Kindness, Clarity, and Insight*, Ithaca, New York, Snow Lion Publications, 1984.

Kautz, W. H., and Branon, M., *Channeling: The Intuitive Connection*, San Francisco, Harper & Row, 1987.

Klimo, J., *Channeling: Investigations on Receiving Information from Paranormal Sources*, Los Angeles, Jeremy P. Tarcher, 1987.

Koestenbaum, P., *Is There An Answer to Death?* Englewood Cliffs, New Jersey, Prentice-Hall, 1976.

Kurtz, P. (ed.), *The Transcendental Temptation, A Critique of Religion and the Paranormal*, Buffalo, New York, Prometheus Books, 1991.

LeShan, L., *The Medium, the Mystic, and the Physicist: Toward A General Theory of the Paranormal*, New York, Viking Press, 1974; London, Turnstone Books, 1974.

Moody, R., Jr., *Life After Life*. Covington, Georgia, Mockingbird Books, 1975.

SUGGESTED READING

Roberts, J., *The Seth Material*, Englewood Cliffs, N. J., Prentice-Hall, 1970.

Rogo, D. S., *The Return from Silence: A Study of Near-Death Experiences*, Wellingborough, Northamptonshire, England, Aquarian Press, 1989.

Spangler, D., *The New Age*, Issaquah, WA: Morningtown Press, 1988.

Sparrow, L. E., *Reincarnation: Claiming Your Past, Creating Your Future*, San Francisco, Harper & Row, 1988.

Sutphen, R., *Past Lives, Future Loves*, New York, Pocket Books, 1978.

Thouless, R. H., *From Anecdote to Experiment in Psychical Research*, London and Boston, Routledge & Kegan Paul, 1972.

Underwood, P., *The Ghost Hunter's Guide*, Poole, Dorset, England, Blandford Press, 1986.

Historical accounts

Barrett, W. F., *Death-Bed Visions*, London, Methuen, 1926.

Frazer, J., *The Belief in Immortality and the Worship of the Dead*, London, Macmillan, 1913.

Gauld, A., *Mediumship and Survival*, London, William Heinemann, Ltd, 1982.

Gurney, E., Myers, F. W. H., and Podmore, F., *Phantasms of the Living*, 2 vols, London, Trubner, 1996 (reprinted New York, Arno Press, 1975).

Hall, T. H., *The Enigma of Daniel Home*, Buffalo, New York, Prometheus Books, 1984.

Harner, M., *The Way of the Shaman*, New York, Bantam, 1986.

Hyslop, J. H., *Science and a Future Life*, Boston, Turner, 1905.

Leonard, G. O., *My Life in Two Worlds*, London, Cassell, 1931.

Lodge, O., *Raymond or Life and Death*, London, Methuen, 1916.

McTaggart, J. M. E., *Human Immortality and Pre-Existence*, London, Edward Arnold, 1915.

Fodor, N., *Freud, Jung, and the Occult*, Secaucus, N.J., University Books, 1971.

Piper, A. L., *The Life and Work of Mrs Piper*, London, Kegan Paul, 1929.

Podmore, F., *Modern Spiritualism: A History and a Criticism*, 2 vols., London, Methuen, 1902 (reprinted as *Mediums of the 19th Century*, Secaucus, New Jersey, University Books, 1963).

Podmore, F., *The Newer Spiritualism*, London, Fisher Unwin, 1910 (reprinted New York, Arno Press, 1975).

Richet, C., *Thirty Years of Psychical Research* (translated by S. de Brath), New York, Macmillan, 1923.

Saltmarsh, H. F., *Evidence of Personal Survival from Cross-Correspondences*, London, Bell, 1938 (reprinted New York, Arno Press, 1975).

de Vesme, Caesar, *A History of Experimental Spiritualism* (translated by S. de Brath), 2 vols, Essex, Anchor Press, 1931.

Webb, J., *The Occult Establishment*, La Salle, Illinois, Open Court, 1991.

Philosophical works

Broad, C. D., *Mind and Its Place in Nature*, The Humanities Press, 1951.

Choron, J., *Modern Man and Mortality*, New York, Macmillan, 1964.

Donnelly, J., (ed.), *Language, Metaphysics, and Death*, New York, Fordham University Press, 1978.

Ducasse, C. J., *Nature, Mind and Death*, LaSalle, Illinois, The Open Court Publishing, 1951.

Ducasse, C. J., *A Critical Examination of the Belief in a Life After Death*, Springfield, Illinois, Charles C. Thomas, 1974.

Guardini, R., *The Last Things, Concerning Death, Purification After Death, Resurrection* (translated by C. E. Forsyth and G. B. Branham), New York, Pantheon Books, 1964.

Hocking, W. E., *The Meaning of Immortality in Human Experience*, New York, Harper & Brothers, 1957.

James, W., *The Will to Believe*, London, Longmans, Green, 1897 (reprinted in William James, Writings, 1902-1910, New York, The Library of America, 1987, and in many other sources).

Smith, B., & Kastenbaum, R. (eds.), *Death and Dying*, whole issue of *The Monist, An International Journal of General Philosophical Inquiry*, 1993, 76.

Kastenbaum, R., & Kastenbaum, B., (eds), *Encyclopedia of Death*, Phoenix, Oryx Press, 1989; New York, Avon, 1993.

Kaufman, W., "Existentialism and Death", in H. Feifel (ed.), *The Meaning of Death*, New York, McGraw-Hill, 1959, pp. 39-63.

Kramer, K., *The Sacred Art of Dying, How World Religions Understand Death*, New York, Paulist Press, 1988.

Lamont, C., *The Illusion of Immortality*, second edition, New York, Philosophical Library, 1950.

Lee, J. Y., *Death and Beyond in the Eastern Perspective*, New York, Interface, 1974.

Leon-Dufour, X., *Life and Death in the New Testament*, New York, Harper & Row, 1986.

Maeterlinck, M., *Our Eternity* (translated by A. Tejxeira de Mattos), New York, Dodd, Mead, 1914 (reprinted New York, Arno Press, 1977).

Maritain, J., *Man's Destiny in Eternity*, Boston, Beacon Press, 1949.

Randall, J. L., *Parapsychology and the Nature of Life*, New York, Harper & Row, 1975.

SUGGESTED READING

Rinpoche, S., *The Tibetan Book of Living and Dying*, Berkeley, CA., Harper/San Francisco, 1992.

Royce, J., *The Conception of Immortality*, Boston, Houghton Mifflin, 1900.

Steiner, R., *Understanding the Human Being, Selected Writings of Rudolf Steiner*, Bristol, England, Rudolf Steiner Press, 1993. Tsanoff, R., *The Problem of Immortality*, New York, Macmillan, 1924.

Scientific periodicals

Omega, Journal of Death and Dying, Baywood Publishing Company, Inc. 26 Austin Avenue, New York, New York 11701.

Journal of Near-Death Studies, Human Sciences Press, Inc. 233 Spring Street, New York, NY 10013-1578.

Journal of American SPR, The American Society for Psychical Research, Inc. 5 West 73rd Street, New York, NY 10023.

Scientific and professional books

Blackmore, S., *Dying to Live, Near-Death Experiences*, Buffalo, New York, Prometheus Books, 1993.

Emmons, C. F., *Chinese Ghosts and ESP, Methuchen*, New Jersey and London, The Scarecrow Press, 1982.

Hansel, C. E. M., *ESP: A Scientific Evaluation*, second edition, New York, Scribner's, 1977.

Kastenbaum, R., (ed.), *Between Life and Death*, New York, Springer, 1977.

Kastenbaum, R., *Death, Society, and Human Experience*, fifth edition, Boston: Allyn & Bacon.

Murphy, G., *Three Papers on the Survival Problem*, New York, American Society for Psychical Research, 1945.

Osis, K., and Haraldsson, E., *At the Hour of Death*, New York, Avon, 1967.

Rhine, L. E., *Mind Over Matter: Psychokinesis*, New York, Macmillan, 1970.

Ring, K., *Life at Death*, New York, Coward, McCann & Geoghegan, 1970.

Ring, K., *Heading Toward Omega*, New York, William Morrow, 1984.

Stevenson, I., *Twenty Cases Suggestive of Reincarnation*, second edition, Charlottesville, University Press of Virginia, 1974.

Stevenson, I., *Cases of the Reincarnation Type*, vol. 3, *Fifteen Cases in Thailand, Lebanon, and Turkey*, Charlottesville, University Press of Virginia, 1978.

Ullman, M., and Krippner, S. (with A. Vaughan), *Dream Telepathy*, New York, Macmillan, 1973.

Wambach, H., *Reliving Past Lives*, New York, Harper & Row, 1978.

Weiss, B. L., *Many Lives, Many Masters*, New York, Fireside Books, 1988.

Wolman, B. B., (ed.), *Handbook of Parapsychology*, New York: Van Nostrand Reinhold, 1977.

Woolger, R. J., *Other Lives, Other Selves: A Jungian Psychotherapist Discovers Past Lives*, New York, Doubleday, 1987.

Zaleski, C., *Otherworld Journeys: Accounts of Near-Death Experience in Medieval and Modern Times*, New York, Oxford University Press, 1987.

INDEX

INDEX